D0097843

DEATH BY LIBERALISM

DEATH BY
LIBERALISM

*The Fatal Outcome of
Well-Meaning Liberal Policies*

J. R. DUNN

An Imprint of HarperCollins*Publishers*
www.broadsidebooks.net

HarperCollins books may be purchased for educational, business, or sales promotional use. For information, please write: Special Markets Department, HarperCollins Publishers, 10 East 53rd Street, New York, NY 10022.

FIRST EDITION

Designed by Eric Butler

Library of Congress Cataloging-in-Publication Data

Dunn, J. R.
    Death by liberalism : the fatal outcome of well-meaning liberal policies / J.R. Dunn. — 1st ed.
        p.   cm.
    ISBN 978-0-06-187380-5 (hardback)
    1. Liberalism. 2. Liberalism—United States. I. Title.
JC574.D866   2010
320.51'3—dc22

                                                    2010011498

11 12 13 14 15   OV/RRD   10 9 8 7 6 5 4 3 2 1

The care of human life and happiness, and not their destruction, is the first and only object of good government.

—Thomas Jefferson to the Maryland Republicans, 1809

CONTENTS

INTRODUCTION

L iberalism kills.

If any two-word phrase ever demanded an explanation, it's that one. Those words simply do not belong together. They defy all logic, all sense, everything we have ever been taught concerning politics, everything we think we know about how our society functions, everything we understand about America's civic culture.

To claim that "liberalism kills" is to say that water burns, that up is down, that ignorance is strength. It is a statement beyond good taste, beyond acceptable argument, almost beyond sanity itself. Whatever its failings and faults, its errors and misjudgments, the high moral stature of liberalism has remained beyond dispute. Liberalism stands as the political expression of humanism, a doctrine epitomizing justice and mercy, the embodiment of human decency in the public sphere. To rank it with killer political dogmas such as communism, Nazism, and fascism is an absurdity, an effort to turn the world inside out.

"Liberalism kills . . . " What can that be other than a cry from the political twilight, an expression of terminal hysteria, the last desperate words of someone with nothing left to say? A pure example of the big lie, vicious and feral, fit only to be passed over in silence.

But it is no such thing. It is a statement of fact, derived from the record, easily demonstrated and impossible to refute. It is no metaphor and no mistake. No twists of meaning or redefinition or conceptual gymnastics are required.

Liberalism kills. It's as simple as that. Liberalism destroys lives, and destroys them in large numbers. It kills blatantly, and in ways that can scarcely be traced. It kills both directly and by proxy. Liberalism kills by commission—through the promotion of programs and policies that violate the safety and security of the public. Liberalism also kills by omission—by denying citizens the protection they are owed by their government and institutions.

Liberalism kills without respect for class, origins, sex, race, education, or any other factor. Death by liberalism is not limited by any set of personal, social, or political characteristics. Not even adherents of the ideology itself remain immune. Liberalism has eaten its own on numberless occasions, without the victims having any idea how or why they were being destroyed.

Death by liberalism occurs in all fields and at all levels of society. Motorists on the roads, workers at their jobs, women in their homes, children taken under the state's protection—all have fallen victim at one time or another. It is implicated in the deaths of hundreds of thousands in this country, while overseas it has contributed to the deaths of millions. It is one of the largest-scale killers active in our time, easily outdoing most deadly diseases, and exceeding terrorism by several orders of magnitude. It has been killing for decades and will continue to kill as long as we allow it.

Liberalism kills for the most part through policy, through courses of action adapted to achieve certain political and social goals. The consequent mortality is neither deliberate nor intentional—barbed wire and the pistol form no part of liberal methodology. The lethality of liberalism is a malignant example of unintended consequences, a by-product of the doctrine's virtues, a result of attempts by its adherents to perfect society and benefit their fellow citizens.

An intractable social or political problem or threat is targeted. It has either gone unaddressed or has defied all previous attempts to solve it. Crime, child abuse, and mental illness can serve as examples. Liberal politicians promise a solution, either through novel technical means, the application of some form of political voodoo not easily comprehensible to the uninitiated, or by other-wise unexplained methods labeled "sanity" or "common sense."

These solutions generally involve the outlay of multiple billions of dollars (read "trillions" as of 2009), along with the establish-ment of a mammoth bureaucracy to oversee the process. After years spent in preparation in the form of studies, meetings, con-sultations, and planning sessions, all of which require trainloads of cash, a solution at last is put into effect. But then . . .

Then things start going wrong. The new knowledge turns out to be in error, the magic no more than empty ritual, liberal sanity not quite as balanced as was claimed. Soon enough, the problem is worse than it ever was. It's as if it was feeding on the attempts to confront it, gaining strength from all that money and effort being thrown into the battle against it. In response, the departments are enlarged, the budgets expanded, and the effort redoubled. But the problem continues growing, in direct symbiosis with the civil establishment created to overcome it.

In a certain number of cases, people start dying. Dying in larger numbers than they did before government interference started. Dying, often as not, as much due to the effects of that interference as to anything directly associated with the problem itself. These deaths are unplanned and unintended, a form of mass negligent homicide, a kind of soft governmental lethality.

The number of fatalities varies. A few dozen in the case of biodiversity programs, a few thousand in the case of child protec-tion agencies, hundreds of thousands in the case of federal fuel standards and criminal justice reform, and truly celestial numbers when the action is transferred to the international stage.

Almost without exception, so much time has passed that those responsible have moved on. The lethal outcome is disassociated from any form of accountability or guilt. To an onlooker, the catastrophe appears to be the result of accident or bad luck. (This is a major reason why the process has occurred unnoticed. To most people, a society's political system is what it is, to be accepted in the same sense as climate or geology. The effects of many of these policies are of such magnitude as to be difficult to comprehend as the end product of human action.)

Horribly enough, the bureaucratic structures established to oversee these policies continue generating mortality long after failure has become manifest, even after the problem itself has faded from significance. Some of them continue killing to this day.

By this process, mass mortality has become a core element of modern liberalism, a product of its most deep-rooted beliefs and ideas, probably inseparable from the doctrine as it exists, and unlikely ever to be eradicated. To accept liberalism, in its current form, is to accept death on a massive scale.

How did this happen? How did liberalism fall so low? It's not as if it started out as a destructive force, like fascism, communism, and similar ideologies. Liberalism began as an attempt to solve the problem of self-government, an effort to establish a successful democratic system where the ancient Greeks and Renaissance Italians had failed. And to succeed on a much higher level—in the modern context, in societies in which change was the only constant, and not merely as involved city-states, but in polities stretching across entire continents.

The liberalism formulated by Edmund Burke and adapted by our country's founders was the liberalism of individual rights, economic freedom, and the rule of law.

It had distinct and limited aims: to establish a stable government, to minimize corruption and faction, to secure the governmental succession (a trivial problem to us, but one that stymied previous civilizations for millennia), to assure fair representation, and to protect individual rights, including economic and property rights.

These challenges were addressed with astonishing swiftness and at little social cost. The American Revolution, the world's first—and, James Fazy's Genevan coup aside, perhaps the only—liberal revolution, was one of the least brutal on record. So encouraging were the results of the first epoch of American governance (nearly matched by Great Britain, which learned a lot from its former colony), that the goals of liberalism were continually expanded throughout the nineteenth century, the definitions of rights broadened, the franchise given ever-wider expression.

If liberalism represented an ideal, it was an ideal based on practice and experience. The precepts of liberalism were continually reworked across decades and generations by some of the greatest minds of the modern era. Jefferson set down the principles of liberal administration. Madison and Hamilton worked out the practical applications. Tocqueville examined the social and political results of the first generations of liberal governance. Acton strove to set the allowable limits of liberal use of power.

Many still believe that today's liberalism is the same thing as the realistic liberalism of the nineteenth century. Modern proponents like to trace their doctrine back to the founders (and some of them back to Socrates, or for that matter Jesus Christ). But no such claim can be made. What operates under the label today is something utterly different, something scarcely in the same category. Classical liberalism, the liberalism of Burke and Madison, was a doctrine. Modern liberalism, whatever modifier might be added, is an ideology.

Rationalism was the snake in the liberal Eden. Rationalism can be simply defined as the conviction that all problems can be solved

by means of unsupported reason, without the aid of traditional beliefs, insight, intuition, or God forbid, faith. In the nineteenth century, rationalism expressed itself in the contention that everything
under the sun, including social and political affairs, was susceptible to scientific analysis, to being broken down to its constituent
elements and subject to any number and variety of manipulations.
When politics met rationalism, the result was ideology.

Ideology was the fruit of attempts to turn politics, that most
human of activities, into a scientific discipline. Ideologies were intellectual constructs in which elements of human society were factored (always in grossly simplified form) and processed to match
a fixed set of concepts. The world in all its complexity was viewed
as a machine in which certain inputs would always and invariably
lead to the same results. Human individuals, in this conception,
were no more than parts.

By means of ideology, political thinkers hoped to gain overall
control of society in order to direct it along the paths they chose—
always, needless to say, in the service of justice and humanity.

Ideological thinking was rampant in the nineteenth century.
The early (and truly bizarre) systems of Claude Henri Saint-Simon
and Auguste Comte set the basis for later figures such as Karl
Marx and Friedrich Engels, who in turn laid the foundations for
the mass ideologies—fascism, Nazism, and communism—that
left such a mark on the twentieth century.

At first, liberalism was in no way influenced by these new systems. Why should it be? The doctrine was going from strength to
strength in the later decades of the nineteenth century. Defusing
sectarian and ethnic conflicts, establishing new standards of political equality, humanizing the harsher aspects of industrial capitalism. But as the century turned, social and economic problems
increased in complexity and immediacy. No longer were the answers simple and straightforward. Many observers declared that
the Age of Liberalism—and with it democracy and capitalism—

had reached the end of its string. They called for new ideas and new methods. Liberals throughout the West were deeply impressed by the apparent achievements of the ideological states—Fascist Italy, Nazi Germany, and the Soviet Union. The brute techniques of the ideologies, their policies, planning, and social engineering, seemed to be a workable alternative.

Unacknowledged among these techniques was that of democide, the murder of citizens by their government. When a part goes wrong in a machine, the part is removed and discarded. So it was with the human beings making up the new ideological states. An individual who did not fit in, who was an irritant to the state, or who simply failed to meet specifications, was dealt with in the same fashion as a broken part. In time, such treatment was extended to families, groups, and entire peoples. Democide became a key technique of the ideological states, with their Gulag, their death camps, their artificial famines, and their massacres.

Killing became a common practice of twentieth-century government, democide a characteristic government activity. The number of deaths brought about by government during the period has been estimated at over 260 million. Democide was one of the major causes of death in the century past, second only to natural causes.

Liberalism never reconciled itself to democide. No greater affront to its basic philosophy can be imagined. But the internal logic of ideology compels its adherents toward lethality whether they desire it or not. In the end, American liberals merely demonstrated that malice and bloody-mindedness were not necessary to democide. Ineptness, carelessness, and arrogance were enough.

In adapting ideology, American liberals violated the basic premises of the democratic system. Democracy became less democratic, liberalism became less liberal. And as it abandoned its core principles, liberalism became an ideology of failure.

The planners and policy-makers bit off more than they could

chew. They became deluded as to their abilities and, like the dictators who served as their models, began to plan on a level beyond the merely human.

It is no surprise that they failed. The response to their early failures was to intensify their efforts, to continue down the same road with even fiercer determination. But the failures simply grew greater, more costly, more difficult to ignore or explain. They covered the entire range of the American social and political landscape: race relations, social welfare, educational reform, affirmative action, urban renewal, industrial regulation, judicial reform, environmentalism.

Some of these efforts failed catastrophically, at a terrifying price in human lives. In this, too, American liberals were following the example of their totalitarian models. Ideological systems without exception leave vast numbers of corpses in their wake. While there were no death camps in the U.S., no Gulag, no killing fields, ideology creates its own pressures leading to lethality. Those who died as a result of policy, and planning, of techniques and concepts borrowed from the most repellent states on earth, of attempts to change the world and society through mass directed effort, differ in no real sense from those who died in Nazi Germany, the Soviet Union, or Maoist China. It is no exaggeration to call it the American democide.

Those are the facts, and no amount of protest, denial, or indignation is ever going to make them go away. Liberalism has a secret history. In these pages we will uncover it. We will trace how liberalism went astray, how a doctrine based on the noblest of intentions became an ideology that causes unnecessary, large-scale, premature mortality among American citizens and other innocents across the globe. We will demonstrate how water came to burn, how ignorance became strength. We will discover how liberalism learned to kill.

DEATH BY LIBERALISM

Liberalism is the supreme form of generosity; it is the right which the majority concedes to minorities and hence it is the noblest cry that has ever resounded on this planet.
—*JOSÉ ORTEGA Y GASSET*

Liberalism is totalitarianism with a human face.
—*THOMAS SOWELL*

1

PROMETHEUS IN GRAY FLANNEL

How Liberalism Went Wrong

The twentieth century was not supposed to turn out the way it did. It was supposed to be liberalism's great age, the epoch in which liberal ideas and practice would spread across the globe. All the ancient dreams—of justice, egalitarianism, internationalism, and progress—would come to pass. Problems that had withstood the efforts of ages would disperse like fog. All errors would be corrected, all promises fulfilled, all visions would become reality.

It didn't quite happen that way. The liberal dream hit an obstacle right out of the gate: the ideological dictators, the bandit rulers who rose like specters out of the ruins left by WWI, extended their control across Eurasia, and finally moved against the Western democracies themselves. Far from embodying any liberal utopia, the twentieth century became, in the words of historian Jacob Burckhardt, "the epoch of the booted commandoes."

The booted commandoes—the gangster rulers who transformed the twentieth century into the Age of Massacre. They were far from unique in history—their kind can be found in any era. The Roman military emperors, the Caesars and Severans, the medieval Carolingian kings, the Renaissance mercenary condotti-erre looting and subverting the republics of Italy. But never before were they so numerous, widespread, or powerful as in the century just ended.

They started as minor figures on the fringes, Mussolini as the nail-hard ruler the Italians deserved, Lenin the café revolutionary, Hitler the lunatic who attempted a coup with an army dispatched from a beer hall. But within a decade, they dominated the world stage. A few years later they were threatening to take control of the globe itself.

It required the most ferocious war in history to destroy the Axis. Another forty years of semi-warfare accounted for communism. Today little remains of the mid-twentieth century dictatorships beyond a few isolated pea patches on the margins of third-millennial civilization—Cuba, North Korea, Burma. But behind that victory lie shattered nations, the numberless and un-pitied dead, and somewhere amid the ruins, the dream of a liberal world.

IDEOLOGY AND TYRANNY

The jackboot dictators had advantages that previous tyrants lacked. They had technology, the tank replacing the warhorse, the dive bomber replacing the trebuchet, modern communications replacing horse-borne messengers. They had managerial innovations to assist in the control of their societies, their armies and secret police, and their camp networks.

But they also possessed one particular tool denied the ancient dictators. Alexander had his phalanx, Genghis Khan his horsemen—the men in jackboots had ideology.

Ideology is one of the great instrumentalities of the modern era, and one of the least understood. Like many obnoxious developments, it originated with the French Revolution. (Its progenitor, the philosopher A.-L.-C. Destutt de Tracy, coined the term as a catchy name for his "science of ideas." Rarely has an individual of such lasting influence been so thoroughly forgotten.) Ideologies comprise total intellectual systems, complete descriptions of the world along with complex social and political programs for manipulating it.

Ideology provided the dictators with a means of mobilizing support and instilling revolutionary zeal. For the bureaucracy (almost always kept intact by revolutionary upstarts), it provided an easily applied system of control. For intellectuals, it offered an alternative to despised bourgeois values. For the masses, it provided a pseudo-religious substitute for traditional creeds.

Ideology in power gave rise to a new type of political entity, the totalitarian state, in which the state controlled not only the political sphere, but all other aspects of public life. In Mussolini's words, "All within the State, nothing outside the State, nothing against the State." In politics, all that existed was the party, usually devoted to the semidivine figure of the führer or duce. In the economic sphere, totalitarianism was expressed through centralization, planning, and "rationalization" of national economies. The intellectual world, including the arts and education, was thoroughly regimented through the procedure termed "thought control." By mid-twentieth century, nearly half the world's population was living under some kind of totalitarian government.

IDEOLOGY AND DEMOCIDE

At the time, many predicted universal victory for the ideological states, more organized, more efficient, and more aggressive than the democracies. But in the end, the irresistible force of totalitarianism broke on the immovable object of human nature. The new tyrannies required hive insects. They had to settle for human beings.

The new dictators did their best to assure compliance. Technical and managerial advances provided unprecedented capabilities for detecting dissent, ensuring obedience, and annihilating internal enemies. The totalitarian states utilized the new tools to the utmost, in the process generating a new class of crime: democide, mass murder instigated by government.

We are all familiar with one form of democide: genocide, the willful annihilation of an ethnic group or race. But genocide is only a single aspect of the democidal spectrum, which includes the mass murder of dissidents; mass mortality due to slave labor; mass starvation due to seizure or withholding of food supplies; and deaths caused by ill-planned or ineptly executed government policy (this last is sometimes identified as "morticide," a term that lacks the force of the original coinage).

According to democide's sole scholar, Dr. R. J. Rummel (you'd think that a topic of such importance to the health and future of civilization would be of interest to more than one individual), democide accounted for up to 262,000,000 deaths over the past century. The number of human beings murdered by governments is on the order of six times greater than those killed in all the wars fought during the same period.

Individual instances of democide mark the century's greatest episodes of mass mortality, far outweighing any natural disaster (excepting only the Spanish influenza of 1918–19). Examples include the Ukrainian famine of 1932–34 (also known as the Holodomor, or "Hunger Death"), which killed upwards of 7 million people; the Soviet purges of 1937–39, which accounted for perhaps 10 million Soviet citizens; the Holocaust, with its tally of 6 million Jews (the Nazis also murdered at least 5 million others, including gypsies, Poles, and Slavs—Rummel puts the total even higher, suggesting that Hitler is answerable for up to 20,946,000 murders, when POWs, slave laborers, homosexuals, and victims of euthanasia are figured in); the Chinese Great Leap Forward of 1959–61, which may account for up to 45 million dead; and the Cambodian Year Zero, which killed 2.5–3 million people between 1975 and 1978.

Democide was almost completely a product of the ideological states. The U.S.S.R., the People's Republic of China, and Nazi Germany are by themselves guilty of half of all democidal murders. When associated nations such as Japan, Vietnam, North Korea, and Cuba, along with imitators such as Franco's Spain or the Mexico of Cárdenas are added, the share of the ideological dictatorships becomes overwhelming. Few incidents involving conventional states even begin to match these atrocities—the million killed in the Indian partition massacres of 1947 is the single exception.

Acting almost alone, the ideological dictators transformed the century into an abattoir. Mass murder attained the level of policy. Ideological tyranny became the typical form of government, and democide the typical expression of that form.

The ideological tyrants may have vanished, but their influence remains. The dictators set the standard for governance in the twentieth century. They became what we would call "change agents," a transformative force acting above and beyond their own desires or intentions. The transformation they wrought was convoluted and obscure, in some ways a return to medievalism, in others a leap into an unheralded future. In Churchill's words, "a new dark age made more sinister, and perhaps more protracted, by the lights of perverted science."

Ideology was tyranny's poisoned gift to modern civilization. Its influence has spread throughout Africa, Asia, and Latin America. Without exception, the results in nations as varied as Argentina, Uganda, the Congo, Rwanda, Burundi, Mozambique, Syria, Iraq, Afghanistan, Burma, and Venezuela have been catastrophic.

But fringe states were not the only nations to fall for ideological enchantment. Not even the democracies remained untouched. Not even the United States proved immune.

LIBERALISM MEETS IDEOLOGY

Ideology entered American politics with the New Deal. The Great Depression was an event all but unique in history. There have been deeper depressions, and depressions that lasted longer (such as the century-and-a-half medieval depression following the Black Death), but none had greater impact or caused more damage. The Great Depression was an economic crisis with the effects of a natural disaster.

The stock market crash triggered a slide of an intensity unseen before or since.* Between 1929 and 1933, the U.S. GNP was nearly halved, dropping from $103,828,000,000 to $55,760,000,000. Exports fell by more than 60 percent. Thirteen million people, a quarter of the labor force, were thrown out of work.

Governmental response on the part of both Herbert Hoover and Franklin D. Roosevelt was a tangle of traditional methods of amelioration, flat-out error, and ideology, derived in equal part from fascist and communist models.

Roosevelt himself was no ideologue but a practical politician willing to accept solutions no matter where on the spectrum they originated. But he surrounded himself with ideologues, from the sentimental leftist Eleanor down to Rexford G. Tugwell and Adolf Berle, core members of his Brain Trust responsible for formulating economic policy.

Tugwell and Berle were open admirers of the U.S.S.R. and Fascist Italy. "It's the cleanest . . . most efficiently operating piece

---

*Including September 2008. The Dow lost 89 percent of its value between 1929 and 1932. The current recession hasn't even approached this number.

of social machinery I've ever seen," Tugwell said of Mussolini's fascist utopia. "It makes me envious." This attitude was fully reflected in the Brain Trust's policy objectives. The New Deal involved a wholesale adaptation of European ideology, emphasizing centralization, government control, and collectivization.

The keystone of the New Deal program—and the first imposition of ideology on American society—was the National Recovery Administration, the NRA. An attempt to rationalize the national economy from the largest corporations to the smallest corner stores, the NRA was based on corporatism, the economic system of Mussolini's Italy. The NRA revealed its fascist roots in more ways than one. It was run by a generalissimo (Hugh Johnson, a businessman and ex-army officer); it featured a prominent propaganda component (including the famous "blue eagle"); and it boasted a secret police force to root out violators.*

It was also a disaster. Participating companies used NRA regulations to ruin competition through price-fixing, product standardization, and exclusion of outsiders, effectively cartelizing their industries. In 1934 an investigating committee chaired by Clarence Darrow condemned the NRA as "monopolistic, irresponsible, grotesque," and other choice adjectives. Finally, on May 27, 1935, the Supreme Court stepped in, deciding in *Schechter Poultry Corp. v. United States* that the NRA was an unconstitutional "attempted delegation of legislative power" by Congress to the president.

Another Tugwell brainstorm, the Agricultural Adjustment Administration (AAA), attempted to do for farmers what the NRA had done for business. The AAA adapted a Soviet-inspired policy of confiscation, destroying excess production in order to drive up prices.

---

*In New Jersey, for instance, a tailor spent time in jail for underpricing an ironing job by five cents. (A judge set him free and gave him a pair of pants to press.)

For two years, in a country where hunger was a serious problem and starvation an actual possibility, the federal government at
a cost of over $700 million plowed under fields of grain, slaugh-
tered and condemned over 6 million pigs, and burned the entire
Southern cotton crop, sending masses of destitute blacks fleeing
north in search of simple survival.

The Supreme Court shut down the AAA on much the same
grounds as the NRA. The administration's "farm support"
program became a major symbol of New Deal failures. (Some
elements remain in effect a lifetime later—farmers and agribusi-
nesses are annually paid large amounts for not planting crops.)

So it went. New Deal programs materialized based on one alien
methodology after another. Population resettlement by the Resettlement Administration (RA), which planned to send urban
unemployed to rural areas. (The program was canceled before
the worst possibilities came to pass.) Mobilization of labor in the
Civilian Conservation Corps (CCC), the Works Progress Administration (WPA), the Public Works Administration (PWA), and
so on through the alphabet. Even a full-bore government propaganda program in "Federal One," the WPA's arts section, which
relentlessly pushed the glories of the New Deal through theater,
art, radio, and music.

It all failed in the end. All the frenetic activity and titanic expense accomplished nothing. Through 1935 and '36, the economy seemed to be healing. Factories and businesses reopened, the
banking system stabilized, the GNP, though far below its 1929
peak, began to inch up.

Then FDR, evidently channeling Herbert Hoover, decided to
raise taxes. Almost instantly the jury-rigged "recovery" collapsed.
Unemployment shot to 7 million by autumn of 1937. In October
the markets once again crashed. By January 1938, unemployment topped 11.8 million, nearly half a million more than when

Roosevelt was sworn in. FDR sat before his cabinet pleading. "Is there no one who can tell me what to do?"

No one could tell him anything. No one could tell him because every last one of them, Brain Truster, fellow traveler, and proto-fascist, had been wrong from the start. The New Deal had been based on a mirage: none of the ideological states had dealt with the Depression in the way that the New Dealers believed.

In Germany, Finance Minister Hjalmar H. G. Schacht (the "H. G.," oddly enough, stood for "Horace Greeley") kept interest rates low and financed enormous public-works programs (including the renowned autobahns) through deficit spending, a policy that today would be called "Keynesian." Unemployment plunged faster in Germany than in any other industrialized country. (Japan's finance minister, Takahashi Korekiyo, utilized similar means, pulling the country out of its slump by 1932.)

Fascist Italy gained nothing from Mussolini's corporatism. During the thirties, Italian industrial production increased only 15 percent, while real wages fell 20 percent. Per capita private consumption remained below the 1929 level straight into WW II. Italy entered the war as an economic basket case, a fact that soon became apparent.

The Soviet answer to economic problems was simple: slave labor. Almost all construction, mining, logging, and much industrial work were performed by the millions arrested by Stalin's secret police. During the Great Purge (1937–39) close to 10 percent of the Russian populace went into the Gulag. Many never returned. The cost of Soviet industrialization may have been as high as 20 million lives.

So Nazi Germany prevailed through conventional economic methods. Fascist Italy didn't prevail at all. The U.S.S.R. did so astride a bottomless pile of corpses. The New Dealers short-circuited the recovery, sabotaged the economy, and destroyed liberal political culture in pursuit of models that didn't exist.

THE COST OF IDEOLOGY

In imitating the practice of the ideological states, liberals hollowed out their own political doctrine. Liberalism's basic principles—individual freedom, freedom of trade, and rule of law—were undermined or cast aside. No point in American history witnessed greater efforts at regimentation. The combination of communist-derived "mobilization" and fascist corporatism left no room for individualism. Under the NRA and AAA, the country suffered the largest-scale effort at economic centralization ever attempted in the West. If not for the Supreme Court's intervention, the United States would either have undergone complete economic chaos like that which struck Germany in the early 1920s, or permanent stagnation on the Soviet model. As for law, New Deal legislation was not adequately debated by Congress, was passed under duress, and was applied by bureaucrats unchallengeable through customary means.

The remaining shell of liberalism filled up with elements originating with the European ideologies. Not the camps or mass executions—the New Dealers were sincere in hoping to bring about good and humane results, a terrible thought in itself—but the attitudes and practices that made those crimes possible. Roosevelt and his followers truly believed they could mine the most vicious systems in the human record without evil consequences.

Liberalism was transformed into a mirror-image of itself. Respect for law became lawlessness, a conviction that rules did not apply to those who made them. Faith in progress became grandiosity, as plans and visions grew ever more baroque. Belief in principle became obsession with policy, in the conviction that events could be controlled by clever planning. Above all, adherence to democracy, to equality before the law, was contorted into a delusion that the people of America were no longer fellow citizens but only units, raw materials awaiting use by the planners and centralizers.

Liberalism, the doctrine of the humane, the moral, and the enlightened, had at last metamorphosed into an ideology. America's liberals had eaten of the fruit of the tree, and nothing would ever be the same again.

THE NEW LIBERALISM MATURES

While the New Deal planted the seed, World War II germinated it.

Among other things, the war clearly demonstrated that nothing at all was wrong with the American economy. WWII was largely a conflict of industrial production. America's titanic industrial strength, its status as the "arsenal of democracy," was a key factor in the defeat of fascism, assuring that the war was won in relatively short order, with the least number of casualties, and without unduly straining Allied economies and societies.

Even prior to direct involvement, the U.S. was a major source of aircraft, weapons, and resources for nations across Europe. As the Nazi threat became apparent following the failure of Munich's "peace in our time," tariff barriers fell worldwide, enabling the U.S. to work its way out of the slump in the classic manner. But for the poor decisions of the Hoover and Roosevelt administrations, the same result could have been obtained during the early 1930s.

But the legions of New Deal bureaucrats believed otherwise. They lived by an intricate myth in which failure had been banished. Rather, FDR and his stalwart reformers had spent the decade battling entrenched reactionary interests—first poor Hoover, then corrupt businessmen, at last a vicious and senile Supreme Court—on behalf of a helpless American proletariat. This *Grapes of Wrath* version of events, elaborated by left-wing academics and historians, remained the accepted narrative of the Depression for the next fifty years.

The myth first took root among the young bureaucrats thronging the war agencies, a fractal-geometry jumble of interlocking, opaquely titled departments that made the New Deal bureaucracy look straightforward by comparison. Having grown up during the Depression, this second generation viewed FDR as a semidivine figure, and his policies as something on the order of the Tablets of the Law. Their ranks included such figures as Alan Cranston, Arthur Schlesinger, Jr., and James Reston in the Office of War Information, John Kenneth Galbraith and Robert L. Heilbroner in the Office of Price Administration, and Eugene V. Rostow in the Lend Lease organization.

The war bureaucrats needed no introduction to the new liberalism—the ideological variety was the only kind they knew. They took its tenets of collectivism, centralization, and government control as givens. They in no way acknowledged that the New Deal had failed, nor did it matter. As they saw it, the validity of the new liberalism was being proven through its success in war. It wasn't the GIs, sailors, and airmen, or even Rosie the Riveter in the nation's defense factories who were forging the way to victory. It was the bureaucrats behind desks in Washington, sending out memos in triplicate.

WWII became the touchstone for postwar government programs, encompassed in the formula, "If we could win World War II, why can't we do X"—put your social, economic, or political problem here. (The modern version is, "If we could put a man on the moon, why can't we—?") This overlooks the fact that war is unique in human affairs. War is a simple proposition. The tribe gathers as many rocks and sharp sticks as possible and carries them to a place where they can be thrown at the enemy. The process remains the same when tribes become nations and empires, and rocks and sticks become artillery shells, missiles, and

A-bombs. Everyone knows their role, and everyone (excepting the odd traitor or types like Seward Avery, the Montgomery Ward chairman famously carried out of his office during WWII for defying government dictates) fulfills it without complaint.

Compare this to the complexity of the simplest large-scale peacetime project—say, constructing a dam or an apartment development. The interests that have to be reconciled, the tempers soothed, the grievances addressed. Such processes cannot be carried out through duress. That's the reason why politics is an art rather than a science and why we have creatures known as "lawyers." War and peace are separate realms of human activity, with different requirements. The new liberals failed to make this distinction, and as a result, operated in a continual crisis mode throughout the postwar period, with a parade of "wars" against poverty, drugs, and inflation.

But while the war further distorted liberalism, it also acted to preserve it. The New Deal would have been no more than another anomalous historical period, like Reconstruction or the Progressive era, if it wasn't for the reprieve the war offered. It was WWII that set the attitudes and concepts of the New Deal in concrete, endowed it with a new horde of followers, and provided it with a legend of success. The war institutionalized the new liberalism, assuring its survival into the postwar period.

It takes roughly a generation for a new paradigm to sweep out the old. The task of the new-model liberals during the early postwar era was to maintain the gains already established, preserve doctrinal tenets, and expand liberal influence. In the late forties, ideological liberalism entered into a missionary phase.

This missionary work took the form (though no liberal would have admitted it) of selling the new ideology, persuading the public that not only was the ideological brand a legitimate descendant of classical liberalism but the same thing, that the new form was, if anything, the culmination of liberal development.

The U.S. was going through large-scale social changes, still not well understood. (Attempts to characterize the 1950s as the "decade of conformity" or the "decade of fear" are simplistic at best.) A number of profound shifts, delayed by the Depression and the war and compressed into a handful of years, was occurring in sexual mores, minority rights, and the status of various elites. Having shed many traditions, the American public needed a new intellectual framework. In the absence of competition, ideological liberalism was the only game in town.

Postwar liberalism became the consensus view of the educated urbanite. It was during this period that the contemporary conception of liberalism was established—just, virtuous, incorruptible, infinitely superior to all other doctrines. The ideology of all right-thinking, civilized, and sane (one of their favorite adjectives) Americans. So great was the gulf between the liberal and everyone else that it resembled—as seen by liberals—that between the Eloi and the Morlocks in *The Time Machine*, with the Morlocks played by an assortment of anticommunists, Southerners, Catholics, Evangelicals, and career military officers.

The same period saw the launching of a number of large-scale social programs based on New Deal principles. Prominent among them were federal welfare, urban renewal, and the establishment of a national educational system.

Few today are aware that federal welfare began as a New Deal effort. Like many such programs, welfare was a limited attempt to address a particular challenge that metastasized into something even more destructive than the original problem. Welfare began with the Social Security Act of 1935 as Aid to Dependent Children (ADC). The program was flawed from the beginning, featuring as it did no restrictions, financial or otherwise. All comers were allowed to apply for assistance, and no one could be cut off for refusing to accept employment, failings that guaranteed program inflation. The level of federal reimbursement to the states rose from the original 33 percent until, with the advent of Medicare in 1965, reimbursement under some circumstances reached 100 percent.

By the early 1960s, the program was rife with corruption on all levels, ranging from "welfare queens" with multiple accounts to state padding of welfare rolls. Even worse was the effect on communities, particularly minority communities. The black illegitimate birthrate, a steady 20 percent for decades, rose from 22 to 28 percent during the 1950s, in clear response to rising benefits. It eventually shot up to over 70 percent, a rate unparalleled in modern history. Accompanying ballooning illegitimacy were related social problems arising from the absence of responsible adult males: juvenile crime, drug use, and the abandonment of education and employment.

Confronted with failure, liberals simply shifted the grounds of debate. Welfare was no longer a matter of attacking poverty. It was transformed into a means of obtaining "social justice." Welfare checks became "transfer payments," intended to level income inequalities. Welfare was no longer charity, it was an "entitlement," a right somehow overlooked when the Constitution was being written, but a right all the same. The reality of deteriorating neighborhoods, crippled families, and blighted lives was lost amid the spiraling abstractions of policy debate.

Similarly, urban renewal, a nationwide program to "revitalize American cities," ended up doing more damage to the physical structure of the United States than even the most ferocious storms and earthquakes, while educational reform, designed to ensure that all American children were educated to the same high standard, resulted in the dumbing down of generations of students while turning the school system into an adjunct of the teachers' unions.

Failures of such magnitude as to wreck cities, destroy the aspirations of entire social classes, and dismantle public education would raise second thoughts in a stone. But America's liberals didn't even slow down. The see-no-evil response to the New Deal's failures had become a key element of the liberal mentality. American liberalism had attained a state of ideological blindness, a not at all uncommon condition. (Solzhenitsyn wrote of faithful Bolsheviks in the Gulag who moaned, "If only Comrade Stalin knew!") Like medieval Christianity or modern Islam, ideologies are total systems requiring total commitment. Failures, which may call basic premises into question, cannot be acknowledged for fear of threatening the entire structure of belief. Instead they are either ignored, dismissed as unimportant, or blamed on someone else. Cognitive dissonance is to some extent a necessary feature of the ideological mentality.

No objective observer could fail to see liberalism's fiascoes for what they were, fail to recognize the cause, or fail to be chilled to the bone by how much worse it could become if such efforts were expanded into other areas of national life.

As the 1950s passed into history, ideological liberalism was coming into its kingdom. The old Democratic Party warhorses were dying off. Liberals controlled the party organization, including its powerful urban machines and patronage systems, taken over without any evident moral qualms. Congress was effectively theirs. They had controlled the bureaucracy since the 1930s. The Supreme Court had fallen with the appointment of Chief Justice Earl Warren, a disturbing example of the phenomenon of the liberal Republican (his role in WWII's Stalinesque Nisei relocation should have barred him from serving in any public capacity whatsoever). John F. Kennedy, the new Democratic president, was the last of the old liberal presidents and the first of the new, mixing concerns such as anticommunism with more ideological elements. (His successor, Lyndon B. Johnson, with his faux–New Deal "Great Society," was the first complete presidential product of New Deal politics.) The new liberalism's second generation—

Schlesinger and Galbraith, Robert S. McNamara and John T. McNaughton, the Bundy brothers, Dean Rusk, and many others—would be taking positions at the very apex of government.

Not a single element of society would be overlooked under the new dispensation: criminal justice, health care, education, race relations, the economy. All would come under close examination, all would be reworked, all would be transformed. The new liberalism would rid the nation of crime, free the insane, rescue abused children, refine the nature of birth and death, even heal the planet itself. The old dreams of reason had returned, in all their unmatched glory.

Their goal was utopia. They would never have admitted it, these logical, placid products of the most intense specialist educations. Utopia was not a concept they recognized, a word they cared to use. But the impulse was undeniable. It was the impulse of Plato and Thomas More, of Tommaso Campanella and Edward Bellamy. With one enormous difference: the new liberals believed they could bring it to life. They could almost see it, in all its order and harmony, only a short stretch of days ahead, nearly close enough to touch.

What they could not see was the simple truth that utopias are deadly.

Half a world away, Mao Tse-Tung had decided to surpass the West economically in one bold move—the Great Leap Forward. Chinese agriculture was collectivized in 1957 with the establishment of twenty-six thousand agricultural communes. In 1958, the peasants were directed to discard all customary farm practices in a quest for higher yields. Spacing between plants was cut to zero. Three, four, and even more seeds were planted in the same hole. Peasants were encouraged to eat as much as they pleased, in the certainty that more was coming.

But the next harvest ushered in catastrophe. Across the country, crops failed almost without exception. The 1959 harvest was only 170 million tons, nowhere near enough to feed the country. In 1960 it dropped to 144 million tons. Almost all reserves had been wasted. Throughout the vast reaches of China, the nation began dying.

Rationing was introduced, but more on the order of a wish than anything firmer. In many areas open warfare broke out as the army and the Communist Party seized whatever food remained. In other areas cannibalism, China's ancient curse, appeared in all its horror.

In as chilling an example of ideological blindness as exists in the historical record, the Great Leap Forward continued for another two years, until a group of moderates under Deng Xiao Ping forced its cancellation. (They paid a high price for that action during the Great Cultural Revolution.)

The bill for this exploit was on the order of 45 million lives. A number that would have emptied the U.S. Northeast starved to death in the worst famine in history. A famine triggered by human meddling.

The American liberal elite probably heard nothing of the Great Leap Forward—little news came out of China in the 1950s. They would not have recognized themselves in its distorting mirror, and would have rejected any suggestion that their own policies resembled those of the Chinese Politburo.

But both systems had origins in the reductionist rationalism of the nineteenth century. They shared the same tools of bureaucracy and centralization. Their leaders possessed the same presumption, the same arrogance, the same view of human beings as raw materials.

All that differed was the level of application. The Chinese, like the Germans and Soviets, were more radical and more unwavering, so disaster was both quicker and more thorough.

Similar processes will give similar results. But far from acknowledging the possibility of failure, American liberals pushed on as if no such thing existed. Operating at ever higher levels of risk while ignoring the consequences, oblivious to the fact that programs could not only fail but fail catastrophically, fail in ways that would make the New Deal seem trivial. Fail in ways that killed.

For decades the United States had avoided the new form of political murder—democide, in which governments act as executioner and gravedigger for the people. The great democidal frenzies—in Spain, the U.S.S.R., China, and countless other nations—had no impact on this country. That wave of blood had broken against the rock of American democracy. In the most murderous of all epochs, in the midst of the Age of Massacre, the United States abided above it all.

But as the mid-century faded into the past, that immunity was about to end. Thanks to pride, and blindness, and good intentions of the worst sort, democide was coming to America.

Solon being asked, namely, what city was best to live in, "That city,"
he replied, "in which those who are not wronged, no less than those
who are wronged, exert themselves to punish the wrongdoers."
—PLUTARCH, "SOLON," PARALLEL LIVES

2

AMERICAN NOIR

The New Liberalism Takes On Crime

The great crime wave of the late-twentieth century is a disaster that did not have to happen.

For three decades, this nation's criminal element, with a hard core of perhaps only a few hundred thousand, held the country hostage. Crime rates skyrocketed, increasing several hundred percent across the board. Criminals ran law-abiding citizens off their own streets, gained effective control of many neighborhoods, and violated the peace of entire cities. The number of victims is incalculable, the amount of damage—financial, social, and personal—beyond reckoning.

This chain of events was historically unprecedented. In the past, criminals had gained ascendancy in limited areas—San Francisco in the early 1850s, New York City's Five Points in the mid-nineteenth century, and Cicero, Illinois, in the 1920s—for short periods before the forces of the status quo acted to either isolate them or shut them down. As a frontier culture, Americans knew how to handle crime. Justice was swift, punishment was certain, and if formal law enforcement faltered, the citizenry was prepared to act.

Each of those elements failed during the great crime explosion. The criminal justice system broke down completely. The police were consistently undermined. The citizenry were actively restrained and threatened with legal sanctions if they made the most basic effort to defend themselves or their property.

The long nightmare ended through a return to traditional means of enforcement, often reinstated under new names and through political subterfuge. It left behind a society utterly changed, with many of its basic assumptions damaged; a society less trusting, less open, and less free.

How could this have happened? Those who lived through it, and are aware of it as a discrete historical event—and many are not, viewing it as a bad period endured and best forgotten—often consider it to be some kind of inexplicable spasm caused by forces beyond human comprehension. Historians tend to shy away from it, treating it as another strange product of that strange decade, the 1960s. Criminologists and sociologists have their standard run of recomplicated explanations, reflecting more the fashions of the moment than any style of objective reasoning.

But the crime explosion didn't just happen. Like urban renewal and welfare, it was the result of policy, a deliberate attempt to remake the criminal justice system in the image of an ideal. What, precisely, that ideal may have been remains unclear. Were American liberals aiming at a perfectly just society? A society without crime? Some sort of new relationship between criminals and the law-abiding majority? It's impossible to say. While the goals of urban renewal and welfare reform were straightforward—to remake the urban centers and eliminate poverty—the criminal justice effort was vagueness itself. No clear picture ever emerged from the journal articles, papers, and speeches of the academics, lawyers, jurors, and politicians involved, and no one has been much inclined to revisit the question. All that is certain is that they had no idea of what the actual consequences would be, and no intention of doing the damage they did.

CRIME CONTROL

Criminal justice was in no crisis state in the 1950s. Crime was handled with techniques proven effective for decades under the rubric of "crime control," a term that speaks clearly for itself. The system had failings, as all systems do. These were identified by government crime commissions as early as the 1920s: widespread brutality by police forces, low-level corruption, racism, and a growing alienation between police and the public. Progress had been made in overcoming these flaws (except the last) thanks in large part to growing professionalism within law enforcement.

As with urban decay and poverty, crime was to be conquered using the tools of the new liberalism: centralization, bureaucracy, and social engineering. Plans to reform the system were vast and sweeping. They were also, not to put too fine a point on it, more than a little strange. American liberals planned to rectify crime by decriminalizing criminals.

Rehabilitation of criminals had been attempted previously through the Pennsylvania and Auburn systems of the 1820s and later during the Progressive era, without much in the way of results. It was revived in the twentieth century through the efforts of the pioneering Chicago School of Sociology. Beginning in the 1920s, Chicago School criminologists such as Clifford R. Shaw, Henry D. McKay, and Frederic Thrasher spent years and sometimes decades studying crime in Chicago neighborhoods. Their conclusions were that crime was caused by a breakdown of the social network, that the community rather than law enforcement was the most effective method of regulating crime, that incarceration was unsound, and that rehabilitation of criminals should be made paramount.

American psychiatrists, prominent among them Karl A. Menninger, concurred. Criminal behavior, according to Menninger, was a form of mental illness best handled by treatment. He dismissed punishment as no more than a form of revenge: "The scientists, and penologists and sociologists I know, take it for granted that rehabilitation—not punishment, not vengeance in disguise—is the modern principle of control."

Both schools of thought promoted a denial of personal responsibility. Crime was a product of outside forces, beyond the control of the individual offender. As Konrad Lorenz, a Nobel laureate, world-respected expert on aggression, and diehard critic of the reformers, put it, "all men are born equal and . . . all moral defects of the criminal are attributable to defects in his environment and education." Society's role was not punishment, or even correction, but to make right the "root causes"—social, economic, and psychological—driving criminal behavior.

The rehabilitation thesis appealed to the educated public, who viewed criminals with a combination of sentimentality and romanticism. The two groups of major concern in light of crime were teenagers and blacks. Youth gangs had been a problem since the end of WWII, while thanks to the civil rights movement, blacks were receiving public attention for the first time since Reconstruction. In neither case was severity considered an option. The gangs were viewed as "just kids" who were "misunderstood." Outside of the South, blacks were victims of a strange, unvoiced notion that allowing black criminals to run loose would somehow make up for years of discrimination and neglect.

Romanticization originated with intellectuals who enjoyed posing as rebels. Chief among them was Norman Mailer, whose 1956 essay "The White Negro" speculated about the beneficial aspects of murdering shopkeepers. The Beats, the decade's premier nonconformists, boasted two murderers, Lucien Carr and William Burroughs, while Neal Cassady, immortalized as Dean

Moriarty by Jack Kerouac in *On the Road*, was a career criminal. A similar attitude was reflected in TV shows and films of the period, including *The Wild One*, *Twelve Angry Men*, *The Defiant Ones*, and *Compulsion*, which portrayed lawbreakers as sympathetic figures oppressed by a domineering society.*

Given such an atmosphere, spread of the rehabilitation thesis comes as no surprise. Already dominant in the criminal justice system through exposure in schools and journals, it went on to capture the sophisticated public, losing considerable intellectual content during the process. Where a criminologist might say that "crime has it roots in social disintegration, in which a community's controlling mechanisms lose their capability of enforcing compliance," the public heard, "It's all society's fault." Where the Chicago School found that "incarceration is often inferior to strict and carefully monitored community control," the public understood that "prisons don't change anything."

Sentencing was the first element affected. Crimes that might have drawn light sentences instead resulted in probation, while more severe offenses drew less time, often further cut by generous parole and "good behavior" policies. It was in no way unusual for punishment to be set aside completely in favor of "treatment." In one notorious case, an underage murderer was hospitalized and then released as "cured." He went on to kill three other people, each time being subject to further "treatment," before it occurred to anyone to lock him up for good.†

---

*Public idolization of charismatic criminals was also commonplace. Caryl Chessman, a serial rapist and sociopath sentenced to death in 1948, wrote a bestseller, *Cell 2455, Death Row*, persuading large numbers of people to buy his claims of innocence. Chessman went to the gas chamber on May 2, 1960, but not before setting the pattern for Leonard Peltier, Jack Henry Abbott, and Mumia Abu-Jamal. Even William F. Buckley, Jr., was drawn in by one such figure, the killer Edgar H. Smith.

†This case was recounted by Frederick Hacker in 1960, ironically in a lecture to the Menninger Foundation.

• •

Nevertheless, sentencing guidelines, state parole policies, and federal interference with local criminal justice establishments soon nationalized these practices. Slowly but steadily, the prison population began to fall. For reasons that remain unknown, crime also fell marginally during the late 1950s and early sixties, convincing reformers that they were on the right track.

At that point, the Supreme Court stepped in.

MAPP V. OHIO

Dorlee Mapp was a single black mother who ran a boardinghouse in Cleveland. On May 23, 1957, the police appeared at her door on suspicion that she was involved in an attempt to assassinate Donald King, a man active in the local numbers rackets. She denied them entry on the advice of her attorney. A few hours later they returned, bursting in as Mrs. Mapp was descending the stairs. Flashing a sheet they claimed was a search warrant, the police brutalized Mrs. Mapp, then went on to ransack the premises without permission. In the basement they found what at the time was considered "obscene material" (probably pretty tame compared to current newsstand smut). Mrs. Mapp was arrested, tried, and found guilty of possessing pornography.

That's the story as told in law and criminal justice classes. A more perfect reflection of 1950s liberal attitudes, featuring racial discrimination, police misbehavior and brutality, and a clear miscarriage of justice, would be difficult to find.

Or to top for inaccuracy. To start with, "Donald" King is actually Don King of the exploding hair and the army of champion boxers. Dorlee Mapp herself was not unacquainted with the Cleveland numbers game. After King's house was bombed (they play for keeps in Cleveland), she fell under suspicion as the girlfriend of Virgil Ogiltree, the suspected bomber. Spotting Ogiltree's car in front of Mapp's boardinghouse, the police failed to gain entry. After being reinforced, they burst inside, waving the "search warrant." Dorlee Mapp snatched it away and attempted to hide it ("in her bosom," as the Court discreetly put it), triggering a struggle with the cops. Subduing Mapp, the police went on to bag Ogiltree and discover the dirty books.

This little tussle between a female numbers racketeer and inept Cleveland cops (the "search warrant" disappeared, and has long been dismissed as bogus. Why, with the evidence they had, couldn't the cops have obtained a real one?) might never have reached the Supreme Court but for the stubbornness of Dorlee Mapp, who pushed it through several appeals. *Mapp v. Ohio* would never have made it into the textbooks without transparent collusion between the Warren Court and the American Civil Liberties Union.

Much has been said in liberal circles about the fact that Chief Justice Earl Warren was a Republican, nominated by Dwight D. Eisenhower (who later regretted doing so), as if there's no such animal as a liberal Republican (in current terminology, a "Republican in name only," or RINO) or that the two episodes closely associated with Warren's name—the WWII Nisei relocations and the Warren Court—failed to reveal a taste for rampant, untrammeled power.

But in the *Mapp* case, the responsible party was Supreme Court Justice Tom Clark. Although the appeal turned on questions of obscenity, Clark was interested in opening up the case. Encountering Justices William Brennan and Hugo Black in an elevator, he proposed that they use *Mapp* as an opportunity to extend the exclusionary rule, a federal law demarking the grounds on which evidence could be presented in a court of law.

Mapp v. Ohio was not high-grade lawmaking. Arguments from both sides were substandard (that of Ohio State Attorney

Gertrude Bauer Mahon is considered a legendary example of legal incompetence), confusing the issues and threatening to forestall Clark's dramatic move. But then ACLU attorney Bernard Berkman was granted leave to speak—a first before the Supreme Court—giving Clark the precise grounds he required to expand the exclusionary rule to cover the states. The June 1961 decision freed Dorlee Mapp and plunged the country into the "procedural revolution."

The exclusionary rule became a major tool of defense attorneys in criminal cases. Attempts have been made to bar evidence on the grounds that paper clips rather than staples were used on search warrants, that Wite-Out was used and then written over, and that items discovered varied slightly from what was listed on the warrants. Many of these ploys were successful. Possibly no other single judicial decision has been responsible for freeing more criminals.

REFORM KICKS IN

But *Mapp* was only the first step. Over the next five years, the Court produced decisions any one of which would have caused a national earthquake. All together, they shook American law enforcement to its foundations. *Gideon v. Wainwright* (1962) guaranteed legal representation to defendants in criminal cases. *Escobedo v. Illinois* (1964) guaranteed an arrestee meaningful contact with his legal counsel, and *Miranda v. Arizona* (1966) established that suspects must be notified of the right to remain silent and of their right to an attorney. (The ACLU played a large role in these decisions, as they had in *Mapp*.)

They were all squalid little cases, of no importance beyond the legal purpose for which they served. Clarence Earl Gideon was a petty thief. Danny Escobedo had shot his brother-in-law. Ernesto Miranda was a rapist and kidnapper.*

Some of the decisions—*Gideon*, for instance—were commendable, even long overdue. But carried out all at once, without preparation, without guidance, without serious forethought, the procedural revolution acted as dynamite to the criminal justice establishment. The immediate effect of the decisions was a confused court system, demoralized police forces, and an angered and fearful public. For the first time since the New Deal, the Supreme Court was exposed to severe criticism, with "Impeach Earl Warren" becoming a slogan of the day.

The Supreme Court had put itself in the position of a referee overseeing the day to day operations of the police and the lower courts, a role for which it had neither qualifications nor constitutional sanction. From that point on, it was a rare session that failed to produce a decision tinkering with a previous decision. The results were often trivial and occasionally ludicrous, exposing the Court and the criminal justice system as a whole to ridicule and contempt. (The nadir was perhaps reached with 1987's *Arizona v. Hicks*, in which a thief was freed because a detective moved a piece of expensive stereo gear to check the serial number—without a search warrant. That decision was authored by the usually sensible Antonin Scalia.)

A majority of the public viewed the "procedural revolution" as amounting to a get-out-of-jail-free card, and the record suggests they were right. Estimates of cases lost due to the *Miranda* ruling

---

*The defendants' fates were uniformly squalid as well. Dorlee Mapp—whom one legal scholar praised as "the Rosa Parks of the Fourth Amendment"—served a nine-year term for heroin possession. Danny Escobedo became a drifter and was arrested for parole violations and involvement in a stabbing in 2001. He remains in custody. Ernesto Miranda was murdered in a barroom brawl in 1976. His attacker claimed his Miranda rights, remained silent, and went free.

alone range from 10 to 38 percent. A 1996 study by Paul G. Cassell and Bret S. Hayman found that crime clearance rates, roughly 60 percent prior to 1965, dropped a full 9 percent in the three years following *Miranda*. Their estimate of 1995 violent crimes unsolved due to *Miranda* stand between 56,000 and 136,000.

The Supreme Court's ill-considered program put the seal on the developments of the previous decade. America's criminals had the sympathy of the educated classes. They were serving extremely light sentences—in some cases, none at all. Their "control" consisted of a system of rehabilitation that, where it actually existed, was essentially in the business of boosting criminal self-esteem. The courts were weary and overworked, the police disgusted and cynical. All this was occurring simultaneously with the racial climate going south, the country cycling into one of its periodic stages of antiauthoritarian defiance, and the arrival of the first wave of the male Boomers, a large cohort of young men passing through their teens, the age group most prone to involvement in criminal activity. It wasn't at all difficult—unless you were a criminologist—to grasp where events were headed.

AND CRIME KICKS BACK

But before all hell broke loose, there occurred one of those historical incidents that means something, as the historian John Lukacs has suggested, because we believe it does. In March 1964, a young Queens woman named Kitty Genovese was stalked and tortured to death on the very steps of her apartment building. Her ordeal lasted over half an hour, her assailant actually leaving at one point before returning to finish the job. As she wept and screamed for help, her neighbors—a later count put the number at thirty-eight—listened and did nothing. Some watched through their windows, as if at a television drama. At one point, a man shouted for the killer to desist. No one called the police until it was nearly over. The killer, Winston Moseley, walked off into the darkness, and would never have been found if he hadn't been picked up on an unrelated burglary charge several days later.*

Though very young at the time, I recall clearly that the incident was discussed for days. No one knew what to make of it, but everyone seemed to realize that something fateful and unprecedented had happened, that the cold wind of chaos was blowing over our heads, that the country was moving deep into unknown territory.

In retrospect, 1964 looms as the critical year, the dividing line between the old world and the new. Violent crimes increased nationwide by nearly fifty thousand. Murders, which had actually dropped since 1960, jumped from 8,640 in 1963 to 9,360 the next year. Rapes shot even higher, from 17,650 to 21,420. Robberies increased from 116,470 to 130,390, while assaults jumped from 174,210 to 203,050, an astonishing 17 percent increase. (It needs to be kept in mind that these statistics, drawn from the FBI's Uniform Crime Reports, have been demonstrated to seriously underestimate crime levels. Victimization studies consistently show higher levels of criminal activity.)

Senator Barry Goldwater, in his ill-starred presidential campaign of that summer and fall, was the first candidate to treat crime as a political issue. Goldwater's warnings were dismissed as the ravings of a right-wing Neanderthal. The country's liberals knew better.

Authorities claimed that crime in fact hadn't risen at all, that the apparent jump was explained by improved record-keeping. This explanation works only if you believe that the public checks statistics to ascertain whether their neighborhoods have actually

---

*Moseley was sentenced to death but had his sentence reduced to life imprisonment by a New York court in 1967. A few years later he escaped and took a number of hostages, one of whom he raped. He remains imprisoned today.

grown dangerous. A concurrent claim was that fear of crime was a cover for white racism, a contention that overlooked the fact that the bulk of criminal activity was occurring in black neighborhoods. Such theories became something of a scholarly industry in ensuing years. They included the demographic thesis—that the crime explosion was a by-product of the teenage Boomer cohort, even though crime began surging in 1964, four years late, and ebbed and flowed thereafter with no relation to youth numbers. (Crime scholar James Q. Wilson has charted variations between white and black youth crime, revealing that they change according to their own internal dynamic, with no reference to demography. "Detroit," wrote Wilson, "had about a hundred murders in 1960, but over five hundred in 1971, yet the number of young persons did not quintuple.") Another theory held that the increase was due to a new ease in obtaining illegal drugs. In other words, crime was increasing because crime was increasing.

Following his election in 1964, Lyndon B. Johnson responded to Goldwater's charges in time-honored fashion—by appointing a commission. It included people such as civil rights activist Whitney Young, Yale president Kingman Brewster, and former attorney general William P. Rogers, although the actual work was done by lawyers and academics under the guidance of James Vorenberg of Harvard Law School.

The commission's report, *The Challenge of Crime in a Free Society*, was heavily informed by systems analysis, with much emphasis on inputs and outputs, and illustrated by a rococo series of flow charts. It contained over two hundred recommendations, the most important calling for centralization of the criminal justice system and less incarceration in favor of "community programs."

The report set in concrete the liberal agenda on crime. Further centralization created a channel for bad ideas to spread nationwide. Emphasis on rehabilitation simply reinforced failure.

Johnson, who had started his political career under the New Deal (his "Great Society" was simply an expanded and turbocharged version) accepted the report's conclusions in toto, and the War on Crime joined the War on Poverty as part of his attempt to remake American society.

Shortly thereafter, the Law Enforcement Assistance Administration was established, with the mission of allocating "several hundred million dollars a year" to law enforcement agencies across the country in support of the commission's recommendations. As is true of all Great Society programs, it's next to impossible to trace how the money was actually spent. But it can be said with certainty that not a dime had any effect on the public safety. (According to news reports of the time, some funds went to purchase army-surplus armored personnel carriers, in preparation for threatened uprisings by black radicals or drug-crazed yippies.)

Increased funding hastened the deterioration of the criminal justice system by transforming it into a full-bore bureaucracy, with all the habits and practices of a bureaucracy. Paperwork became the major focus, process rather than results the goal. Plea-bargaining, already seriously abused, became the primary method of resolving cases—in some jurisdictions, virtually the sole method. In May 1978 in New York City, 87 percent of all criminals brought before the bench walked due to plea arrangements. That particular month was in no way exceptional. Experienced criminals learned to game the system, reducing light sentences even further. From the bureaucracy's viewpoint, the case was cleared no matter what the outcome.

Prison levels dropped throughout the decade, even as crime rates skyrocketed. The American prison population, both state and federal, peaked at 220,149 in 1961. It fell annually thereafter, bottoming out at 187,914 in 1968. Criminologists continued to argue that incarceration lacked any deterrent or educational effect. What rehabilitation advocates overlooked was the most straightforward effect of imprisonment: incapacitation. A man sitting in jail is manifestly not stealing a car or mugging a passerby. Incapacitation is the single major purpose of imprisonment, and as such unanswerable. Not surprisingly, it seldom came up in public debate.

Nor did the plight of the victims. It is truly disturbing how thoroughly crime victims were written out of the criminal justice equation by reform advocates. Karl Menninger, sympathetic when writing about criminals, was uncharacteristically dismissive where victims were concerned: "This childish outcry has an appeal for the unthinking. Of course no victim should be neglected. But the individual victim has no more right to be protected than those of us who may become victims." The only way the rehabilitation thesis could be sold was to rebrand the criminal as victim—victim of society, victim of circumstance, victim of his own psyche. As a victim, he had a claim on his fellow citizens that overwhelmed all others, even those of the people he had injured. The "real" victims became no more than counters in the game that criminal justice had become.

Romanticization of the criminal expanded with the revolutionary fever of the late 1960s. Law journal articles began to appear extolling criminals as a "revolutionary vanguard" acting as the "first line of defense for the Bill of Rights." A representative figure was Ramsey Clark, at that time serving as U.S. attorney general, who in later years became better known for his volunteer efforts in representing Saddam Hussein. "There are few better measures," said Clark, "of the concern a society has for its individual members and its own well being than the way it handles criminals." George Jackson, a lifer shot to death during an attempted escape from San Quentin prison in 1971, was one of many praised as revolutionary saints. How seriously this attitude distorted criminal justice during the period is anyone's guess.

• •

As the 1960s waned, a new penological concept was promoted—prisoner rights. The ACLU established a prisoner rights project in 1970, and in ensuing years numerous lawsuits, frivolous and otherwise, were filed with the intent of lightening the prison regime. Many were successful. (I have been unable to verify the story that one felon persuaded a federal judge to order a train to slow to a crawl when passing the prison so as not to disturb the prisoner's sleep, but the case of the lifer who successfully sued the prison administration for denying him kosher food is unquestionably true.)

DEEP MIDNIGHT

The decade ended with crime levels still mounting. Tension increased unbearably with the 1968 assassinations of Robert F. Kennedy and Martin Luther King, Jr. A year later Charlie Manson (himself a recently released convict) and his merry band of drug-addled cutthroats opened new horizons in mass murder. But even these crimes were eclipsed during the upcoming decade.

Murders surpassed 16,000 in 1970, going on to reach 20,710 in 1974. Rapes began the decade at 37,990 before establishing a new benchmark with 51,400 in 1973. Robberies exceeded assaults for the first time in 1970, 349,860 to 334,970. But assaults soon sprang ahead, leading 393,090 to 376,290 in 1973. By 1976, assaults exceeded a half-million annually, at 500,530. At the decade's end, the total of official violent crime victims each year reached 1,208,030. Over a half-percent of the American population was being victimized every year.

Faced with such numbers, the police began manipulating records. In 1983, Chicago mayor Jane Byrne revealed that her police force had been falsifying crime figures for twenty years or more, categorizing nearly half of all felony reports as "unfounded." Similar dodges were pulled in Baltimore and New York City, where crimes were deliberately knocked down a category or two—assaults being transformed into muggings and so on. Other police forces took more direct action, dumping bodies just outside their jurisdictional limits to cut down the murder rate. (The police, at least, knew they had something to cover up. The Supreme Court continued to act as if it existed in a vacuum, unaffected by what was occurring in the streets outside its chambers. In June 1972, the Court issued its decision in *Furman v. Georgia*, declaring the death penalty "cruel and unusual" and halting executions for over two years.)

Crime took on the aspect of a natural phenomenon, on the order of a hurricane or a plague, something beyond control or understanding. Pathetic little tricks became common among the public—"no radio" signs in car windows, the "mugger's five" carried separately to offer as a kind of fee to the neighborhood's reigning demons.

All of us who lived through that period have a story to tell. Many have more than one. Mine include the aged man strangled by a burglar in a first-floor apartment of my building (one of those incidents that was "lost"—it went unreported in newspapers and, so I was told, appeared in police records as a suicide), the young woman whom I comforted seconds after she had been raped at gunpoint, the college student shot in the face and left to die in his car six blocks from where I was living, for the mistake of stopping at a dope dealer's corner to ask for directions.

It was said of Josef Stalin's U.S.S.R. that no family failed to see a member vanish into the Gulag. Much the same can be said of America's great crime wave. It is easily possible that no American family exists that was not in some way victimized. According to Alice M. Kaminsky, author of *The Victim's Song*, who lost her son to violent thugs on a crowded New York subway platform, one in three families nationwide suffered a murder. The scale of lesser crimes can be readily imagined.

A WORLD OF VICTIMS

So it went for thirty years. One commentator characterized it as the country's worst disaster since the Civil War, and in truth, the crime explosion had many of the consequences of a war. Several large cities were destroyed by criminal activity, including Newark, Paterson, and Camden in New Jersey; East St. Louis, Missouri; Detroit, Michigan; and the South Bronx. Other cities were heavily damaged. American blacks, the intended beneficiaries of many criminal justice "reforms," suffered the worst. Most crime was black-on-black, turning inner-city neighborhoods into combat zones. What should have been an epoch of triumph—the overthrow of segregation, the victory of the civil rights movement, the redemption at last of promises a century old—was destroyed by dope, and violence, and gunshots on blighted streets.

The 1980s dawned to a marginal drop in crime rates. Authorities predicted a further decrease as the enormous Baby Boom cohort petered out. But it was an illusion. Fueled in part by the appearance of crack cocaine, crime roared back in 1986, matching and then exceeding the previous decade's levels. Murders climbed back to 20,613; rapes to 91,459; robberies to 542,775; and assaults to 834,322.

The public began showing signs that its endurance was breaking. A volunteer patrol group, the Guardian Angels, distinguished by their red berets, appeared in New York and then in other cities. Though as much a vehicle for the ambitions of their founder Curtis Sliwa as anything else, the popularity of the Angels was a clear sign of the depths of public frustration, and they often did decrease criminal activity in the areas they patrolled.

In late December 1984 Bernhard Goetz, an eccentric and reclusive electrical engineer, was surrounded by four young black men on a New York subway. Drawing a revolver, he shot all four. Many commentators praised Goetz as a heroic figure. But the liberal elite revealed that they had learned nothing in the previous two decades. Goetz, a slight and soft-spoken individual, was portrayed in the media as a vicious thug carrying out a vigilante action against "harmless" young men. (All four had been armed with sharpened screwdrivers.) The attackers' halos dimmed slightly when one of them, James Ramseur, was arrested shortly after his release from the hospital. In short order, all except the one man crippled by Goetz's gunfire were again enmeshed with the law. Nevertheless, Goetz was found guilty of criminal possession of a weapon and later lost a related civil suit.

The Goetz case was critical in revealing how close to the edge the country actually was. Several other vigilante-style actions occurred in the incident's wake, with fears expressed in the media and the criminal justice bureaucracy that they would spread even further, particularly in light of the knowledge that New York subway crime dropped precipitously following Goetz's action. But even as the Goetz incident played out, long-term solutions were already in motion.

BROKEN WINDOWS

In 1982, the *Atlantic Monthly* magazine published "Broken Windows," by James Q. Wilson and George L. Kelling, one of the most influential pieces ever written about crime. Kelling, a psychologist, had been consulting with a New Jersey police department concerning foot patrols, concluding that while patrols might not directly lower crime, they contributed to a sense of security among the public. Working with Wilson, a political scientist (the most influential work on crime in recent decades has been produced not by criminologists but by practitioners of unrelated disciplines such as political science and, particularly, economics), Kelling formulated a theory of public order illustrated by the metaphor of broken windows: if a shattered window is left unrepaired, soon all of a building's windows would be shattered. If repaired quickly, no further damage would occur. By extension, if petty offenses such as loitering, loudness, and public drunkenness were controlled, then more serious crimes would be discouraged.

Kelling got the opportunity to put the theory into practice in 1984, as a consultant to the New York Metropolitan Transit Authority, operator of the very subways in which Bernhard Goetz was forced to the wall. With the backing of MTA president David Gunn, Kelling targeted quality-of-life crimes such as graffiti and vandalism, slowly cleaning up a nearly derelict system. In 1990, William J. Bratton took over as chief of transit police, extending Kelling's reforms to such crimes as fare-jumping. The effect on subway security was palpable. The strategy was adapted under the name "zero tolerance" by Rudolph Giuliani when he became mayor in 1993. Giuliani first targeted the notorious "squeegee men," itinerants who gathered at points where cars were forced to pause, such as tunnel entrances, to extort money from drivers for "cleaning their windshields." The mayor scattered the squeegee men and then moved against such offenses as public intoxication and jaywalking. Within months, the "intractable" New York City crime rate, which had defied the efforts of mayors for three decades, began to fall.

"Broken Windows" became the most widely ordered reprint in the 130-year history of the *Atlantic*. Kelling and Wilson's ideas were adapted by cities across the country, with impressive results. While many critics questioned their actual effect on overall crime, Wilson countered that "when the police work to restore order and do so in a decent and lawful fashion, they have produced an important public good. We doubt it is necessary to justify that result." With public order maintained, further progress is possible. Without it, nothing is.

A revolution in sentencing was also taking place. The philosophy of "indeterminate sentencing," which left it up to parole boards to decide when to release a convict, resulted in most prisoners serving only a fraction of their sentences, some as little as 10 percent, very few as much as half. Most of the released convicts soon re-offended (the recidivism rate was 50 to 80 percent). Efforts at "rehabilitation" had no effect whatsoever. In 1984, Washington State enacted the first truth-in-sentencing law. Other states followed, and in 1994 the Violent Crime and Enforcement Act, which authorized federal funding for new prisons, restricted such aid only to states that had TIS laws in effect. By 1998, twenty-seven states and the District of Columbia had qualified, with another thirteen states utilizing TIS for certain offenses. Results were evident almost immediately. In states with TIS laws, arrests for murder dropped an average of 19 percent, rape and sexual assaults dropped 19 percent, and robbery 16 percent.

A second innovation (in truth a revival of an old practice under another name) involved habitual-offender laws, commonly known as "three-strikes laws." The state of Washington was again the pioneer with 1993's Initiative 593, which mandated a life sentence for a third felony. California followed the next year. (California's Proposition 184 was encouraged by the murder of twelve-year-old Polly Klaas, raped and strangled by a drifter who should never have been freed.) By 2004, twenty-six states and the federal government had adapted three-strikes laws.

No other recent innovation has caused more controversy, due to a handful of high-profile cases in which felons were "unfairly" given life sentences for "trivial" offenses. In one case, a California criminal earned life for stealing a slice of pizza. Most accounts failed to note that he had taken it at knifepoint from a twelve-year-old. In similar instances—the theft of golf clubs or a sackful of videos—critics overlooked the fact that career felons usually commit dozens of crimes for each one for which they're caught. Two Supreme Court decisions, *Lockyer v. Andrade* and *Ewing v.*

California, found that these laws did not violate Eighth Amendment restrictions against cruel and unusual punishment. And the record was hard to argue against: after California's law was passed, crime rates dropped 43 percent statewide over five years, a full 10 percent more than national figures.

From 1990 to 1997 prison population grew at a rate of 7 percent a year, from 689,577 to 1,100,850. Over 50 percent of that number were violent offenders. New prison space was required, and bond acts were passed across the country authorizing construction. The number of federal and state prisons grew from 592 in 1974 to 1,023 in 2000. Prisoners in custody continued to rise through the first years of the new millennium, peaking at 2,267,787 in 2004 before dropping to 2,193,798 in 2005. Such high numbers aroused considerable criticism, which often revealed serious misunderstanding of the mechanism at work. Fox Butterfield of the *New York Times* was one of several commentators who endured ridicule for his inability to grasp why more people were in prison at the same time that crime was falling.

The new policies were fought tooth and nail by the liberal establishment. In New York, Giuliani's effort was attacked by politicians, advocacy groups, and the media on behalf of squeegee men, graffiti artists, drug dealers, and the like. Liberals continued in their insistence that "root causes" must be solved before crime could be tackled. The crime wave, from this point of view, was deserved punishment for the primal sins of American society.

Little question remains concerning the effect these new (or revived) strategies had on criminal activity. Violent crime dropped across the board. By 2005, murders had fallen to 16,692, two-thirds of their 1990s peak; rapes had fallen to 93,934; robberies to 417,122; and assaults to 862,947. These numbers stood in sharp contradiction to expert predictions of a decade previously, foreseeing an overall leap in crime due to the appearance of "superpredators"—the remorseless offspring of Boomer criminals.

If the superpredators existed at all, they saw in the millennium from behind bars.

THE PRICE

The American crime explosion was a rare historical expression of one of the deepest of social nightmares: a society given over to the control of its worst members. The liberal elite had turned the country into a continent-wide laboratory in order to demonstrate the truth of some very simple propositions: that reason does not explain everything, that barbarism remains very close to the surface, that you do not meddle with the constituent elements of a society without paying a very high price.

But what was the overall price? How many victims of the criminal justice revolution were there?

It's impossible to know with certainty. Involving as it does an entire nation over several decades of time, the situation is far too complex to allow for an exact answer. The precise figure must remain beyond our grasp. But it is possible to obtain an approximation. Under the old system of crime control, murder rates were generally stable, remaining within a particular limited range relative to population growth. During the early 1960s, for instance, murders cycled between eight thousand and nine thousand annually. Only in 1964, with the full impact of the procedural revolution, did they begin to skyrocket. By taking 1960 as the base year, and indexing annual population growth, we can get an approximate figure for America's murder deficit—the number of murders that would not have occurred if the original criminal justice methods had been maintained—for the forty years following 1964.

That figure is 263,568.

Again, this is an approximation—too many factors are involved over too long a period for anything approaching real accuracy. But the total is unquestionably of that scale. And it is unquestionably a product of the liberal criminal justice reform program. No other explanation fits. The nightmare begins just as the "reforms" are initiated, grows as they take hold, and abates only when traditional methods of law enforcement are reintroduced through "broken windows" and sentencing reform.*

Over a quarter of a million Americans, dead to no purpose. That is the equivalent of a medium-sized city, a regional center like Fort Wayne or St. Petersburg. It is a full two orders of magnitude larger than the casualties of 9/11. If an enemy were ever to kill that number of Americans, we would scour the earth to track them down. But this was self-inflicted. This was homegrown.

They were from all across the country, from all walks of life. All races, all religions, all backgrounds. Many would probably have been proud to call themselves "liberals." They were our friends, and neighbors, and family. They included Kitty Genovese, and Sharon Tate, and Rosemary LaBianca, and Richard Adan, and Polly Klaas, and Eric Kaminsky, and a lost student bleeding out on a dismal New Jersey street corner, and a forgotten old man strangled with a curtain cord in his own home, one of 9,600 others who died needlessly in the year 1975.

And this in no way addresses the victims of rape, robbery, assault, and lesser crimes, many of them crippling, physically or mentally, their victims for life. Or the second-order victims—the aging women who will never hold their grandchildren, the small children who can't understand why Momma or Daddy won't come

---

*Anyone who doubts this progression can take a look at the U.K., which under the Blair Labour government copied many American mistakes while adding a few of their own, among them a policy of prosecuting and imprisoning crime victims who defended themselves. As a result, Great Britain currently has one of the highest crime rates in the industrialized world, easily overshadowing that of the United States.

home. The husbands and wives who fold and box and give away the clothes and belongings of their murdered spouses or children and try to face a world turned hellish. There is no method of accounting for these, no way this side of eternity that their number can ever be calculated.

All these people were victims of policy—a policy created in blindness and conceit, in light of a distorted, too-optimistic analysis of human nature. A policy put in place by stealth and subterfuge, and kept in operation in defiance of all evidence of moral disaster. The bodies filled the morgues, gunfire and sirens echoed across urban nights, entire cities fell into chaos, and still the process continued, unmodified and unchanged. It is said that human stupidity is the only actual evidence we have for the existence of infinity. But we must not forget the reality of human despair.

We are not out of the woods yet. Many cities—New Orleans, Detroit, and San Francisco among them—have refused to adapt the new law-enforcement policies, and their citizens are paying the price. The Supreme Court continues making decisions difficult to understand. (For example, the 2005 case *Roper v. Simmons*, in which Christopher Simmons, who gratuitously murdered a woman by throwing her off a bridge, was spared the death penalty due to the fact that he was seventeen at the time of the offense.) The country's murder deficit, which dropped almost to a thousand in the first years of the new millennium, has begun increasing once again.

And, lastly, rehabilitation theory, though refuted as forcefully as any such concept in history, retains its hold on activists, lawyers, judges, and academics across the country. A cursory Internet search utilizing the words "criminal rehab" will turn up dozens of criminal rehab advocacy sites based in every state in the Union.

In 2005, the violent crime rate rose marginally from 1,360,088 to 1,390,695, the first rise in five years, after a nearly continual decline since 1993.

So much of left-wing thought is a kind of playing with
fire by people who don't even know the fire is hot.
—GEORGE ORWELL

3

THE DARKER SIDE OF GREEN

The Demonization of DDT

S uppose you knew of a disease that had been killing people
for millennia. A disease perhaps responsible for taking more
lives than any form of death other than old age. A disease that
has killed anywhere from 150 to 300 million people over the past
century, most of them children.

Now, suppose you had access to something that could stop this
disease. Not a cure as much as a preventative, something that could
break the chain of transmission. A compound proven to work
through decades of use, one that has eliminated the disease from
vast tracts of the earth, saving millions of lives in the process.

You'd bend heaven and earth to assure that the disease was
stopped, wouldn't you? And you'd consider anybody who stood
in the way to be something on the order of a clinical psychopath.

Of course you would. But you'd be wrong.

THE ANCIENT ENEMY

The disease in question is malaria. One of the oldest of killer diseases, malaria was well-known in ancient China, where records

of its effects go back nearly five thousand years. In Sumeria and Egypt, fevers with symptoms matching those of malaria ran rampant four thousand years ago. So deadly is the disease that it was known to stop entire armies. In 452, malaria prevented Attila the Hun from taking Rome. During WWI, it paralyzed Allied forces in Greece for nearly three years. In WWII, it killed over sixty thousand American troops in North Africa and the Pacific, the largest number to die from any single cause apart from combat.

The hundreds of millions killed by malaria have included some of the towering names of history. It has been implicated in the death of Alexander the Great. Oliver Cromwell very likely died of it. Lord Byron was a victim. Others include Alaric, king of the Goths, the emperor Titus Caesar Vespasianus, and Dante, the poet of eternity.

Malaria is a blood disease caused by a parasite. It has a weirdly complex life cycle requiring both insectile and warm-blooded hosts. The malaria carrier, the *Anopheles* mosquito, feeds on a warm-blooded victim, injecting the malaria parasite at the same time. The parasite enters the victim's liver, where it resides for a period of weeks to months before emerging into the bloodstream. There it infects red blood cells, reproducing until the cells at last burst, unleashing a wave of new parasites to hunt down more cells, and in the process filling the victim's bloodstream with toxins causing unbearable symptoms of fever, chills, and weakness.

Malaria comes in four types, *Plasmodium falciparum* and *Plasmodium vivax* being the most widespread. *P. falciparum* is by far the worst, resistant to many medical treatments and with a terribly high fatality rate. According to one medical authority, malaria epidemics caused by *P. falciparum* "can be among the most lethal forces of nature."

Malaria is endemic throughout the tropics. Over a billion people are subject to the disease, and between 350 and 500 million suffer an attack each year. Two to 3 million die, most of them in Africa, up to 90 percent of them children under five years of age. Repeated bouts of malaria are crippling, resulting in permanent weakness and disability. Malaria alone may well be responsible for much of the poverty prevalent in Third World countries.

DDT

The single most critical factor in taming this killer was a chemical called dichloro-diphenyl-trichloroethane, better known as DDT. The Austrian chemist Othmar Zeidler discovered DDT in 1874 but failed to come up with any use for it. In 1939, Paul Müller of the J. R. Geigy Company was researching insecticides when he tested DDT and found that it killed virtually all types of insect pests. The company began marketing the chemical a year later, to the Swiss Army among others. The Swiss were so impressed that they took the risk of smuggling DDT out of Nazi-occupied Europe to the United States.

In 1942 the American Research Council for Insectology tested DDT on behalf of the U.S. Army. The results were so spectacular that it was immediately ordered into production. DDT was effective, nonpoisonous, cheaply manufactured, easily stored and transported, and appeared to have no environmental effects apart from killing insects. It was the perfect solution for a military operating in some of the most disease-ridden regions of the globe.

DDT's first major test occurred in Italy. Typhus was a deadly by-product of war, a lice-borne disease that thrived when people were packed together with inadequate hygiene, a situation typical of refugee and prison camps and armies on the march. During World War I, a major typhus outbreak killed millions across Europe, including over 3 million in Russia alone. In October 1943, another such epidemic appeared imminent when typhus broke out in Naples. Brigadier General Leon A. Fox, later the U.S. Army's chief physician, turned to DDT. During January

1944 over 1.3 million people were dusted with the chemical. In less than three weeks, the epidemic was under control. From that point on, DDT was used on all fronts, saving millions of lives, particularly those of prisoners freed from concentration camps.

Malaria was first targeted later that year. The Allied Control Commission began spraying the town of Castel Vortuno in May 1944, treating the inside walls of the town's buildings in hopes of curtailing mosquito activity. A similar program was carried out in the Tiber area near Rome. Over the next two years, DDT spraying resulted in the eradication of the disease in central Italy.

Using the same techniques, a campaign to rid the U.S. of malaria began in 1947 under the auspices of the Centers for Disease Control (CDC). Once common as far north as Boston, malaria had disappeared from the Northeast, but was still a problem in many of the rickets-belt states. The campaign sprayed houses in rural areas in the thirteen states still reporting malaria. By 1949, over 4 million buildings had been treated. Two years later, for the first time in its history, the United States was declared malaria-free.

Similar campaigns occurred worldwide. Under the sponsorship of the Rockefeller Foundation, spraying was carried out across the Mediterranean. Malaria was effectively eradicated in Italy, and in Greece was reduced to 5 percent of previous levels. In short order Egypt, Hungary, Bulgaria, Romania, Yugoslavia, Poland, Spain, and Portugal eliminated the disease.

Eradication programs accelerated during the 1950s. India, which had suffered nearly a million malaria deaths in 1945, whittled them down to a few thousand by 1960. According to Indian medical authorities, control of malaria in and of itself increased national life expectancy from thirty-two to forty-five years. Sri Lanka (at that time called Ceylon) had also endured hundreds of thousands of malaria cases, with eighty thousand deaths in 1934–35 alone. In 1963, only seventeen cases were reported.

In May 1955 the World Health Organization (WHO) inaugurated the Global Malaria Eradication Campaign, combining DDT spraying and antimalarial drugs in an attempt to eliminate the disease worldwide. By the mid-1960s, many of the campaign's aims had been achieved, with malaria wiped out across broad regions of Asia and Latin America. At the time, it must have seemed that a final destruction of the parasite was within reach.

But difficulties cropped up. Ill-advised mass aerial spraying, often for agricultural purposes, gave rise to several varieties of resistant insects, including mosquito species. For various reasons, countries such as Honduras and Indonesia proved difficult to clear. And, strangely enough for a "global" initiative, most of sub-Saharan Africa had been omitted due to lack of financing and infrastructure.

All the same, the antimalaria program could look back on an astonishing record of success. Much of the earth was now malaria-free. Numerous other insect-borne diseases, such as plague, typhus, and yellow fever, were in decline. DDT had saved a minimum of 100 million lives, and perhaps as many as 500 million. In less than twenty years DDT had blunted one of humanity's greatest scourges.

ENTER RACHEL CARSON

Rachel Carson was a well-known naturalist and the author of two best-selling books, *The Sea Around Us* and *The Edge of the Sea*. She had worked for the federal government's Fish and Wildlife Service as one of the few mid-twentieth-century women holding scientific degrees, a B.A. in biology from the Pennsylvania College for Women (today known as Chatham University) and an M.A. in zoology from Johns Hopkins.

In 1958 Carson received a letter from fellow writer Olga Huckins. A short time earlier, Huckins's private bird sanctuary had been sprayed for mosquitoes, resulting in a mass die-off of birds.

Carson thought the story might be worth a magazine article. What she found convinced her that something extremely serious was in play. Several other cases of bird deaths were on record, including that of every last robin on the Michigan State University campus. Mass fish kills had also been reported. DDT was the implicated cause.

Carson began work on the book that became *Silent Spring*. It took her four and a half years to write, under difficult circumstances, including the death of her mother and several illnesses culminating in a diagnosis of breast cancer. At first, Carson's burden was eased by the presence of a skilled collaborator, Edwin Diamond, the science editor for *Newsweek*. But Diamond pulled out early, concerned with the course the book was taking.

He had good reason. Carson had become convinced that DDT embodied a malignant threat to her beloved natural world. In her eagerness to make this case, certain facts went out the window while certain unsupported assertions were invited in. The Huckins spraying also included fuel oil meant to curtail mosquito breeding, which in itself would have threatened birds in the vicinity. The Michigan State campus had also been treated with a fungicide containing arsenic. The fish kills were freak events caused by overspraying. None of this appeared in the book.

Carson added cancer to the mix, implying that a specious "rise" in cancer rates during the 1950s, attributable to improved detection programs, could actually be blamed on pesticides. As "evidence" she presented a pair of cases in which exposure to DDT allegedly led to cancer: a woman who sprayed for spiders and died of leukemia a month afterward, and a man who sprayed his office and was diagnosed with aplastic anemia a week later. From these Carson derived a universal threat of cancer, particularly involving children.

Pure speculation played a large part in Carson's argument.

This was especially apparent in the opening chapter, "A Fable for Tomorrow," a horror story depicting an idyllic small town which is, without warning, overcome by an unseen force that kills local birds and threatens all other forms of life. Carson also suggested that DDT leaking into the ocean would kill off phytoplankton, depriving the earth's atmosphere of oxygen.

Science gone too far, cancer epidemics, a threat to children, apocalyptic imagery . . . If all this sounds familiar, it should. With *Silent Spring*, Carson was creating a new literary genre, the environmentalist tract. All unknowing, she was setting the pattern for countless books dealing with apparent threats against the environment. Every last crusader against smog, ozone depletion, cell phones, or global warming—to mention just a few examples— was to pattern his work on *Silent Spring*. Al Gore, who wrote the introduction to the thirtieth anniversary edition in 1992, learned all he knows from Rachel Carson.

Including what to omit. As Tina Rosenberg of the *New York Times* pointed out, nowhere does Carson mention the hundreds of millions of lives saved by DDT. Quite the contrary—Carson went to some lengths to downplay the pesticide's beneficial effects, claiming for instance that the U.S. Army used DDT to treat "head lice," a complete misrepresentation of the Italian spraying campaign. DDT had to be an utterly dark element, with no redeeming qualities.

CARSON'S IMPACT

Silent Spring first appeared as a three-part series in the *New Yorker* before publication in book form in the fall of 1962. Advance sales reached forty thousand, and the book spent thirty-one weeks on the *New York Times* bestseller list. Comment was widespread, with over fifty newspaper editorials and twenty independent columns devoted to the book.

Carson's book appeared at one of the most anxious moments of the postwar period. The country had recently weathered a widespread uproar concerning fluoridation of water supplies. The thalidomide tragedy was fresh in the public mind. A sedative prescribed to pregnant women for morning sickness, thalidomide proved to have teratogenic properties leading to extreme birth defects, including a characteristic malformation in which seal-like flippers grew in place of arms. (A law inspired by the episode strengthening the Food and Drug Administration, the Kefauver-Harris Act, was passed on October 10, 1962, only weeks after *Silent Spring*'s publication.) The previous year had also seen considerable disquiet over nuclear testing, following revelations that radioactive isotopes such as strontium-90 and iodine-129 had become widespread in the atmosphere. Publication was almost simultaneous with the Cuban missile crisis of October 1962. At no other time would the public have been better primed to welcome such a book as Carson's.

Political ramifications were not slow to appear. Before the year was out, some forty bills regulating pesticides were pending in state legislatures. In Washington, Democratic senator Abe Ribicoff made a Senate speech opposing pesticides. He approvingly quoted *Silent Spring*: "We have allowed these chemicals to be used with little or no advance investigation of their effects on soil, water, wildlife, and man himself." (Carson later made several appearances before appreciative congressional committees.)

The president's Science Advisory Committee was asked to study the problem. The committee's report was in complete agreement with Carson. Government spraying programs against such pests as gypsy moths, Japanese beetles, and fire ants came in for severe criticism and most were shut down shortly afterward. Although the report called for further research, its tone echoed that of *Silent Spring* in its hostility to pesticides, their users, and the industry that had created them. Recommendations included a call for restriction and eventual elimination of DDT.

The record makes it clear that environmentalism, despite its later association with the counterculture, was a direct creation of the liberal establishment. The *New Yorker* was (and still is) the flagship magazine of liberal urban middlebrows. Abe Ribicoff, a perennial presidential hopeful, was a popular and well-liked liberal politician. The Science Advisory Committee featured many notable scientific thinkers of the period. CBS was the most senior and respected of the Big Three networks.

Environmentalism was never an extremist cult but an expression of the concerns and interests of mainstream liberals. It was a concrete and deliberate manifestation of their doubts concerning the methods and products of industrial capitalism. Whatever associations environmentalism gained with patchouli and lava lamps over the coming decade, it remained in essence a liberal initiative. Its spokesmen, the Ehrlichs and Commoners among them, were products of the liberal educational system, its organizations, the Audubon Society and Sierra Club, liberal in tone and practice (despite such deviant offshoots as Earth First! and Earth Liberation Front), its doctrines and policies those of the liberal elite. That has remained true throughout its development from a movement to a mass ideology to something resembling a secular religion. It remains true today—as witness its current spokesman, Al Gore, foundered liberal politician turned Green messiah.

DDT AT BAY

As the 1960s wore on, Carson's contentions became subject to serious scientific examination. Her critique was based largely on the concept of biomagnification, a process in which small amounts of a compound become concentrated after being ingested by an organism. A few parts per trillion in the air or water could conceivably be magnified to a substantial number of parts per million within an animal's metabolism. Carson was on firm ground here—such substances did exist, DDT among them, concentrating itself in the fatty tissues of animals and birds that preyed on insects. The question remained of what impact this had.

Studies were not all kind to Carson's thesis. DDT was not a carcinogen. No single case of cancer was attributable to the compound among all the millions who had come into contact with it, including the army medics who had dusted masses of threatened Europeans, those same surviving Europeans of all ages, sexes, and states of health, and the thousands who had worked in DDT plants or in spraying programs across the world. Noted entomologist J. Gordon Edwards opened his lectures on DDT by swallowing a spoonful, and he lived to a ripe old age.* There would be no cancer epidemic triggered by DDT. (All the same, the cancer allegation went on to be used against half the chemicals in production, ranging from dioxin to that deadly poison Alar.)

What about animals? The four-footed variety seemed to share human immunity. The fish kills were caused by massive overuse amounting to spills, and could be avoided with due care. Which left the question of birds, Carson's primary concern. It was quickly established that songbirds remained unaffected. But raptors— falcons, ospreys, and eagles—were another story. Two papers— "Decrease in Eggshell Weight in Certain Birds of Prey," published by British researcher D. A. Ratliffe in *Nature* in 1967, and "Chlorinated Hydrocarbons and Eggshell Changes in Raptorial and Fish-Eating Birds," by Daniel Anderson and Joseph Hickey in the October 1968 issue of *Science*—established that raptors were subject to egg-thinning that severely cut down the number of their

---

*Edwards, an early champion of DDT, produced some of the most well-researched and footnoted pieces defending the pesticide. Unfortunately, they cannot be cited, due to the fact that they appeared in LaRouchite publications such as *Executive Intelligence Review*. This is probably attributable to naïveté—Edwards was a legitimate scientist of high repute, with a museum at San Jose State University named for him.

offspring. The mechanism was interference with the bird's calcium metabolism, leading to eggs that were either soft or brittle. Both papers contended that the "catastrophic decline" in raptor population since WWII could be explained only by DDT.

The difficulty with these claims was that raptors had been in decline long before DDT appeared. The bald eagle, to take one example, had been considered a varmint, with government bounties paid on it until the 1940s. This policy was reversed with the national bird on the very brink of extinction. Conversely, raptor populations rebounded even as DDT use moved into high gear worldwide. (Currently numbering over sixteen thousand nesting pairs, the bald eagle was removed from the endangered list in 2006.) But even given the validity of the eggshell findings—and they have never been disproven—this is an awfully small return for all the controversy, and one easily corrected by proper restrictions on DDT use.

But it made no difference to the public. DDT had been ideologized—given a character that had nothing to do with its actual nature but which made it a focus of public fears. Like an endless number of substances in the years since, DDT had become evil made manifest, an unmitigated threat demanding banishment from the natural world.

Rachel Carson was beyond caring. She had died from complications of cancer in 1964. Her demise served to burnish her halo—many believe to this day that her illness was in some way connected to DDT, giving her the aura of a martyr. Through sheer accident of history, a dishonest and ill-conceived book had made the staid, straitlaced lady scholar a secular saint.

THE BAN

Use of DDT declined throughout the 1960s. From a peak level of 80 million pounds in 1959, American DDT spraying fell to 13 million pounds in 1971. But even that steep decline was not enough for the budding environmentalist movement, which wanted nothing less than complete abolition. In 1971 the Environmental Defense Fund (EDF), an advocacy group founded specifically to seek such a ban, arranged for hearings on the issue before the newly established Environmental Protection Agency (EPA).

The EPA was founded at the behest of President Richard M. Nixon in one of his attempts—like affirmative action and curtailment of the space program—to win over Democratic liberals. Watergate revealed how well that stratagem worked.

The hearings, presided over by Judge Edmund Sweeney, were not the environmental movement's finest hour. Judge Sweeney ran a taut ship, and was better prepared than the EDF expected. Environmentalist witnesses had a rocky time of it—at several points the judge admonished them over the shabbiness of their evidence. Several were so angered they refused to complete their testimony. (One such witness, Dr. George Woodwell, was forced to admit that the "average" DDT levels he'd obtained were actually taken from a spot where a DDT tank truck had been standing.)

After seven months, 125 witnesses, and 9,362 pages of testimony, Judge Sweeney ruled against the EDF, finding that DDT was not a carcinogen, caused no detectable harm to humans, and was generally benign if used with care. While that should have ended the matter, environmentalism is an ideology, and ideologues never give up.

The EPA was headed by William D. Ruckelshaus, a liberal Indiana Republican who after several terms in Congress had switched from politics to life as a career bureaucrat. On August 31, 1970, Ruckelshaus, speaking as assistant U.S. attorney general, told an appeals court that "DDT has an exemplary record of safe use, does not cause a toxic response in man or other animals, and is not harmful."

What changed his mind is something he never saw fit to clarify.

But less than a year later, in May 1971, he told the Audubon Society (of which he was a member) that "I was highly suspicious of this compound, to put it mildly," going on to outline how he intended to force it off the market.

Ruckelshaus declined to attend the hearings. He declined to so much as skim the testimony. All the same, on June 14, 1972, he issued an order canceling existing federal registrations of DDT products, except for public health, quarantine, and marginal crop purposes.

An appeal was lodged by the pesticide industry, and quickly denied by Ruckelshaus. He answered protests from the agricultural sector by recommending the use of parathion, a proven carcinogen and nerve poison fatal to a large variety of wildlife and capable of causing respiratory arrest leading to brain damage in humans.

The EPA's ban* ended the use and the manufacture of the compound that the National Association of Scientists had praised in such terms as "To only a few chemicals does man owe so great a debt as to DDT. . . . In little more than two decades, DDT has prevented 500 million human deaths, due to malaria, that otherwise would have been inevitable."

Ruckelshaus was later revealed to have solicited donations for the Environmental Defense Fund on his personal letterhead, and after leaving the EPA worked closely with the organization, facts curiously absent from his official bio. He prospered in later years, sitting on the boards of several global corporations. When recently asked about the ban by the *New York Times*, he said, " . . . if I were a decision maker in Sri Lanka, where the benefits from use outweigh the risks, I would decide differently. . . . We're not making these decisions for the rest of the world, are we?"

---

*Despite insistence to the contrary by numerous environmentalists, it was in fact a "ban," the precise term used by the EPA in publicizing the decision and easily verified by accessing the agency's website.

MALARIA RETURNS

But as Ruckelshaus must have known, it wasn't that simple. Where America led, other nations tended to follow. Within a few short years, DDT was banned or restricted in most industrial countries, leaving only a single plant in the free world producing DDT, at Cochin, India.

International use of DDT was phased out over the next ten years. Although interior residential spraying (known by the charming abbreviation "IRS") left next to no environmental footprint and had proven extremely effective everywhere but on the African savannah, that didn't matter. The wealthy northern countries had turned against DDT and that was the end of it. Most nations suffering from endemic malaria were underdeveloped and could not afford to mount aggressive antidisease campaigns on their own. Donor nations went to great lengths to discourage use of pesticides no matter what the circumstances. By the early 1980s both the United States Agency for International Development (USAID) and the World Health Organization had ceased supporting efforts involving DDT.

DDT was replaced by treated bed nets and schemes such as "integrated vector management." Bed nets could be very effective, with up to a 45 percent prevention rate, if properly used. But few African huts featured fixtures to hang nets from, and the nets required reapplication every few months, factors that complicated their use. Vector management was a Rube Goldberg system of "strategies" applied "synergisticially" to control the local mosquito population and was distinguished mainly by the fact that it seldom worked.

As a result, malaria surged worldwide. That possibility should have been foreseen. Fair warning had already been given by events in Sri Lanka. After nearly eradicating the disease, the Sri Lankan government discontinued DDT use in 1964. Malaria immediately reappeared in force. By 1968, over 600,000 cases were reported.

The next year, that figure was exceeded in the first quarter. Total cases for 1969 reached 2.5 million, nearly as many as occurred before DDT was introduced.

The same pattern was duplicated across the developing world. Latin American countries were forced to give up DDT or face cuts in aid. Mexico dropped DDT as a requirement of participation in the North American Free Trade Agreement (NAFTA). Belize in Central America was threatened with aid cuts by USAID officials unless it complied. Malaria cases took off across the continent, going from near zero to 1.8 million. Only in Ecuador, which continued using DDT in defiance of the developed North, did malaria remain under control. (Malaria was not the only problem. Latin America also experienced a return of dengue fever, known historically as "bonebreak fever" for the unbearable level of joint pain it inflicts. According to Dr. Donald Roberts of the Uniformed Services University of the Health Sciences, more that 250,000 cases were recorded annually. Nearly 10,000 of them involved a new hemorrhagic variant that caused victims to bleed to death.)

Africa presented a particularly challenging situation due to the fact that the African *Anopheles* mosquito was "anthropophilic"— it preferred preying on humans to anything else. According to medical authorities, this unique propensity was "the most important single factor responsible for the stability and intensity of malaria transmission in tropical Africa today."

Africa's special problems were a matter of little account to the international community. Countries such as Mozambique and Zambia that used DDT were forced to abandon it. Denied the most effective means of fighting the disease, malaria-control efforts across the continent fell apart, their collapse assisted by corrupt governments, widespread social disorders, and civil wars. By the early 1990s such efforts were moribund. Outside of South Africa, which like Ecuador continued spraying, malaria raged unchecked across Africa.

Particularly tragic was the situation in Madagascar. Effectively wiped out in the highlands area during the 1960s, malaria was kept at bay for twenty years by judicious spraying. But when DDT was eliminated, a generation never touched by the disease and lacking any immunity died by the tens of thousands.

The world at large paid no attention. A survey of newspapers and newsmagazines during the period uncovers few major stories or even references to the disease. Hundreds of millions were suffering, millions dying, entire regions being overwhelmed, and the subject simply did not arise. It wasn't that it went down the memory hole as much as it never got out. Western elites, thrown into turmoil by the fate of the bird population of an imaginary village, could not summon the least grain of sympathy for the dying populations of entire continents.

According to the WHO, at the end of the 1990s, "more people are now infected [with malaria] than at any point in history." An indifferent world looked on as the tropics were racked by a preventable disease. Every thirty seconds, a child died shivering.

THE BAN REDUX

DDT remained an environmentalist target. In 1999 the World Wildlife Fund (WWF) began lobbying the UN to include DDT in the pending Persistent Organic Pollutants treaty (known genially as POP), in the hopes of halting manufacture and use worldwide by 2007. The WWF was joined by a coalition of 260 advocacy groups including Greenpeace and Physicians for Social Responsibility.

Shortly before this effort began the WHO had in 1998 initiated a global antimalaria campaign under the title "Roll Back Malaria." The campaign's goal was to halve the incidence of malaria by 2010. This was to be accomplished through the accepted mix of bed nets and vector management.

But events were unfolding that would derail both the Greens' and the WHO's original plans. Under environmentalist pressure, South Africa had abandoned DDT. Its replacement, pyrethroids, were more expensive but, the government was assured, just as effective. Through careful residential spraying, South Africa had kept malaria cases to below 10,000 a year, and sometimes much lower—in 1995, only 4,117 cases were recorded.

Three years later, pyrethroid-resistant mosquitoes appeared in KwaZulu-Natal province. In 1999, malaria cases shot to at least 27,238. A year later, they increased to over 62,000. Facing a horror on the same scale as had occurred in Madagascar, South Africa resumed spraying DDT. Within months, the malaria rate dropped 80 percent.

The South African experience utterly changed the debate. No longer could DDT's capabilities be dismissed. No other pesticide was in the same league, no other method of control as effective. If malaria was to be contained, DDT had to be part of the strategy. South Africa was no small country that could be threatened or manipulated. It was a regional superpower, the subject of close international attention and support after the fall of the apartheid regime.

A number of African nations, backed by advocacy groups such as the Malaria Foundation International and the Institute of Economic Affairs, had been pressuring the UN to allow an exemption for DDT. In the wake of the South African decision, they redoubled their efforts. Their persistence was rewarded in the final round of negotiations (carried out, ironically, in Johannesburg) when DDT was found to be a unique case, its use allowed for public health purposes.

But if the African nations at last had the prescription, the problem remained of getting it filled. Despite the POP treaty, none of the international aid institutions—including the Global Fund to Fight AIDS, Tuberculosis, and Malaria; the World Bank; and

USAID—was willing to finance DDT use. The stumbling block was the WHO guidelines, which still recommended inadequate net and vector management methods. While the WHO paid lip service to DDT use "under the proper conditions," these conditions never seemed to arise, no matter how widely the disease raged or how many victims it claimed.

Another five years passed before the stalemate was broken. In June 2005, President George W. Bush announced the President's Malaria Initiative (PMI), to take over from the WHO's stalled Roll Back Malaria effort. The U.S. planned to spend $1.2 billion in an attempt to meet the WHO's original goal: halving malaria cases by 2010. The unspoken quid pro quo was a complete shakeup of the international malaria establishment.

The backstairs infighting must have been worth seeing, involving as it did the appointment of a new WHO malaria chief, Dr. Arata Kochi, the departure of much of WHO's malaria staff, and an entirely new emphasis for the war against malaria. Dr. Kochi had made his reputation in the fight against tuberculosis, establishing himself as a man who suffered fools neither gladly nor otherwise. He applied the same tactics to malaria, overturning accepted doctrines of disease control, excoriating drug companies for wasting the potential of ACT treatment (derived from artemisinin, a very effective herbal-based malaria drug developed by the Chinese), and on September 15, 2006, ending the de facto prohibition of DDT.

There was little protest from environmentalists. On the contrary—to hear them tell it, they were delighted. A spokesman for the World Wildlife Fund said, "You've got to use it. In South Africa it prevented tens of thousands of malaria cases and saved lots of lives." Greenpeace, which a year earlier had been ablaze to shut down India's sole DDT plant, said, "If there's nothing else and it's going to save lives, we're all for it. Nobody's dogmatic about it."

Forty-four years after *Silent Spring*, thirty-five years after the EPA ban, and a quarter-century after the WHO ceased supporting its use, DDT, the most effective insecticide ever formulated, went back into action. Mozambique served as a model. Rather than utilize the mass mobilization methods of the international aid organizations, the Mozambicans trained a handful of people in each community in spraying techniques, then sent them home with the necessary supplies to spray their neighbors' houses once or twice a year. In this fashion, mosquito spraying becomes part of the local way of life. With the program in place, Mozambique could protect its population for a cost of $1.70 per house per year.

With funding of $99 million a year from the U.S., new multiple-drug therapies based on artemisinin, and the venerable bed nets, there was a good chance that malaria could at last be brought under control.

THE COST

Liberalism prides itself as being the rational doctrine. Problems and challenges are examined with a cool eye, decisions are made rigorously and without emotion, action is taken with forethought and discretion. This, we are assured, is one of the elements— perhaps the major element—that separates liberalism from other political formats, that renders it superior to all other methods of political action.

But you'd look long and hard to detect any vanishing trace of logic, rigor, or discretion in the DDT saga. Without a single exception, every last sector of the liberal establishment was tried and found wanting. The media, the academy, the scientific community, the politicians, the bureaucrats, all collapsed one after the other into a form of mob hysteria that not only still prevails (see global warming), but has become part of the very essence of liberal identity and belief. American liberals allowed themselves to be stampeded by a book, and as a result millions suffered and died.

The crowning irony is that Rachel Carson never called for the banning of DDT. "We must have insect control," she said shortly before her death. "I do not favor turning nature over to insects. I favor the sparing, selective and intelligent use of chemicals. It is the indiscriminate, blanket spraying that I oppose." But in *Silent Spring* her rhetoric outran her ideas, and her followers took it as a given that this malignant threat to all that was natural must be abolished. And for that reason, Carson takes her place beside Marx and Engels in that small elite of writers who triggered mass death by their words alone.

What was the cost? The commonly quoted number, derived from multiplying estimated yearly deaths by thirty years, is 30 to 50 million. But not all of these victims could have been saved. Those living deep in the forests of the vast African and Latin American heartlands, or in states ruled by careless and inept dictatorships, or in otherwise collapsed societies, would have been doomed in any case. But if the money had been spent, if the effort had been made, if the single useful compound had been available, then the ancient parasite would often have been cheated of its prey, and many who died would have lived. We have no idea how many millions that number encompasses, but it must be very high.

It would have been a great thing to have defeated malaria in the mid-twentieth century. It would still be a great thing. What better way to open the new millennium? The final eradication of malaria lies within the realm of possibility. And if it is at all possible, it must be done. Polio, smallpox, and any number of lesser diseases have been conquered. There is no reason why this insult to human dignity should remain immune.*

---

*Late in his presidential campaign, Barack Obama pledged to "rid the world of malaria by 2015." It was a typical Obama moment—the steps he was "pledging" to take were already being accomplished by the Bush program. Only DDT went unmentioned.

With consistency, beautiful and undeviating, human life, from its commencement to its close, is protected by the common law. In the contemplation of law, life begins when the infant is first able to stir in the womb. By the law, life is protected not only from immediate destruction, but from every degree of actual violence, and, in some cases, from every degree of danger.
—JAMES WILSON, OF THE NATURAL RIGHTS OF INDIVIDUALS, 1790–92

4

ROE V. THE PEOPLE

Abortion as Democide

On January 29, 2010, Scott Roeder was found guilty of first-degree murder in the shooting death of Dr. George Tiller, a Kansas abortionist specializing in late-term abortions. Roeder perpetrated the shooting during Sunday service on May 31, 2009, as Tiller was acting as an usher for the Reformation Lutheran Church. He had stalked Tiller at the church several times previously (Tiller, who had been repeatedly attacked by antiabortion opponents, lived his life behind the protection of bodyguards, armor plate, and elaborate electronic security systems), waiting for the right moment to strike. As Tiller stood in the vestibule, Roeder approached him, put the barrel of a .22-caliber pistol against his forehead, and pulled the trigger.

The Tiller shooting was the latest of six abortion-related assassinations since 1993. The number of abortions that occurred during the same period is difficult to calculate. Tiller himself had performed something on the order of sixty thousand abortions in his career. Yet pro-abortion activists had been quite successful in utilizing these crimes to portray the abortion conflict as one opposing gun-wielding religious fanatics against blameless women's health-care providers. For their part, extreme pro-life advocates viewed abortion as a crime against the laws of nature and God demanding immediate and total expiation.

Both were shadow interpretations of one of the most divisive and irreconcilable conflicts to engulf this country since the heyday of slavery. Both were based not on the record or any identifiable set of facts but on the preconceptions held by either side. Neither reflected the original intent behind legalized abortion, which had nothing to do with women's rights on one hand or with subverting moral law on the other. Legalized abortion was instead yet another bold liberal reform program that promised no end of beneficial results and delivered only societal distress, political conflict, and pain, injustice, and death to millions of nameless infants and countless troubled women, not to mention George Tiller himself.

Liberals have long claimed a monopoly over compassion in the public sphere. Self-styled empathy is basic to liberal identity. Liberals are the Good Samaritans of American political life. No opportunity to display humanity is too small, no effort too great. They nest in trees for months to checkmate the logger. They travel to northern Labrador to defend baby seals. They walk the meanest streets to hand out clean needles. Threatened species, ethnic minorities, the homeless, refugees, migrants, professional criminals . . . virtually no outcast group finds itself beyond liberal protection.

With one exception: the millions of unborn children aborted over the past four decades. They alone fail to qualify. They alone find themselves outside the circle of liberal compassion.

How can this be explained? What is it about abortion that causes American liberals to abandon their professed core beliefs?

The common response is "*Roe v. Wade*," but that merely represents a sharpening of terminology. What is it about *Roe* that lends it such power? How does a court case nearly forty years old endure as a central element of the liberal creed, something they're willing to defend to the edge of rationality and beyond, something on which they've pegged their entire political future?

THE WORLD BEFORE *ROE*

Justification for *Roe v. Wade* lies in claims of necessity: American women before *Roe*, the story goes, were living a nightmare existence that could be relieved only by immediate and complete liberalization of abortion laws.

Prior to *Roe*, we're told, life in the U.S. presented a bleak prospect to the woman in trouble. Abortion was banned in all fifty states. A woman seeking to end her pregnancy had few alternatives. She could turn to home remedies, the dread "coat-hanger abortion," or she could brave the back alleys to seek out a local abortionist, usually unsavory, sinister, and incompetent. Either way, the casualty rate was horrendous. According to estimates by the University of California School of Public Health, five thousand to ten thousand women died of complications from abortions each year prior to 1966.

Little evidence exists to support this picture. Former abortionist Bernard Nathanson estimates the actual mortality figure at less than 250 annually. Perhaps far less: in 1966 the Denver hospital system began keeping records of how many women were treated for complications to abortion. The total was twenty-seven, none of whom died. The major cause of death in such circumstances was sepsis triggered by bacterial infection, a complication treatable with antibiotics. The means of obtaining abortions had also changed. Most large cities possessed surreptitious abortion networks, many run by women (the one in St. Louis was operated by mainline Protestant ministers, a far cry from the defrocked M.D. with a pint in his back pocket).

A number of states had liberalized their abortion laws, beginning with Colorado in 1967. That bill was a bipartisan effort sponsored by Democrat Richard D. Lamm and Republican John Bermingham. It was also an early example of the chicanery typical of such efforts. The sponsors kept the bill hidden until the governor, a practicing Roman Catholic, was out of state, then rushed it through committee to present him with a fait accompli upon his return.

Colorado was soon followed by California, North Carolina, Maryland, and Georgia. By 1972, seventeen states had some kind of provision for legal abortion, ranging in permissiveness from the Colorado model to New York State's complete freedom of action up to twenty-four weeks. A slow social transition was taking place, which if allowed to continue might have evolved into a workable modus vivendi. But it wasn't allowed to continue.

BLACKMUN RULES

The man responsible was Supreme Court Justice Harry A. Blackmun. Born in 1908 to a middle-class St. Paul, Minnesota, family (his father was a shop owner), Blackmun's early life embodied the not-uncommon tale of the average boy who works his way to the top. Attending Harvard under scholarship, he went on to Harvard Law School while supporting himself with various odd jobs.

After two decades in his own law practice, Blackmun became general counsel for the Mayo Clinic, a position he held for nine years. There he gained deep respect for doctors, along with sympathy for the challenges facing the profession.

In 1959, Blackmun was appointed to the Eighth Circuit Court of Appeals. In 1970 he was selected by Richard M. Nixon to replace Justice Abe Fortas on the Supreme Court. He was Nixon's third choice after Clement Haynsworth and G. Harrold Carswell. An acute irony lies in the fact that Blackmun was evaluated by the assistant attorney general William H. Rehnquist, later to oppose him on many occasions as a fellow member of the Court. Rehnquist thought Blackmun competent but unexceptional.

Little doubt exists that Chief Justice Warren Burger had a hand in Blackmun's selection. The two were unusually close, having met in kindergarten and grown up together (they were known as the "Minnesota Twins"). Though no man ever looked more the part of a judge, Burger was deeply unsure of himself, requiring constant reassurance from others, from Blackmun above all. Such dependence tends to breed resentment. All the same, during his first term, Blackmun voted with the chief justice 89 percent of the time. That easy agreement began to unravel with *Roe v. Wade*.

The Supreme Court's entanglement with abortion began with a nearly forgotten 1961 case, *Poe v. Ullman*, the fruit of a Planned Parenthood campaign to overturn a Connecticut law prohibiting the sale of contraceptives. The carefully wrought case collapsed when it developed that no actual legal dispute existed—no crime had been committed, no law broken, and no arrests made. The Supreme Court had little choice but to dismiss the case.

But Planned Parenthood's efforts were not totally wasted. Writing in dissent, Justice John Marshall Harlan suggested that the Connecticut statute deserved to be rendered void as an " . . . invasion of privacy in the conduct of the most intimate concerns of an individual's personal life." Harlan's dissent marked the first appearance of the "right of privacy" argument, which was to serve as the cornerstone of abortion-related jurisprudence. (It comes as no surprise to learn that the existence of such a right, undiscovered in two centuries of constitutional scholarship, was suggested by ACLU attorney Melvin L. Wulf.)

Planned Parenthood soon succeeded in getting themselves arrested. Estelle Griswold, executive director of the Connecticut chapter, and Dr. C. Lee Buxton, an M.D. and professor at Yale Medical School, opened a branch office in New Haven, where they sold contraceptive materials to several married couples. Duly arrested and found guilty, they were fined $100 each. They immediately appealed, working their way up the appellate ladder to the Supreme Court.

The *Griswold* decision, written by Justice William O. Douglas, was handed down on June 7, 1965. Accepting the "privacy rights" baton from Justice Harlan, Douglas reversed the lower court's verdict, in the process producing what was likely the most ridiculed line ever to appear in a Supreme Court decision: " . . . specific guarantees in the Bill of Rights have penumbras, formed by emanations from those guarantees that help give them life and substance." Since Douglas couldn't actually locate a "right of privacy" in the Constitution, he divined one, in much the same manner as a holistic healer analyzing a patient's "aura."

Not even the concurring justices were willing to sign on to Douglas's convoluted chain of reasoning, in which the "emanations" of the First, Third, Fourth, Fifth, and Ninth Amendments converged in the Due Process clause of the Fourteenth Amendment, still seventy years in the future when the Bill of Rights was written. In accepting Douglas's conclusions while sidestepping the means by which he reached them, the justices demonstrated a willingness to overlook specious logic and bizarre jurisprudence for the purpose of overturning "an uncommonly silly law" (in the words of dissenter Potter Stewart). *Griswold* blazed the trail for *Roe* in more ways than one.

Like *Griswold*, *Roe v. Wade* was a planned operation from the start. And, like *Griswold*, it very nearly failed to come off. Texas attorneys Sarah Weddington and Linda Coffee, representing "Jane Roe," actually won their original case before the U.S. District Court, with the state's restrictive abortion law judged unconstitutional. But the court refused to provide injunctive relief (rather a moot point, considering that "Jane Roe" had given birth months earlier). In 1971, Weddington and Coffee appealed to the Supreme Court.

Only seven justices were sitting, Harlan and Hugo Black having recently retired. Weddington fumbled her presentation, providing no serious constitutional argument. State's attorney Jay Floyd took the proceedings less than seriously, amusing himself with remarks about "lady attorneys."

The final roadblock appeared after the court had actually voted to modify the Texas verdict. Chief Justice Burger's selection of Blackmun to write the decision created serious disquiet among the other justices. Blackmun was a relative newcomer, widely suspected of lacking the experience and knowledge to handle a decision of such gravity. And so it proved. Blackmun produced a mess that satisfied no one. The case was rescheduled for October 11, 1972.

The long recess appears to have benefited all concerned. The Court was once more at full strength, with the addition of new justices William H. Rehnquist and Lewis F. Powell, Jr. Weddington presented a more compelling case (perhaps she'd read up on the "right to privacy"). And Blackmun, for his part, was able to produce a decision at least acceptable to his colleagues.

Little in the way of legal exegesis is required in evaluating *Roe*, because little of legal substance exists. Blackmun's central finding is encompassed in a single short paragraph, extending the *Griswold* privacy claim to cover abortion. No further argument is presented, merely a note to "see Griswold v. Connecticut," along with related cases.

Blackmun then provides a lengthy, detailed history of abortion, extending from the ancient world through British practice and on to modern times. These pages appear designed to support

Blackmun's contention that "restrictive criminal abortion laws" are of "relatively recent vintage," robbing them of the power of antiquity. When he discovers contrary evidence in the Hippocratic Oath, he dismisses it as representing "only a small segment of Greek opinion," in full contradiction of the oath's profound influence over the centuries. Some commentators have suggested that this lengthy passage (numbering six pages, or over a quarter of *Roe*'s wordage) was interpolated as a cover for the decision's lack of legal rigor.

Blackmun again required only a single paragraph to deal with the unborn child's human status: "The word 'person,' as used in the Fourteenth Amendment, does not include the unborn." Chief Justice Roger B. Taney did not put it more succinctly in *Dred Scott*: " . . . the black man had no rights which the white man was bound to respect."

Finally, Blackmun introduces the concept of "trimesters," a term with no medical or biological significance. (Trimesters evidently had their origin in the fact that the nine-month term of pregnancy is easily divided by three. Blackmun was lucky human gestation didn't last ten months.) Trimesters were a legal construct created to delineate the balance between a woman's privacy rights and the state's "compelling interests" in matters of reproduction. During the first trimester, decisions regarding abortion were solely up to the woman ("and her physician"). During the second trimester, the state could regulate abortion in "ways that are reasonably related to maternal health." During the final trimester, the state could "regulate, and even proscribe" the procedure, except in cases involving "the preservation of the life or health of the mother."

But *Roe* was not the sole abortion case decided that morning. Also on the docket was *Doe v. Bolton*, brought by nine physicians, seven nurses, five clergymen, and two social workers on behalf of an indigent young woman recently abandoned by her husband and pregnant for the fourth time. "Mary Doe" had applied for an abortion to the state of Georgia's Abortion Committee but had been turned down.

In writing the *Doe* decision, Blackmun not only enjoyed the pleasure of being the first to apply *Roe*, but also achieved the perhaps unique distinction of undercutting his own previous decision within minutes of it being announced. Contrary to decades of feminist rhetoric, *Roe* does not grant an absolute right to an abortion. No one, wrote Blackmun, "has an unlimited right to do with one's body as one pleases."

In *Doe*, Blackmun negated that assertion with two sentences: " . . . medical judgment may be exercised in the light of all factors—physical, emotional, psychological, familial, and the woman's age—relevant to the well-being of the patient. All these factors may relate to health." With those words, the "health exception," under which abortion could be carried out at any time up to the hour of birth, was expanded to a point where anything at all could be asserted as a medical reason for an abortion. Much of what people find excessive about *Roe* actually has roots in this section of *Doe*.

ROE'S IMPACT

Together, the two decisions of January 22, 1973, marked a social revolution of a magnitude not often seen. Decades of debate, centuries of jurisprudence, and millennia of moral teachings were overthrown in a moment. Seldom has a democracy confronted as serious a social transformation with so little consideration or thought. With all the padding stripped away, *Roe* amounts to three substantive paragraphs: the evocation of *Griswold*, the denial of humanity to the fetus, and the trimester format. An assertion, a dismissal, and instructions—what amounted to a diktat, arrived at without public participation, released without general consent.

The Court concurred with Blackmun, seven to two (including Chief Justice Burger). Little reaction was anticipated. Burger predicted the ruling would have no "sweeping consequences." Blackmun himself believed that a tidy round of lawmaking by state legislatures would wrap things up.

A major flaw of liberal thinking—and of the modern mind-set as a whole—lies in what G. K. Chesterton termed "chronological snobbery," the contention that the more ancient the concept, the more it is based on irrationality and ignorance, and the easier it can be set aside. Nothing could be further from the truth. A precept with millennia of practice behind it is one based on the firmest foundations imaginable. You meddle with it at your peril, and with due regard for the consequences.

Roe v. Wade challenged exactly such a precept, and the consequences were dramatic. There is not a single aspect of American society that does not bear its mark. *Roe* distorted the relationships between men and women, husbands and wives, parents and children. Politician and voter, clergy and worshipers, government and people—and we could go on. *Roe* set a blaze that to this day still ravages our culture. And everywhere and without exception, its influence has been one of failure.

A LEGAL VACUUM

Roe's failure as a legal case is widely acknowledged (though it has not, strangely enough, had any effect on its status as a precedent). Both abortion cases were based on deceit, particularly as involved the plaintiffs. Norma McCorvey, the case's "Jane Roe," was a poor woman leading a scuffling existence when she encountered Weddington and Coffee. She agreed to participate only because the attorneys promised her an abortion once the case was over. As it happened (and as the lawyers must have realized), Mc-Corvey's child was approaching its first birthday before the case cleared even the district court. McCorvey had little contact with her lawyers and heard of the *Roe* decision on the news. (McCorvey later became a Christian and an opponent of many abortion procedures, and is no less than scathing in her opinion of the *Roe* attorneys.)

Even more disturbing was the treatment of "Mary Doe." Sandra Cano (at that time known as Sandra Besing—some sources have this as "Bensing") was another young woman in sorry circumstances, with a husband in jail and two children removed by welfare officials. She needed help above all, and that's what she was offered by ACLU lawyer Margie Pitts Hames. Unfortunately, Hames's definition of "help" consisted of involving Cano in abortion litigation without her knowledge and arranging for an illegal abortion without her consent. Three days before the scheduled procedure, Cano fled to relatives in Oklahoma, refusing to return until assured that no abortion would be forced on her. Cano remained part of the suit as plaintiff Doe. Around her, Hames constructed an entirely fictitious case, based on the claim that Cano had first been denied an abortion by the hospital committee, then succeeded on reapplication, only to abandon the effort due to lack of funds. No record of any such train of events exists. It appears that Hames was that rarity even among lawyers—an attorney willing to risk lying to the Supreme Court. The truth was not revealed until Cano spoke out in 1989. Hames should have been disbarred. The reason that she wasn't is likely to remain a secret of the legal profession.

Two justices also acted problematically: as a lawyer in Richmond, Virginia, Lewis Powell had been obliged to intervene when the girlfriend of a young associate bled to death after an abortion. Though dependably conservative on most topics, Powell considered the nation's abortion laws to be "atrocious" and was eager to see them overturned. The second was Harry Blackmun. In 1966, Blackmun's daughter Susan, discovering she was pregnant, quit college to marry her boyfriend. The marriage slowly collapsed, failing completely at the height of the *Roe* litigation. (Years afterward, honest Harry Blackmun declared, "People misunderstand. I am not for abortion. I hope my family never has to face such a decision.")

While perhaps not rising to a level requiring recusal, as critics have asserted, these revelations suggest that both justices might have thought better of involving themselves.

Neither Powell nor Blackmun were thinking as judges while considering *Roe*. Neither was thinking in terms of law. They were thinking of their friends and loved ones, of personal situations utterly divorced from the interests of the public and society at large. Adequate legal decisions can scarcely be made under such circumstances.

It is clear that adequate law was not made. Two justices dissented from the *Roe* decision. Byron White's dissent was a superb polemic, the response of a civilized man provoked to open outrage: "I cannot accept the Court's exercise of its clear power of choice by interposing a constitutional barrier to state efforts to protect human life and by investing mothers and doctors with the constitutionally protected right to exterminate it."

Justice William Rehnquist's dissent was something else altogether. Displaying the cool tone and clarity of thought that were to serve him well as chief justice, Rehnquist poked a number of embarrassing holes in the *Roe* thesis, undercutting the "right to privacy" argument by pointing out that abortion involved a transaction that is "not 'private' in the ordinary usage of that word." The decision's use of the "compelling state interest" claim ignored what the Fourteenth Amendment actually had to say about the concept. "The fact that a majority of the States . . . " Rehnquist wrote in response to Blackmun's historical passage, "have had restrictions on abortions for at least a century is a strong indication, it seems to me, that the asserted right to an abortion is not 'so rooted in the traditions and conscience of our people as to be ranked as fundamental.'" Lastly, Rehnquist pointed out that *Roe* violated a long-accepted tenet of Supreme Court procedure: " . . . a statute found to be invalid as applied to a particular plaintiff, but not unconstitutional as a whole, is not simply 'struck down' but is, instead, declared unconstitutional as applied to the fact situation before the Court."

Rehnquist's dissent was echoed and elaborated by conservative thinkers such as Robert Bork, Antonin Scalia, and Samuel Alito. More surprising are the searing criticisms of the decision from reliably left-of-center figures such as Laurence H. Tribe and Ruth Bader Ginsburg. Writing in the *Harvard Law Review*, Tribe accused Blackmun of creating a "verbal smokescreen" behind which any "substantive judgment . . . is nowhere to be found." Ginsburg was equally harsh, stating that *Roe* had gone too far and that a limited decision might have proven more acceptable. (Ginsburg's thesis is common among liberal legal scholars and serves as the basis for the volume *What Roe v. Wade Should Have Said: The Nation's Top Legal Experts Rewrite America's Most Controversial Decision*. It's difficult to imagine another court case receiving such treatment.) When Ginsburg joined the Court in 1993, Blackmun was suspicious at first, until finally convinced that Justice Ginsburg was willing to overlook her own analysis for the sake of saving *Roe*.

No court decision as thoroughly undermined as *Roe* can stand unmodified. Over the years, many of the decision's claims have been restricted on purely procedural grounds. In *Harris v. McRae* (1980), the Court found that the Hyde Amendment, which prohibited federal funding of abortions, was constitutional. *Webster v. Reproductive Health Services* (1989) upheld a Missouri law requiring that physicians conduct tests for fetal viability on pregnancies of twenty weeks or more, and forbidding use of public funds and facilities to carry out abortions. *Planned Parenthood of Southern Pennsylvania v. Casey* (1992) upheld a twenty-four-hour waiting period along with parental consent for minors. Going a step further, it replaced *Roe*'s "strict scrutiny" standard for review of abortion laws, in which any restriction was examined under presumption of error, with the less stringent "undue burden" standard. In *Ayotte v. Planned Parenthood of Northern New England* (2006), the Court reinstated a law requiring parental notice and a forty-eight-hour waiting period for minors despite the lack of a health exception. (*Casey*, widely anticipated as an opportunity to overturn *Roe* completely, was a disappointment in pro-life circles. When Justice Blackmun's papers were released five years after his death, it was revealed that *Roe* had in fact been in jeopardy until Justice Anthony Kennedy got cold feet and threw in with Blackmun.)

By the 1990s, it was evident that the *Roe* decision was being whittled away steadily. The sole surviving major element was the "central holding"—that abortion was a fundamental right not to be abrogated by act of government. Everything else—even the trimesters—was nullified or under attack.

Harry Blackmun had become a querulous figure, putting excessive time and effort into defending his single, horribly flawed victory. "And I fear for the darkness," he wrote in a 1992 decision, "as four Justices anxiously await the single vote necessary to extinguish the light!" His friendship with Warren Burger had ended long before, transformed into a thing of impersonal notes and scarcely veiled insults. When Burger died in 1995, Blackmun barely responded. On his retirement he was lauded for one thing alone—his role in *Roe v. Wade*. The name of Harry Blackmun will forever be intertwined with the subject of abortion.

A POLITICAL DISASTER

Politically, *Roe* was a disaster without parallel for liberalism. At the time the decision was handed down, liberals were engaged in the destruction of Richard Nixon's presidency while riding a wave of popularity due to public weariness with the Vietnam War. A decade later they were confronted with a resurgent social conservatism spearheaded by a religious revival they scarcely understood, a revival triggered in large part by *Roe v. Wade*.

Roe was supposed to end the debate over abortion, with the high court's grandeur and standing overcoming dissent and instituting the new dispensation with iron finality. Nothing of the sort occurred. Instead, Burger's "sweeping consequences" arrived with a vengeance. A pro-life movement already existed in response to state liberalization of abortion laws. *Roe* supercharged this movement, transforming it from a disorganized local phenomenon to an affair of national consequence. At first the movement was largely Catholic. The American Church was swift to condemn the newly liberalized procedures, and the Church faithful provided a large and willing reservoir of recruits in the campaign against abortion clinics springing up in the wake of *Roe*.

The pro-life movement assured that abortion remained a hot-button issue, made it clear that it was not simply going to go away, and put politicians on notice that there was a price to be paid for supporting *Roe*. The movement drew a line and announced that the "culture of death" would not advance one inch further.

But pro-lifers were unable to retake the ground already lost. The media successfully portrayed the movement as a peculiarly Catholic obsession of little interest to outsiders. They were aided by nominally "Catholic" politicians who claimed to be fully faithful in all things apart from this single exception, concerning which they voted their "consciences."

All that changed late in the 1970s with the arrival of Evangelicals in pro-life ranks. Born-again Christians had long avoided involvement in politics due to a belief—not altogether mistaken—that it represented an occasion of sin. This quietism ended with a late-1970s federal attempt to interfere with private Evangelical schools. Another crucial development was a campaign carried out by theologian Francis A. Schaeffer and Dr. C. Everett Koop, later Ronald Reagan's surgeon general. Schaeffer and Koop published *Whatever Happened to the Human Race?*, a book calling for greater Evangelical Protestant involvement in the fight against abortion. The book was followed with a twenty-city lecture and film tour that inspired thousands of born-agains to confront abortion.

The movement marked the first time the two Christian denominations had worked together. The Evangelicals, many of them graduates of Bible schools, were often more theologically sophisticated than their Catholic brethren. They were also more intense. The born-agains saw abortion as a blood crime demanding atonement. Picket lines were not enough—they craved direct action against abortion clinics and the evil they represented. A watershed moment occurred when Randall Terry, a Binghamton, New York, Evangelical, began organizing sit-ins at a local clinic. He went on to collaborate with Rob and Paul Schenk, Assembly of God ministers from Tonawanda, New York, in actions against clinics in nearby Buffalo. Terry envisioned a civil disobedience campaign in the tradition of Martin Luther King, Jr. Through nonviolent action, abortion could be ended in much the same way that the civil rights movement ended legal segregation.

In 1986, Terry founded Operation Rescue to carry the campaign to the national level. The strategy was to concentrate as many protestors as possible against the clinics in a single city. Clinics were blockaded, with sit-ins carried out inside while other protestors turned away women seeking abortions. When protestors were arrested, they identified themselves as "Baby Roe" or "Baby Doe." The aim was to clog the jails and courts, shutting down city administrations.

Operation Rescue targeted Wichita, St. Louis, Tallahassee, Atlanta, and numerous smaller cities. At first the program had some success. A few abortion clinics closed altogether, while others were forced to invest in barriers, elaborate security devices, and trained security personnel. But Operation Rescue gained no sympathetic media coverage of the kind that had aided the civil rights movement. Portrayed as religious fanatics "bothering pregnant women," Operation Rescue protestors failed to enlist the support of the public at large. The response of local authorities was often little short of brutal. Joan Andrews was the most notable example. Arrested over fifty times in abortion protests, Andrews was given five years in a Florida lockup for attempting to unplug a piece of abortion-related equipment, a harsh sentence by any measure. In prison she suffered ferocious hazing and was denied adequate medical care for a chronic condition, treatment that commentator Nat Hentoff compared to life in a Third World dictatorship.

Opposition by the authorities guaranteed failure over the long term. Nowhere did Operation Rescue shut down the abortion industry. Frustration mounted, along with an inclination to open violence, abetted by the unstable types that any burgeoning movement attracts. (Including Scott Roeder, who was active for years in extreme pro-life circles and in the late 1990s served a term for possessing bomb components, for what purpose remains unclear.) Dozens of assaults and hundreds of death threats were followed by at least thirty-six clinic bombings and over eighty acts of arson. Assassination was the final step, justified by such splinter groups as the Army of God. At least six doctors or clinic workers were killed by gunfire or in bombings.* Pro-lifers were

---

*Abortion supporters sometimes claim that an attempt was made on Justice Blackmun, but evidence fails to support this assertion. The bullet that pierced the window of Blackmun's Virginia apartment in February 1985 was found by the FBI to have been traveling in a downward trajectory when it hit, which meant that it had been fired from too far away to have been aimed.

in danger of embodying the media stereotype of a latter-day John Brown, embarked on a half-crazed mission of retribution.

The abortion wars ended with the passage of the Freedom of Access to Clinics (FACE) act in 1994, providing for stiff penalties against anyone blockading, threatening, or attacking an abortion clinic (and, in an act of naked diplomacy, churches and other houses of worship). The FACE act was signed into law immediately by President Bill Clinton. Operation Rescue ceased its campaign against clinics and broke apart a short time later amid internal turmoil over tactics and leadership.

The pro-life movement turned to the conventional tools of lobbying, education, and, most effective, abortion-prevention counseling. Within a few years over 2,300 pregnancy crisis centers were in operation, providing a sympathetic ear to distraught young women along with information concerning alternatives to abortion. So deeply did the centers cut into abortion-clinic operations that many were threatened with legal action. The crisis centers were a direct assault on the main claim of the abortion establishment: that it provided the sole alternative for pregnant women.

While liberals won tactical victories against the pro-life movement, they made these gains in the process of losing the war. Working- and middle-class urban Catholics steadily abandoned the Democratic Party. The party's abortion stance was a major factor in the loss of the Evangelical South, Democratic hunting grounds since the days of Reconstruction. Abortion played a large role in the birth of the Christian social conservative colossus, a clear example of liberalism creating its own worst nightmare. Abortion also crippled second-stage feminism, as feminists raised the procedure to a near-sacramental level. Feminist ritualism as regards abortion only repelled the average woman. The end result was to send feminism spiraling into irrelevance.

• •

Liberals wasted energy and effort on defending abortion under any and all circumstances. No bill even vaguely related to the topic is passed without obsessive vetting and endless debate. Scarcely a political or judicial appointment can be made without the appointee being interrogated on his opinions concerning abortion. (Often to ludicrous effect, as when Pennsylvania Republican* Arlen Specter demanded that Supreme Court appointee John Roberts agree that *Roe* was a "super-duper precedent.")

In the end, the consequences may prove fatal. James Taranto of the *Wall Street Journal* has postulated the existence of a "Roe effect." According to Taranto, liberal support of abortion—which extends to utilizing it as a method of birth control—may well mean that liberals are breeding (or not breeding) themselves and their supporters out of existence. An impressive array of charts and statistics seems to demonstrate a close correlation between the drop in liberal voters and the number of abortions in liberal districts. While Taranto is noted as a comic writer, he doesn't seem to be joking in this case.

Clearly, abortion is one of the worst political bargains on record. In taking up the defense of abortion as a major element of domestic policy, American liberals hung a millstone around their collective neck.

A FAILED POLICY

Abortion's most grievous failure involves policy. As in the case of criminal rehabilitation, abortion was promoted as a magic formula that would automatically solve all kinds of intractable problems. Illegitimacy would vanish, with a corresponding drop in child abuse, child murder, and abandonment. Teenage motherhood would dwindle. Poor families would no longer be overwhelmed

---

*At the time, anyway.

with unplanned-for children. Marriages, unburdened by the un-
controlled arrival of children, would be strengthened. The eugenic
element went unmentioned but was far from overlooked—a
liberalized abortion regime promised fewer "subnormal" or deformed children.*

Almost none of these problems was in any sense ameliorated
by *Roe*. By all available indications, the majority have been made
worse.

Statistics dealing with children and family matters are an open
scandal in the United States. Many serious concerns are less than
adequately measured on a national or state level. Take, for example, the annual number of "discarded" infants (what the average
person would think of as "abandoned," that is, infants left in
Dumpsters, restrooms, and other public places): the yearly total
in the U.S. has been "estimated" in the low three figures (105
for 1998), which is a blatant absurdity—Great Britain, with a
third of the population, records over five thousand such incidents
annually. Other statistics are badly collected, collated, and recorded. The bureaucracy acting in "support" of families, consisting in large part of poorly managed state-level "youth and family
services," requires complete overhaul, and the sooner the better.

But enough statistical material exists to give us a general picture of the trends in question. First and above all is the number of
illegitimate births. In 1970, the last census year prior to *Roe*, the
figure was 398,700, high enough, to be sure. But by 1980, it had
shot up to 665,747. From there, it rose relentlessly: by 2005, it had
reached 1,523,674.

---

*This is what Justice Ginsburg was referring to in her July 7, 2009, remarks to
the *New York Times*: "Frankly I had thought that at the time *Roe* was decided,
there was concern about population growth and particularly growth in populations that we don't want to have too many of. So that *Roe* was going to be then
set up for Medicaid funding for abortion. Which some people felt would risk
coercing women into having abortions when they didn't really want them."

One way of putting that figure in perspective is to note that it comprises 36.8 percent of all births, over a third of the 4,140,419 children born in the United States. Another is to note the 1950 figure: 141,600, or 3.9 percent of all births. In a little over fifty years, the number of illegitimate births has increased by a factor of ten.

Related figures dealing with child and family-related pathology have followed similar curves. According to the Department of Human Services, child victims of neglect and abuse consistently approach the one million mark. In 2005, these totaled 899,000 children. This represented a substantial drop from 1995, when over a million children were in some way brutalized or mistreated. Unfortunately, it represents a rise from 1999, when 826,000 children suffered.

Child deaths due to abuse—child murders, not to put too fine a point on it—have tracked a far simpler curve, increasing consistently from year to year. In 1995, the number was 996 killed. In 1999, this had grown to 1,100. In 2005, the number was 1,460. Considering the number of media reports of such crimes, this is almost certainly an underestimate.

There are other categories that might interest us, but these will do. They reveal a social train wreck in motion, a nation lacerating its upcoming generation without even being aware of the fact. The vastness of this catastrophe is almost beyond comprehension, its future course mercifully vague. It need only be mentioned that the majority of children involved are black.

Abortion does not bear total responsibility for this situation. There are numerous other factors of varying degrees of importance, interacting in ways we cannot fully grasp. But abortion is a key element. There is no way to arrive at an adequate explanation for this disaster without implicating the practice of casual abortion.

Our current dilemma is a classic example of unintended consequences. Easy availability of contraceptives triggered a boom in premarital sex, the storied "sexual revolution." But stupidity, lack of foresight, and runaway passion led to commonplace sloppiness in contraceptive use. The natural consequence was a rise in pregnancies. At the same time came the demise of the "shotgun marriage"—marriages in which the man was forced to "do the right thing" on behalf of his pregnant girlfriend. (During my childhood, the thought of having to explain that term would have been unimaginable.) Women now had an alternative—they didn't have to carry to term. So how could the man be held responsible? But a significant number of women, faced with the prospect of terminating a child, could not take that step. So the illegitimacy rate skyrocketed, along with associated social pathologies.

Abortion's central failing lay in easing male responsibility, always a mistake. Few situations exist where the average male, offered the opportunity to continue roaming, will not happily take it. As George Gilder, among others, has pointed out, women are responsible for civilizing males. They do so by luring men into the comfort and security of family life. This ritual dance has gone on since our days on the Serengeti, and in many ways defines our humanity in relation to the opposite sex. Easy abortion has in many cases curtailed it. The losers have been men and women equally.

But women have often paid the higher price, in the form of single motherhood, in raising children while also earning a living, in the loneliness and awkwardness of continuing the search for sex and affection long after the matter should have been settled. Abortion, we are assured, was intended to set women free. Apart from certain members of the upper middle class, such an argument would be difficult to sustain.

Other pathologies have followed in *Roe*'s train. There are women who use pregnancy to pressure their boyfriends or husbands, aborting the child after it has served its purpose. There are women who use pregnancy to test relationships, or to test their own fertility. There are, on the other hand, heartless males who order their women to "get rid of it," with the implied threat that it's either them or the child. Recent years have witnessed an increasing number of incidents in which minors have been forced into abortions by the men who abused them, in order to destroy the evidence of statutory rape.

None of these forms of misbehavior was available before the appearance of casual abortion. Create opportunities for bad conduct and people will take advantage of them. As for those of us who believe that government's role ought to limit such opportunities where possible . . . there's no real place for us in Roeland.

Finally, there is the existence of Post-Abortion Syndrome, an emotional and psychological reaction to abortion characterized by guilt feelings, anxiety attacks, and depression. Abortion is a traumatic event, and, like all such, incurs psychic cost. This is often aggravated by denial, since abortion victims are not encouraged to discuss their ordeals. In some cases the reaction can be of the utmost severity. Studies have found that women who have undergone abortions attempt suicide at a rate six to nine times higher than the average. After fighting a lengthy rear-guard action, the psychological establishment has admitted that such a syndrome may well exist, while adding that birth itself can also have adverse psychological consequences. And this is to leave unmentioned the number of women killed in botched abortions, another case for which no useful statistics exist.

Plainly, apart from acting as a form of after-the-fact birth control, abortion possesses no social utility whatsoever. Quite the contrary—there is no aspect of communal life which abortion has not degraded. If abortion had been forced on the country by an occupying army, its consequences would place it in the realm of crimes against humanity.

One exception exists to abortion's overall social failure. The introduction of advanced ultrasound imaging has, along with other tests, made it possible to identify severe and untreatable birth defects early in gestation, allowing the flawed pregnancy to be terminated. This is understandable, and easy to condone—except in the case of Down-syndrome children. Classically known as "mongolism" due to characteristic false epicanthic folds, Down syndrome is one of the milder forms of retardation. Though limited, Down children are highly affectionate and good-natured, a fact that has led a number of mothers to decide to give their afflicted child a chance. Unfortunately, such women are in the minority, and the number of Down children has steadily dropped, leading many mothers to worry that their children will grow up, and age, and at last die alone.

Chalk one up for the pro-choicers.*

So what is the answer? Why are liberals so beguiled by abortion? We have seen that it confers no advantages. Quite the contrary— it's a crippling burden on all levels. It is legally empty, and cannot serve as a precedent for similar action. Politically akin to suicide, it is a practice that has cost more liberal votes than any other single factor.

It is socially an atrocity, giving the lie to claims of superior morality and systematic compassion. Yet American liberals still cling to it. After thirty years and more, abortion continues to occupy a central position in their vision of domestic policy.

If the value of a thing or process acting within a political or social context is not apparent, it does not necessarily follow that it has no value. It means that the value is hidden, that it's expressed in a way not readily visible to casual observation. We have established that, from the liberal point of view, abortion has no value in the legal, political, and social spheres (and we could

---

*The liberal attitude toward such children was clearly revealed in the vitriolic public response to the birth of Sarah Palin's Down-syndrome child, Trig.

go on to the cultural, scientific, and religious as well). So where does its value lie? To answer that we must return to the question of ideology. One of the most attractive elements of the ideological states to the liberal mind-set was dominance, the ability to impose policies through direct compulsion, without debate, without consultation, without compromise.

As we have seen, much of the history of political liberalism over the past seventy years involves attempts to do exactly that. Beginning with the NRA and extending into the postwar era involving matters of criminal justice, economic leveling, and affirmative action, we find endless attempts to ram through suspect programs against the full weight of popular opposition, at first through political means, then legislative, and at last through the judiciary.

None of them ever worked as anticipated. All faltered, miscarried, or collapsed (sometimes only after several decades, as in the case of forced busing). With one exception: abortion, through *Roe v. Wade*, is the sole example of an apparently permanent social transformation brought about by judicial coercion. It marks the only occasion where the liberals brought it off. Other attempts have been made since, involving gay marriage and euthanasia, but none has been national in scope, none has affected the whole of society, none has been maintained over the long term despite all attempts to reverse it.

Roe is the liberal's single home run. It is their high-water mark. It is an expression of control over the very source of life itself, a proclamation of the ability to reach into the womb and shut it down, if they see fit. It is the benchmark of liberal dominance, one they have never exceeded, and one that they will never abandon, as long as they retain the means of defending it.

That's why casual abortion is still practiced nationwide. That's why 45 million potential lives have been extinguished in this country over the past four decades—as a political symbol, an expression of liberal power. Abortion is the purest example of ideological policy ever carried out in the United States.

THE PARTIAL-BIRTH FIASCO

We know that power tends to overreach—which is exactly what occurred with abortion. Partial-birth abortion is the popular term for an abortion method technically known as "intact dilation and extraction" (D&E). This repellent procedure was developed by a physician named James McMahon for the evident purpose of circumventing laws protecting viable infants from being aborted. Labor is artificially stimulated and allowed to continue until the head appeared in the birth canal, at which point a scissors or forceps is jammed into the back of the child's head, a vacuum nozzle introduced into the wound, the brains sucked out, and the skull collapsed.

Partial-birth abortion proved to be the downfall of the "absolutist" interpretation of abortion. It was impossible to justify such a procedure, and public outrage was widespread. The pro-abortion responses—that no such procedure existed and that it was utilized in only a handful of cases—were less than convincing. The first was a variety of word game—practitioners used "D&E" and not "partial-birth." As for the second, the level of record-keeping typical of abortion clinics allowed no such claim to be made with confidence. Annual estimates concerning the procedure varied from "a few dozen" to over 2,200, quite a large range. But this argument overlooked the fact that in the public mind not a single child should ever suffer such a fate. The very existence of partial-birth abortion brought to mind images of the crimes of Josef Mengele that pro-lifers had always insisted were the only true measure of the tragedy of abortion.

For these reasons, among others, politicians had no fears of tackling the issue. Congress twice passed laws prohibiting the procedure, in 1996 and 1997. These were vetoed, as expected, by Bill Clinton. In 2003 the bill was reintroduced, passed, and signed into law by George W. Bush.

Pro-abortion organizations appealed to the Supreme Court. But it was a new era and a new Court. On April 18, 2007, in a 5–4 decision, the Court upheld a Nebraska law banning partial-birth abortion. The decision was the work of Anthony Kennedy, who had written an opinion striking down a similar law seven years previously. Ethical and moral considerations, wrote Kennedy, amounted to compelling state interests in the case of partial-birth abortion. *Gonzales v. Carhart* was the first decision to ban outright a form of abortion, and the first to contain no health exception.

With the turn of the new century, abortion had reached its high-tide mark and begun a slow retreat. Numerous supporters, among them Naomi Wolf, William Saletan, and Dr. Bernard Nathanson, have expressed second thoughts. The new pro-abortion slogan was "Keep it legal, but rare." And it was becoming rarer. According to the Guttmacher Institute, the research arm of Planned Parenthood, 1.29 million abortions were performed in 2003, a dramatic fall from the peak of 1.6 million in 1990.

Casual abortion may well prove to be the pathological symptom of a particular epoch, one that will not survive into a new period. *Roe* may hang on for a decade, perhaps even two, but its days are numbered. The attempt to impose a new social order centered on abortion has proven a failure.

According to Edmund Burke, the true measure of a civilization lies in how it treats its weakest members. By those criteria, we are not yet civilized. But we may get there yet, through the process of democratic consensus, interrupted by decree in the winter of 1973.

If we believe absurdities, we shall commit atrocities.
—VOLTAIRE

5

GAIA'S CHILDREN

The Greens Cash In

The *Silent Spring* template has served the modern environmental movement well. In the wake of the book's appearance and the ensuing campaign against DDT, environmentalism underwent a sea change, metamorphosing from a conventional reform movement working within an accepted social framework into what amounted to a pseudo-revolutionary cult.

Prior to Rachel Carson, environmentalism had been widely known as "conservationism," a word and concept that would be utterly unfamiliar to today's Greens. A product of the Missionary Generation, the turn-of-the-twentieth-century cohort devoted to good works, political reform, and social betterment, conservationism was exemplified by the California naturalist John Muir, a pioneer of nature writing, and Teddy Roosevelt, who, among much else oversaw the beginning of the great American national park system. The conservationists were motivated by respect and appreciation for nature, devoting themselves to the protection of threatened species, the preservation of wilderness areas, and the cultivation of public interest in the natural world. In retrospect, it's possible to envision the conservationist impulse gradually spreading across American society as a whole, instilling a set of values in which pride in nature and concern for its welfare might have become permanent aspects of the American civil character.

Instead we got environmentalism, a chopped and channeled version of conservationism based not on love of anything but on hostility toward American society, contempt for democratic capitalism, and hatred of humanity in general. Conservationism had become, in a word, ideologized. From a doctrine based on careful nurturing and protection of the environment, environmentalism became simply another expression of the adversary culture.

At one time a low-key movement, environmentalism turned aggressive. At one time a movement appealing to the higher civic virtues, environmentalism began dealing in fear and paranoia. At one time closely associated with conservative values, environmentalism became explicitly revolutionary.

The environmentalist method followed the DDT paradigm in detail. A compound, material, or procedure in widespread use was identified as a public threat. As with DDT, the target was depicted in the most horrifying terms conceivable, with particular emphasis on the threat of cancer, teratogenic mutations, and effects on children. Unsourced stories of its deadliness were spread through the media, backed by manipulated statistics and mercenary scientific testimony. The scientific studies quoted in these campaigns were often misrepresented (in many cases they were limited to the megadose effects on white mice and rats) if not fabricated from whole cloth. By this means, public anxieties were deliberately and repeatedly amplified to the point of hysteria.

Materials, compounds, and processes subject to this treatment include nuclear power, PCBs, dioxins, "acid rain," Alar, "secondhand smoke," electromagnetic fields, "noise pollution," ozone depletion, several different (and contradictory) forms of climate change, medical waste, nitrates, phosphates, asbestos, large automobiles and trucks, and beef cattle, to mention only the most prominent examples over the past forty years. (The latest example involves the phthalates, a family of esters used to soften plastics. Repeated massive doses of phthalates can cause subtle changes in the endocrine systems of rats. Simply scale up for humans using plastic sandwich bags. The basic research here was carried out in the cutting-edge scientific center of Bulgaria.) The bombardment became continuous, with several targets often sharing the stage at the same time. Another threat would be ramped up even as the last receded from attention. A sense of public unease became constant, expressed in the outcry that "Everything in the world is dangerous!"

Some of the targets, such as dioxins and PCBs, were perfectly legitimate subjects for inquiry, well deserving of close examination. Some were not quite the threats that the environmental movement claimed them to be. Some were bogus from start to finish.

These campaigns usually resulted in some kind of ameliorative action, often in the form of a ban, not infrequently a de facto ban laid down by acquiescent courts, in which judicial decisions rendered the substance or process too difficult or expensive to use. This was the fate of the American nuclear power industry. A relentless opposition campaign during the late 1970s coincided with accidents at ill-managed plants such as Three Mile Island to result in an effective banning of all new nuclear power plants. This ban remained in place for thirty years, despite the fact that new generations of power reactors have overcome the failings of earlier models (for example, the CANDU and pebble-bed reactors, which cannot melt down in the fashion of Three Mile Island's light-water reactor).

The odd thing about these victories is that they did little to protect either the public or the environment. While conservationists could point to so many thousands of wilderness acres set aside, or to threatened species such as the bald eagle or whooping crane brought back from the verge of extinction, their environmentalist heirs could display no such triumphs. According to their own rhetoric, the world only grew worse the more powerful and all-pervading their movement became—the threats more numerous and deadly, the natural environment more degraded, the future more appalling.

There are reasons for this. Often the changes introduced by environmentalists acted for worse rather than better. Replacement materials and processes occasionally proved more dangerous or destructive than those banned or forced off the market. Second-order effects impossible to predict beforehand negated or even reversed environmentalist efforts. (We'll encounter several examples below.) Like all ideologues, environmentalists were picture painters, constructing vast and elaborate visions of the world that would result from their efforts. When the world went its own way, revealing a different, less attractive image, environmentalists often failed to adjust, instead becoming nonplussed, confused, and despondent—though never quite enough to reconsider either principles or tactics.

As occurred in the case of DDT, the unforeseen effects were frequently lethal. Environmentalism introduced serious danger into American society on a number of levels, often unnecessarily, and with few countervailing benefits. The more integral a part of public life environmentalism became, the worse effects it had. The environmentalists promised a new world. What they delivered was social disruption, a climate of fear, and an unparalleled waste of time, money, energy—and lives.

DEATH BY CAFE

One of the memorable public hysterias of the 1970s involved the "oil shortage." A short-lived 1973 oil embargo imposed by OPEC in response to Israeli victory in the Yom Kippur War dovetailed with environmentalist rhetoric concerning "declining resources" to create a nationwide panic inflamed by irresponsible media coverage and poor government decisions.

Prominent among these was the Corporate Average Fuel Economy (CAFE) Program, passed as part of the 1975 Energy Policy and Conservation Act. The CAFE standards required that both domestic and foreign automobile manufacturers make substantial increases in the gas mileage achieved by their cars and light trucks within a limited period under the threat of stiff fines.

The industry succeeded in increasing vehicle mileage through the single solution open at the time: designing cars with smaller, fuel-efficient engines while shrinking vehicle weight and dimensions so that performance remained adequate.

Environmentalist panics commonly create truly grotesque examples of unintended consequences (for example, the wind farms that produce piles of dead birds wherever they're constructed—paging Rachel Carson!), and the CAFE standards were no exception. Hopes that gas consumption would drop were dashed by the "rebound effect," in which greater energy efficiency leads to greater energy use. Since smaller cars cost less to drive, motorists drove more often. While automobiles became up to 50 percent more fuel efficient, the average number of miles driven more than doubled.

Another expression of the rebound effect involved the family station wagon. A ubiquitous presence in American driveways during the postwar period, the station wagon was killed by CAFE when lawmakers refused to classify it as a light truck with a consequently lower mileage rating. After several years of tinkering, the industry acknowledged that the fuel-efficient station wagon was a contradiction in terms. Needing a vehicle capable of transporting hordes of small children and associated gear, families turned to the SUV, which, while admirably suited to the role, burned more gas than any three station wagons. The SUV soon became the font of all evil among environmentalists and politicians.

The standards also failed in their major political purpose—
that of lowering oil imports. From 35 percent in the mid-1970s,
imports increased to 52 percent by the turn of the century. But the
most serious effect was on highway safety. Cars were made large
and heavy for reasons quite apart from pulling in more cash for
Detroit. As a simple matter of physics, drivers of lightweight cars
face a heightened risk of injury or death. The larger and heavier
the vehicle, the more material it contains to absorb impact along
with greater space to attenuate impact forces before they cause
injury. In contrast, drivers in lightweight cars were as much as
twelve times more likely to die in a crash. Such findings were repeatedly verified by independent studies:

- A 1989 study by Robert Crandall of the Brookings Institution and John Graham of the Harvard School of Public
  Health, neither of them hotbeds of reaction, found that the
  five-hundred-pound weight reduction of the average car increased annual highway fatalities by 2,200 to 3,900 and
  serious injuries by 11,000 to 19,500 per year.
- A 1999 USA Today study found that 7,700 deaths occurred
  for every mile per gallon gained in fuel economy standards.
  Smaller cars accounted for up to 12,144 deaths in 1997, 37
  percent of all vehicle fatalities for that year, while comprising only 18 percent of all vehicles.
- In 2001, the National Academy of Sciences found that
  smaller, lighter vehicles "probably resulted in an additional
  1,300 to 2,600 traffic fatalities in 1993."
- A 2003 National Highway Transportation and Safety Administration study demonstrated that reducing a vehicle's
  weight by only one hundred pounds increased the fatality
  rate by as much as 5.63 percent for light cars, 4.70 percent
  for heavier cars, and 3.06 percent for light trucks. These
  rates translated into 13,608 additional traffic fatalities for

light cars, 10,884 for heavier cars, and 14,705 for light trucks between 1996 and 1999.

As Crandall and Graham put it, "the negative relationship between weight and occupant fatality risk is one of the most secure findings in the safety literature." And the total cost? Depending on which estimates you use, 41,600 to 124,800 deaths since the standards went into effect. This appalling toll of unnecessary and unjustifiable mortality is accompanied by a similar number of serious injuries—which can mean being crippled for life—totaling between 352,000 and 624,000 over the same period.

What was the response from environmentalists and other CAFE supporters? Some reacted with denial, claiming that actual deaths amounted to zero, a contention that would require the repeal of Newton's laws of motion. Others pointed out that traffic fatalities had dropped overall, suggesting that the effect of CAFE was minimal. This argument overlooked the fact that the same period saw the introduction of lifesaving devices such as airbags. Clearly, the drop in highway deaths would have been even more dramatic in the absence of the CAFE standards.

But the most common argument involved the menace of heavy cars and trucks. In a collision, such vehicles tend to annihilate smaller and lighter cars. It was this factor alone, insisted CAFE supporters, that explained high auto casualty rates. The problem with this contention was that most automobile collisions involve only a single vehicle, and the SUV, the main target of environmentalist wrath, was involved in only 4 percent of fatal accidents. In light of such facts, the CAFE adherents' claims come across as weak efforts to camouflage a losing argument.

But where politicians are concerned, weak efforts are often all that is necessary. In 2007, Congress revisited the CAFE regulations, not in hopes of halting the carnage, but to further extend the standards already in effect, an effort directed in large part against that devil's chariot, the SUV. In early 2008, the single standard for light trucks was replaced by a new set of regulations dividing the class into six categories based on size and weight, with each having a distinct miles-per-gallon target. Overall fuel economy is to be raised from 22.2 mpg to 24 mpg. The standards already in place regarding cars were also extended and made more rigorous.

Automobile design is much better understood today than it was in the 1970s. Greater fuel efficiency can be attained by utilizing advanced lubricants, installing computerized valve systems and transmissions, and adopting stop-start engines (which shut down while idling and then restart automatically), all without adversely affecting vehicle weight and sturdiness. It is possible that the new standards can be met without a sudden jump in automotive deaths. Not that any such factors entered into congressional considerations for one moment—no more than they did in the cases of criminal justice or DDT. It's a sad state of affairs when we must rely on automotive engineers to protect us from politicians.

THE BIG RIPOUT

Asbestos is a silicate mineral with the rare property of breaking apart into fibers, as if it were some kind of uncanny, earth-wrought textile. It possesses a number of other valuable qualities as well: it is resistant to heat and flame, does not conduct electricity, and is practically indestructible. Asbestos occurs naturally in deposits throughout the world. Its varieties include serpentine or white asbestos, which is long and curly, easily woven, and is the most widely used form. White asbestos is mined largely in Canada. Amphibole asbestos, which occurs in both brown and blue varieties, is straight and needle-like. Its applications are limited. It is found mainly in South Africa.

Although it has been mined in the United States since the 1850s, asbestos did not come into common use until WWII, when it proved invaluable to the war effort as insulation and fireproofing for the shipbuilding industry and in military base construction around the world.

After the war, asbestos use redoubled as a major element in the postwar construction boom. Its applications seemed endless: along with insulation and fireproofing it was utilized to stiffen cement, in ceiling and floor tiles, in roofing slates, as sound-proofing material, and as an ingredient of paint, plastic, putty, and other compounds. In the United States alone over 100,000 schools, 700,000 public and commercial buildings, and count-less private homes contained asbestos in one form or another. The automotive industry also employed asbestos for use in brake linings.

Asbestos appeared to be the perfect industrial resource: cheap, widely available, easily worked, and harmless. But asbestos had a dark side, one that became apparent decades after its introduc-tion as a ubiquitous material. Mining and industrial operations involving asbestos commonly created dense clouds of loose fibers. Once inhaled, these fibers could lodge within the lungs, poisoning and infecting surrounding tissue. The latency period for asbestos turned out to be on the order of thirty to forty years. By the early 1970s, serious health problems had begun to appear in tens of thousands of workers exposed to asbestos.

Asbestos-related disorders included lung cancer, asbestosis (a chronic form of pulmonary inflammation), and mesothelioma (a particularly hideous cancer afflicting the membranes of the chest and abdomen). Workers in all industries utilizing asbestos on a large scale were susceptible, along with their families, who suf-fered exposure to asbestos-covered work clothing.

Asbestos poisoning was the worst industrial disaster of the twentieth century. Over 170,000 American workers have died of asbestos-related causes, and another 120,000 deaths are likely to occur before the epidemic finally runs out in the 2020s.

Under rational circumstances, the response would have been straightforward: an industry-financed fund for treatment of stricken workers, and a set of stringent regulations including masks, sealed workspaces, and careful inspections for all further operations involving asbestos. But the 1970s was not a rational era. It was the decade of Love Canal, acid rain, and Three Mile Island, when environmental paranoia became a standard fixture of life in the United States. The shadow of Rachel Carson loomed large, and asbestos was given the full DDT treatment.

The wonder material was instantly transformed into a poison in the same class as plutonium and dioxin. There was, medical authorities insisted, "no safe level" of asbestos exposure (an unlikely assumption—naturally occurring asbestos had been blowing around since before humans first trod the Serengeti). Some researchers, led by Dr. Irving Selikoff of Mt. Sinai Medical School, claimed that a single inhaled fiber could lead to cancer.

The media leaped on the story without hesitation. In 1978, CBS News introduced major coverage of the asbestos crisis with three lengthy segments and numerous shorter reports, including several contributions from God's honest man, Dan Rather. All of them relentlessly hammered the "asbestos as plague of mankind" thesis. Accusations of corporate conspiracy were, as ever, a dominant feature. Detailed catalogs of asbestos use were formulated, including claims that asbestos was present in crayons, talcum power, and tampons. Particularly panicky reports appeared concerning the use of asbestos in cement water pipes, even though the mineral had never been implicated in gastrointestinal disorders.

In an anonymous, badly prepared report, the National Cancer Institute and the National Institute for Environmental Health Sciences predicted 2 million excess cancer deaths over the next thirty years, with asbestos responsible for a large proportion of them. This figure was repeated publicly by the Carter administration's secretary of health, Joseph Califano, who added that up to 17 percent of all cancer deaths were attributable to asbestos and that all workers in any industry using asbestos were in danger.

The Consumer Product Safety Commission banned asbestos from products used directly by the public. (This led to tragic consequences on January 28, 1986, when the space shuttle *Challenger* exploded only seconds after leaving the launch pad, killing its entire crew. While blame quickly focused on the solid-fuel booster's O-rings, years passed before it was revealed that the original asbestos paste used to set the O-rings had been replaced due to the ban. The inferior new paste failed in action, allowing superheated gases to burn through the O-rings and ignite the shuttle's fuel.) The industry itself came under legal attack in some of the largest class-action lawsuits undertaken up to that time. Close to a quarter of a million separate lawsuits were filed against asbestos producers, processors, and suppliers. Even the mighty Johns Manville Corporation, which at one time had been powerful enough to found its own town (Manville, New Jersey), was forced into bankruptcy under the legal deluge.

All of which left one question unresolved: What was to be done about the hundreds of thousands of buildings across the country containing asbestos?

The Environmental Protection Agency (EPA) had no doubts. The agency in 1979 issued a handbook on asbestos, the cheerfully colored "Orange Book," calling for the immediate removal of asbestos under all circumstances. The same advice was reiterated in the similarly florid "Blue Book" in 1983.

Frightened homeowners began tearing out any material that looked in the least suspicious or unusual. Real estate transactions were canceled due to the presence of "asbestos"—which often proved to be anything but. Both real and phantom contamination closed down buildings across the country.

It required several years for the development of adequate procedures for asbestos removal. In the interim, hundreds of "rip and run" companies sprang up, winning removal contracts, hiring low-quality, often immigrant labor, tearing out a building's asbestos with no safeguards or precautions whatsoever, then leaving the building, surroundings, and sometimes entire neighborhoods heavily contaminated.

In 1986, Congress passed the Asbestos Hazard Emergency Response Act (AHERA), establishing regulations for asbestos removal as well as requiring schools to prepare plans to "manage"—which at that time meant remove—asbestos found in school buildings. Asbestos removal went into high gear nationwide.

Removal was now rigorously regulated, with work areas sealed and workers required to wear environmental suits. Buildings containing removal sites were usually closed, sometimes for months on end, and their functions transferred elsewhere. All types of public buildings, not to mention other structures, were affected—schools, factories, fire stations, city halls and other government buildings, post offices, libraries, and hospitals, not to mention L. Ron Hubbard's private cruise ship, the *Freewinds*.

But however high the standards, and however effective the containment, there was no hiding the fact that removal released large amounts of asbestos filaments, not all of which could be isolated once work was finished. Buildings subjected to asbestos removal suffered a much higher level of filaments per square millimeter than had previously been the case. As was often true of environmentalist solutions, it seemed that the cure was worse than the disease.

The EPA had begun to back off from its earlier insistence on removal as the only solution. In yet another colorful volume, the "Purple Book," published in 1985, the EPA suggested that managing asbestos in situ might be the preferable alternative under some circumstances.

The EPA's new approach was a response to a widespread scientific backlash against asbestos hysteria. Much the same as with the climate-change debate today, many scientists and physicians were critical of both the unreasoning fear surrounding the issue and the policy of removal as the sole practical solution.

Overlooked in the original panic was the fact that the vast bulk of asbestos used in the U.S.—as much as 95 percent—was a serpentine variety known as chrysotile. The curly shape of chrysotile asbestos assured that it could not penetrate deep into the lungs and was easily washed out by bodily processes. Simply put, chrysotile asbestos was not the cause of the types of disorders suffered by asbestos workers. The essential harmlessness of the chrysotile variety was underlined by a 1986 *American Review of Respiratory Diseases* study of workers and their families in Thetford Mines, Quebec, the main source of chrysotile asbestos. Although the town was saturated with asbestos and surrounded by vast mounds of tailings, women living there remained unaffected. Workers in the mines themselves also remained healthy until exposed to heavy fiber concentrations of 95 to 194 per cc.

Crocidolite (or blue asbestos) was another story. Its needlelike structure assured that it remained in the lungs, causing serious scarring that resulted in pulmonary disorders of the type found in asbestos workers. Fortunately, only 2.5 percent of the asbestos used in the U.S. was of the crocidolite variety, much of it limited to shipbuilding. (A third type, armosite, or brown asbestos, while problematic, was no match for the danger of crocidolite.)

The new findings changed the complexion of the debate, at least among the better-informed. At the same time a consensus was growing among scientists that asbestos removal was a poor strategy in a majority of cases.

Health Aspects of Exposure to Asbestos in Buildings was the title of the proceedings of a 1989 symposium held at the Energy and Environmental Policy Center at Harvard's Kennedy School of Government. The proceedings dismissed the current asbestos hysteria as "out of proportion to the existing public health risk," and also recommended against continuing removal as a policy. The Harvard group was soon joined by a team led by Dr. Brooke T. Mossman, a cell biologist at the University of Vermont's medical school. In a study published in *Science* magazine in January 1990, Dr. Mossman's group found the asbestos hysteria "unprecedented." "As a result of public pressure," the report read, "asbestos is often removed haphazardly from schools and public buildings." The report recommended that removal occur only when strictly necessary. In 1991, the American Medical Association published a review through its Council on Scientific Affairs that concurred with both of these studies.

Later that same year, the EPA, at the urging of Congress, financed a study of the actual risk of asbestos in buildings, a study that should have been carried out a decade and a half previously. The Health Effects Institute's two-volume report found that the health risks of asbestos in buildings were minimal—in fact, ten time less than that of outside air—and that the policy of removal should be abandoned. These findings had been anticipated in yet another colorful EPA volume, the "Green Book," which stated that asbestos in public buildings, including schools, presented no risk and should be left where it was. The governmental aspect of the great asbestos hysteria had come to a belated end.

But panics are not ended by decrees. The damage caused by the great asbestos hysteria remains to this day. The asbestos industry is functionally moribund, perhaps never to be revived. Domestic consumption of asbestos was 803,000 metrics tons in 1973. By 2005, it had dropped to 2,400 metric tons.

Despite efforts by scientists and the newly enlightened EPA (whose administrator William K. Reilly in 1992 went so far as to give a public apology for the agency's role), removal of asbestos continues, at a cost of up to $3 billion a year. The absolute deadliness of asbestos has become conventional wisdom, a concept hammered into the public consciousness, and no longer subject to correction or modification.

In 2004, the cloakroom and press gallery of the U.S. Senate were closed for months after a single filament of asbestos was discovered following removal operations. Tests showed that the number of filaments in the chambers was 99 per millimeter, well above the danger level.

Many questions remain. How much of the asbestos removed during the peak years of hysteria was the relatively harmless chrysotile, the slightly more dangerous armosite, or the deadly crocidolite? We don't know. What about the workers on those projects? How much were they exposed, and to what? Have they been medically monitored since? Did anyone even bother to keep a record of their names? We don't know that either. And the buildings, streets, and neighborhoods where these removals occurred—how much exposure did they suffer? We know that typical removal operations, as one source puts it, "can release substantial amounts of asbestos fibers into the air. Post-abatement fiber levels are occasionally so high . . . that they approach those that asbestos workers were exposed to 50 years ago." Were any records kept, any analyses made, any warnings issued? Again, we have no idea.

We have no idea because that's how panic works. In the mindless fervor to rid the earth of a deadly poison, all safeguards were subverted, all standard procedure thrown aside, all second thoughts dismissed. Thanks to a nightmare triangle of Green advocates, media hacks, and feckless bureaucrats, the public ended up being subjected to the very risks they were most seeking to avoid. The process continues to this day.

ASTHMA VS. THE EARTH

Asthma is the most widespread and well-known respiratory disorder, afflicting up to 17 million Americans. There are very few people in this country who aren't acquainted with at least one person stricken by the disease. Other disorders such as chronic obstructive pulmonary disorder (COPD) and cystic fibrosis raise the total of Americans suffering a respiratory ailment to nearly 40 million, or over 10 percent of the population.

Asthma is a chronic condition in which inflammation of lung tissues triggers bronchospasm, a sudden, drastic narrowing of the bronchial tubes. Symptoms can range from shortness of breath in mild cases to actual suffocation in instances where the bronchial tubes close up completely. Brain damage from lack of oxygen is not unknown. Asthma attacks can be triggered by allergens, smoke, infections, weather changes, stress, medications, or environmental factors.

Asthma is a recognized killer, responsible for the deaths of several thousand victims a year. Paradoxically, the death rate increased for several decades even as treatment improved, rising from a low of near two thousand annually in the early 1960s to a peak of over five thousand in 1996. This rise may in truth be illusory, an artifact of improved diagnostics. In a rare admission for a government agency, the Centers for Disease Control has stated that it remains unsure.

Treatments for asthma range from environmental control measures such as ridding the victim's surroundings of potential trigger factors to an array of medications, largely of recent vintage, formulated to dilate air passages and fight inflammation. While many of these drugs are intended for use in long-term therapy, the most critical class are "rescue medications" introduced to deal with the asthma sufferers' worst nightmare: a sudden attack in a situation where no medical help is available. These drugs, called bronchodilators, include beta-agonists such as Ventolin, Maxair, and Brethaire, and anticholinergics such as Atrovent and Spiriva to open bronchial tubes, along with corticosteroids to battle inflammation.

Rescue medications come in the form of inhalers, in which an inert propellant forces the drugs into the lungs, soothing inflamed tissues and opening blocked passages. Relief is nearly instantaneous, and, with proper use, side effects are minimal. Inhalers were inexpensive and readily available. Easily stored in a purse or jacket pocket, they enabled asthma sufferers to bid farewell to fears of medical emergencies while assuring a welcome return to normal life. Short of an actual cure, inhalers offered asthma sufferers the best of all possible worlds.

An effective treatment, cheap, safe, widely available, and self-administered. Experience tells us there must be a downside. Fortunately, we have alert government bureaucrats to keep a close watch.

The problem lay not with the inhalers themselves, or with the medication, but with the propellant, which turned out to consist of that enemy of all things natural, chlorofluorocarbons (CFCs). The amount in each inhaler was scarcely enough to bother a flea, with the annual worldwide total of all CFCs used in inhalers on the order of ten thousand tons, which sounds large but in relation to the mass of earth's atmosphere is minuscule. But all the same, CFCs in asthma inhalers presented a theoretical threat to the ozone layer. And where environmentalism is concerned, a theory, no matter how unlikely, beats any number of facts.

The ozone layer is a high-altitude atmospheric layer protecting the earth's surface from harmful solar radiation. It was theorized—though never conclusively demonstrated—that CFCs introduced into the atmosphere at the earth's surface could drift into the stratosphere, react with atmospheric ozone, and thin out the layer enough to allow penetration by ultraviolet B (UVB) rays, which could interfere with plant and animal life and cause increased levels of skin cancer in humans.

The sole evidence supporting this thesis was the infamous "ozone hole," a region of seriously depleted ozone over the continent of Antarctica. Ominous reports that the "ozone hole" was spreading, and soon to engulf the southern cone of Latin America before moving on to the equator, were commonplace media fare throughout the late 1980s, and helped ignite an environmental hysteria nearly as frenzied, though not as widespread, as global warming in the millennial era.* It was never explained why this hole formed in the terrestrial region most isolated from CFC sources, rather than in the atmosphere above the sources themselves. As it developed, the "hole" was revealed to be a seasonal phenomenon, appearing like clockwork every Antarctic winter, retreating once again when the sun reappeared.

Despite the weakness of the ozone depletion case, the UN in 1987 convened the Montreal Protocol on Substances That Deplete the Ozone Layer to oversee the phaseout of CFCs. The protocol dealt for the most part with air-conditioning and refrigeration systems. Items such as asthma inhalers went unaddressed, in keeping with the "health exemption," a longstanding convention that substance bans do not extend to lifesaving applications.

But this status quo solution failed to take account of the power of Green absolutism. The lifesaving exemption went on the block with the appointment of Carol M. Browner as head of Bill Clinton's Environmental Protection Agency. Browner was as much an environmental totalist as has ever served in American government. She was a prime mover in the campaign against "secondhand smoke," a claim that environmental tobacco smoke was as deadly as the hazard of smoking cigarettes directly, if not more so. Once public smoking was banned throughout most of the U.S., it was revealed that most of the "research" backing this contention had essentially been fabricated.

In Browner's mind, a ban was a ban, pure and simple, no ex-

---

*So convoluted has environmental rhetoric become concerning such topics that much of the public believes ozone depletion and global warming to be one and the same thing.

ceptions granted. Accordingly, she instructed the American delegation to press for a decision eliminating the health exemption at
the ninth Montreal Protocol meeting. This was duly carried out
as Decision IX/19 Part 5. It was the only substantive amendment
ever made to the original agreement.

The decision was implemented not by the EPA but by the Food
and Drug Administration (FDA), an agency originally established
to protect the interests of patients as regards drugs and medical devices. A new propellant, hydrofluoroalkane (HFA), was
proposed and tested. The most common type of medication, al-
buterol, was reformulated for use with HFA.

In the rush to save the earth, certain aspects of the FDA's usually rigorous and lengthy review process appear to have been set
aside. Industry testing was limited in both number and duration,
and involved only mildly afflicted asthma sufferers.

Introduction of the new inhalers occurred over a period of
several years and was carried out largely by stealth—little or no
effort was made to inform the vast pool of potential users. The
date for the final changeover was set at December 31, 2008. From
then on, CFC inhalers would be illegal and unavailable anywhere
in the home of the brave.

Many asthma sufferers were taken by surprise, learning of the
change only when making their first purchase of the new year. (It
was impossible to mistake the two types of inhalers—the HFA
variety, for one thing, cost eight to ten times more than the old
model.) Only when actual use revealed problems were asthma
patients informed that the dependable old-style devices were now
impossible to obtain.

The response was something close to blind panic. Tens of
thousands of complaints inundated pharmacists, doctors, pharmaceutical companies, politicians, and the bureaucracy. The comments have a nearly monotonous consistency. The new inhalers

offered no relief. The propellant had no push, and the medication was simply not reaching the lungs. (The FDA's response to this complaint, that users should "take a deep breath," suggests that agency understanding of asthma's actual nature was somewhat less than complete.) Air passages remained inflamed and breathing remained stifled. Nor was that the worst case: it developed that thousands of users were allergic to either HFA or the reformulated medication. Many reported a "burning sensation" in their throats and chests, along with vomiting and uncontrollable coughing.

Desperate for relief, some users repeated applications so frequently that they began to suffer symptoms of steroid poisoning, including hair loss and heart palpitations. Emergency room visits and hospitalizations skyrocketed. As a crowning blow, the new inhalers lasted only half as long as the classic models.

One common feature of these complaints was the pathetic pleas that the victims themselves were fervent environmentalists: " . . . as green as they get," as one writer put it, "making all of my life decisions based on what is good for the environment." As if such statements promised some kind of exemption; as if an exception would be made as long as the victim recycled regularly.

Asthma sufferers coped in various ways. A lucky few succeeded in scooping up the last CFC inhalers before they were pulled off the market. Others had small supplies that they carefully hoarded. A few began ordering replacements from foreign sources over the Internet, transforming themselves into criminals in the eyes of the state. Most were forced to fall back on use of the nebulizer, a bulky and impractical alternative that required asthma sufferers to remain close to home, prohibiting lengthy trips, not to mention activities involving strenuous exercise.

Sympathy from the authorities was sparse. Many doctors dismissed the complaints, insisting that their patients had adjusted with little difficulty. (This attitude, strangely enough, was rare among physicians who were themselves asthma victims.)

Little reportage appeared in the major media, while politicians were preoccupied with spending their share of Barack Obama's largesse.

The response from the bureaucrats was utterly cold. The agencies had their agenda, and the sick could kindly step aside. The old, effective devices were history, and would not be reinstated. There would be no investigation, no new tests, no recognition of any problem. In the words of FDA spokesman Christopher Kelly: "People will have to get used to the new inhalers."

Compare this to the FDA's response in 2005, when the asthma and allergy drug Singulair was reported to cause "suicidal thoughts." This alone (no actual deaths were reported) was enough to trigger a full probe into the drug's effects along with widespread public warnings concerning its use.

For the first time on record, the federal government for purely ideological reasons turned its back on a safe, effective medical treatment, in the process putting one-tenth of the country's population in danger of illness, incapacitation, and death. At least one fatality is attributable to the new inhalers. On February 25, 2007, Krimson Leah Hughey of Columbus, Ohio, suffered a serious asthma attack. Her HFA inhaler, at that time an unknown novelty, proved useless. Although her father applied CPR, Hughey sustained severe brain damage from lack of oxygen and died in the hospital less than two weeks later.

Similar fatalities may well follow. A common fear among asthma sufferers is that of dying during an attack. Some will not escape that fate. Asthma deaths dropped steadily from 5,627 in 1996 to 3,816 in 2004, largely thanks to CFC inhalers. We can only await the next set of statistics with foreboding.

But asthma victims can take heart in one thing—it seems that the HFA inhalers are also scourges of nature, providing a scarcely measurable boost to global warming. They may yet join their predecessors on the banned list.

THE RAGE OF GAIA

One truly strange aspect of American millennial culture involves a revival of paganism through the introduction of Gaia, a synthetic goddess-figure representing the earth and combining aspects of both the Earth Mother and mother goddesses such as Hecuba. The concept of Gaia was formulated by James Lovelock, a British scientist who in the 1960s theorized that a hidden homeostatic mechanism existed within earth's biosphere that regulated the environment to assure that temperature, climate, rainfall, and other factors remained within a certain rough mean, never spiraling to life-threatening extremes. As scientists tend to do, he gave this mechanism a catchy name: Gaia.

But then the Greens, most of whom are not noted for close reading of the scientific literature, latched on to the name while dumping the theory, reworking Gaia as a kind of primordial personification of the earth itself, a supernatural entity possessing the looks of Angelina Jolie, the power of Oprah Winfrey, and the temper of Katie Couric. In short order, Gaia became the mythological face of the environmental movement.

In a truly weird development, Lovelock turned his back on his own science, accepted the redacted Gaia, and began publicly referring to "her" as if she were a real entity, with an independent conscious existence, in the process retroactively turning himself into a prophet of the Green Dispensation. And people complain about Evangelicals.

The creed of Gaia has been preached far and wide through the media and all other possible sources. This is no longer our world—it belongs to Gaia now, and we don't even rate as guests, possessing no rights that can't be trumped by the smallest arthropod or mollusk. In the pre-Christian epoch, the world was the property of gods, demons, and various other supernatural entities, with humans acting merely as a kind of resource. (Ovid's *Metamorphoses* was a clear poetic expression of this credo.) With the advent of Gaia, we're halfway back to that status.

Being a pagan goddess, Gaia will have blood—if not burnt offerings. As the new millennium has waxed, no end of dangerous, potentially deadly policies have been passed in Gaia's name.

- Asthma inhalers were far from the only items banned to protect the ozone layer. Other compounds besides CFCs threatened the cloak of Gaia, including a family of chemicals called halons. Nontoxic "clean agents"—that is, chemicals that leave no harmful residue—halons were the most efficient firefighting chemicals ever discovered, and the only ones suitable for certain applications, including aircraft fires. All the same, they are being phased out—a little something to concentrate the mind the next time you experience an in-flight emergency.

- In December 2007, yet another "energy bill" was passed by Congress and signed into law by President Bush. One provision that went undiscussed was the bill's banning of the incandescent lightbulb, on the grounds that it "contributed to global warming." Replacing it by 2014 was the compact fluorescent bulb, which traded better efficiency for poor illumination and light quality. Another drawback was that it contained hazardous quantities of mercury. Attempt to smuggle mercury into the home for any other purpose and the lawsuits would fly like hail, but not in this case. In the event of a broken bulb, the EPA recommends that the vicinity be cleared "for at least fifteen minutes." Try explaining that to a three-year-old.

- As if being poisoned by a lightbulb or burnt to death on an airport runway in fulfillment of government policy were not bad enough, we also face the prospect of being eaten in our own backyards, or worse, seeing it happen to our children.

In the interests of fostering "biodiversity," a theoretical concept with several conflicting definitions, the federal government, in the form of the Fish and Wildlife Service, has established programs to "reintroduce" large predators, including grizzly bears and cougars, into wilderness areas. These programs have the support of Green organizations such as the Sierra Club and the National Wildlife Federation. The argument in favor of this activity is that the animals were once native to certain areas and are simply being returned to where they belong. As this contention could just as easily justify the reintroduction of velociraptors or saber-tooths, it's a good thing they're already extinct.

The grizzly reigns at the top of the North American food chain, challenged solely by the closely related polar bear. Grizzlies at one time populated the entire American West from northern Mexico to Alaska. The bear has been listed as "threatened" in the U.S. since 1975, something of a misclassification, since over sixty thousand of the animals, an unquestionably healthy population, thrive in Canada and Alaska. Nonetheless the federal government, acting without consultation with local authorities, has instituted reintroduction programs for the grizzly. One of these, the Yellowstone program, was so successful that the animal was "delisted" in 2007.

Bear attacks have steadily mounted in areas where reintroduction has occurred. While actual deaths have remained at a low level, this will inevitably change as more bears arrive and population pressures build. Already a large number of bears have been shot after attacking hikers or passersby. (It seems hard treatment for an unknowing animal to be removed from an area where he's perfectly content and dumped somewhere else, only to be shot at a later date.)

The grizzly reintroduction program is yet another example of a policy created for purely ideological purposes. It does the bears no good, the wilderness no good, and the public no good. All it does is satisfy certain environmentalist fantasies of the type entertained by Timothy Treadwell, who spent years attempting to make friends with the grizzlies in Alaska (where they're called "brown bears"), until the bears in 2003 at last grew tired of him and ate both Treadwell and his girlfriend. Despite this sanguinary example, proposals for reintroduction have been made for Colorado, New Mexico, California, and Idaho and southern Montana.

It is easily possible that the grizzly problem will grow to match that presented by the cougar. Also known as the mountain lion and panther, the cougar was pushed out of much of the U.S. as a threat to both livestock and humans until the spread of the Green mind-set created an opening for its reappearance. The cougar burst through it with a vengeance. California banned cougar hunting in 1972. Within twenty years, their numbers had doubled. They also lost all fear of humans. No deaths from cougar attacks had occurred within American borders for nearly a century until April 1994, when runner Barbara Schoener was killed while out jogging through a wooded area of northern California. By no means the petite figure portrayed in many media stories, Schoener was nearly six feet tall, weighed almost 150 pounds, and was in outstanding shape as a lifelong athlete. Nonetheless an eighty-pound cougar killed her, dragged her into the brush, and devoured her. (Two years later, California voters rejected a proposal to renew cougar hunting.)

Since that time there have been over seventy attacks and a half-dozen deaths, a rate of increase that shows no signs of slowing. The response from officials on both state and federal levels has been underwhelming. With a population of thirty thousand, the cat is in no way threatened (although three subspecies are listed as endangered). But it is protected in many areas, with officials behaving as if their hands are tied where misbehaving cats are concerned. Worse still is the attitude, encouraged on all levels of media and government, that the animals belong where they are and that humans "encroaching" on their territory deserve what they get. Despite the cat's numbers and impressive kill rate, plans are being made to reintroduce this master predator in a number of well-populated areas, including Florida.

But even the cougar's record pales beside that of the coyote. A ubiquitous presence across the U.S., the coyote is becoming a sub-urban problem of unprecedented dimensions. Closely related to the dog, the coyote is a low-level predator perhaps a step above a scavenger. It is a useless, vicious animal, one of the few that enjoy killing for its own sake. In inhabited areas it targets cats, dogs, and small children.

The total number of coyote attacks is unknown but must be very high. A study of southern California alone uncovered eighty-nine attacks and seventy-seven stalkings over a period of three decades, almost surely an underestimate. These numbers are very likely matched elsewhere in the country.

In October 2009, the talented Canadian singer Taylor Mitch-ell was attacked by two coyotes while walking through a Cape Breton national park. Though she was rescued by Canadian forest rangers, her injuries were so severe that she died later that night. It appears that these beasts are in the process of losing all fear of human beings.

It would be difficult to find anyone with a good word for this particular pest. All the same, the coyote is treated as if it were some kind of natural marvel, a sterling representative of Mother Gaia. Although no plans exist to reintroduce it—coyotes handle that very nicely themselves—hunting is often discouraged, and some

California towns have gone so far as to establish "coyote feeding stations." (A source of many attack reports, needless to say.)

This is all very strange for a frontier culture, and suggests that the pioneer aspect of the American character may be fading at last. While researching the topic, it occurred to me that a serious response to the predator problem might not arise until a child was ravaged. I was dismayed to learn that not one, but many children have been killed in recent years in such attacks, with little or no response from their communities, the media, or the country at large. In Glendale, California, in 1988, a three-year-old girl was killed in her front yard by a coyote, to little outcry. In 1997, a ten-year-old boy was killed by a cougar in Rocky Mountain State Park in Colorado after racing up a trail ahead of his family. They turned a corner to see the animal dragging his corpse into the brush. The story received the customary three paragraphs in the national media.

Even in the world as it is, one expects more. A people that will not move to defend its children in such extremity is suffering deep moral decay.

Clearly, environmentalism is one of this country's more dispensable postwar developments. The Green movement accomplishes little for the environment or its animal denizens—most contributions on that front are carried out by industry or independent philanthropies. It does nothing to protect human beings—environmentalism is almost certain to have cost far more lives than it has saved. Its actual agenda (which will be covered in detail at a later point) is almost completely divorced from its public rhetoric.

It might be hoped that a reformed version of environmentalism might evolve, one more directly related to conservationism, based not on hysteria, media manipulation, and a huckster's morality but on an honest, rational, and clear-eyed understanding of the natural world and man's place in it. But this is unlikely for two reasons.

• •

How seriously Greens take the Gaia cult is anybody's guess. But it can't be denied that environmentalism has usurped the place of traditional religion for many mentally and emotionally unanchored individuals. It has become a millennial form of pantheism, one that can be accepted as a matter of course, much the same way one accepts a T-shirt slogan or a new MP3 track. Like Marxism before it, environmentalism has its deity, its holy books, its saints, its paradise, its demons, and its Hell. There exists a gaping void in many educated individuals today where a socially relevant form of spirituality should preside. Environmentalism, as the new pantheism, does not fill this void so much as cover it. The pitiful rituals of Earth Day and recycling are no match for religious practices going back to the very roots of history, but they do act to mute the aching that originates within that void. Many feel deep gratitude for this.

The second point is that environmentalism has become a profit center. Al Gore and his multibillion-dollar "carbon offset" schemes, which are based directly on his own predictions of an inevitable climatic apocalypse, spring immediately to mind. (The activists responsible for the "secondhand smoke" and ozone hole campaigns must be kicking themselves for being so shortsighted. Bernard Madoff, too, for that matter.) But similar ventures are operating throughout the country at all economic levels, from contractors making good livings through the removal of domestic oil tanks (and accepting bribes from homeowners for not reporting to state environmental departments that the tanks were corroded and leaking), to speculators making billions erecting wind farms that will have to be torn down again once it becomes apparent that they can't even pay for themselves. (Spain, which has supported "alternate power" programs to a greater extent than any other single nation, subsidizes jobs in the wind industry to the tune of $1.5 million each, amounting to $43 billion in subsidies for power sources providing less than one percent of the country's requirements. Even in the era of Obamanomics, outlays at this level cannot possibly be maintained.) To paraphrase Michael Novak: "A system constructed on greed is based on very solid foundations." Now that the Greens have made their peace with greed, it will be a long time before we see the last of them.

The marvel of all history is the patience with which men and women submit to burdens unnecessarily laid upon them by their governments.
— SENATOR WILLIAM E. BORAH

6

DEATH'S PAVEMENT

Liberalism and Homelessness

One of the most perplexing developments of the twentieth century was a sudden upsurge of homelessness in American towns and cities during the mid to late 1970s that continues to this day. At any given moment, from 300,000 to 600,000 Americans are on the street, a range that has remained constant for over a quarter of a century. The homeless have at times taken over entire neighborhoods and public spaces in large cities—Tompkins Square Park in Manhattan, Pershing Square and the surrounding blocks in Los Angeles, and People's Park in Berkeley, to name only a few. Full communities of homeless have grown up in abandoned buildings and out-of-the-way spots throughout the country. Few cities or towns of any significant size do not possess at least one homeless colony. The homeless have settled in as a semipermanent social problem of the kind that acts as a career opportunity for bureaucrats, a cause for political activists and lawyers, and a source of rhetorical ammunition for politicians.

All this has occurred in the richest country on the face of the earth, one that prides itself, far more than most, on its capacity for building. America built its way out of a supposedly intractable postwar housing shortage within a matter of months in the late 1940s. During the ensuing decade, it constructed a national system of military bases, along with three early-warning networks consisting of hundreds of radar stations. One of those networks was built in the Arctic, under conditions never before encountered. America has erected some of the tallest structures ever built, dozens of stadiums capable of seating 100,000 and more, the largest and most coherent road network in history, and a system of dams across the western states unmatched anywhere. And yet we're stymied by the challenge of building affordable housing for what amounts to six stadiumsful of people.

This is a contradiction on the face of it, one that begs for an explanation that it has never received. As a rule, when you encounter something this strange in the social realm, you can be certain that it is in no way a natural development, but the product of interference—that somebody has been meddling. In the case of homelessness, it turns out to be many somebodies, meddling with quite a lot of things, over an extended period of time.

URBAN RENEWAL

Urban renewal, the first piece in the homelessness puzzle, was a nationwide program aimed at "revitalizing American cities" by clearing and replacing blighted or substandard areas and neighborhoods. The program was a reflection of the "can-do" spirit of the immediate postwar era, the belief that anything was possible given enough effort and money.

The key figure in urban renewal policy was a bureaucrat named Robert Moses, perhaps the most powerful public official in American history. Beginning in the 1930s, Moses held as many as a half-dozen appointed positions in New York City, as well as in state bureaucracies, including chairmanships of parks, transportation, power, highways, and bridges departments. This inter-locking directorate of appointments gave Moses a level of control over public works unmatched before or since. At his peak, Moses was untouchable by mayors, governors, and even presidents. (As Roosevelt learned when he attempted to oust Moses for having the temerity to compete with the New Deal. Public outcry forced FDR to back off.)

Moses had a particular vision of what a city ought to be, based on a small number of rigid axioms: that the automobile was the primary means of urban transportation, that slums should be re-placed by "superblocks"—high-rise structures completely isolated from their neighborhoods—and that urban area use should be kept separate and distinct, with no mixture of commercial and residential usage. Utilizing this framework, he remade much of New York City and the surrounding metropolitan area. In the process he created thousands of acres of parks (9,700 acres on Long Island alone), built thirty-five highways, seventeen miles of beaches, and eighty-four miles of parkways, along with Lincoln Center, Shea Stadium, and the Coney Island Aquarium. But he also destroyed entire neighborhoods thanks to his obsession with expressways, created banks of vertical slums with his high-rise residential towers, and converted New York from a bastion of Victorian and Art Moderne elegance into a city of blank, un-friendly stone façades.

Urban planners and officials across the country made note of the manner in which Moses used his power and saw themselves in the same role. Financing for urban renewal on a national scale became available from the federal government with the Housing Act of 1949. Backed by the federal bankroll, an army of baby Mo-seses went to work. Completely inoffensive neighborhoods were labeled as slums and leveled. Nearly a third of Boston, one of the world's great cities, was destroyed to build an expressway. Mu-nicipalities including Newark, Indianapolis, St. Louis, Detroit, and Columbus became "doughnut cities," their gutted and abandoned centers surrounded by thriving suburbs.

Much in the way of social iniquity was committed under the cover of urban renewal. A favored method of dealing with minorities was to stuff them into high-rises isolated in some peripheral area (often separated from the rest of town by an expressway), a practice that became known as "Negro removal." Skid rows were eliminated in the same fashion, though without any provision for replacement housing. Evidently the down-and-out were expected to drift away on the next departing freight.

Also targeted were marginal areas which, while not quite slums, served as low-rent way stations for people on the way up, the way down, or merely marking time—new arrivals, immigrants, students, artists, and bohos in general. Labeled as "blighted areas," such neighborhoods were commonly bulldozed under, often to be replaced with Mussolini-daydream civic or cultural centers. Lincoln Center, one of Moses' own prestige projects, replaced dozens of blocks of turn-of-the-century brownstones of the type going for several million apiece these days but which at the time comprised the Upper West Side's low-rent district. Similar actions occurred in cities across the country, with the wrecking ball taking down hundreds of thousands of cheap housing units.

It was a project of this type that provided Moses with the opportunity to overreach himself. An attempt to bulldoze Washington Square Park and raze the West Village to make room for yet another expressway introduced him to a nemesis in the form of Jane Jacobs, a freelance architectural critic without a degree to her name. Jacobs organized effective opposition to Moses' new plan, succeeding where presidents had failed. Moses was soon maneuvered into retirement by Governor Nelson Rockefeller. (Jacobs's 1961 critique of the urban renewal mentality, *The Death and Life of Great American Cities*, remains the classic work on the topic.)

Urban renewal as a national program scarcely outlasted Moses, ending when the Pruitt-Igoe homes, a typical high-rise human warehousing project located in St. Louis, was dynamited in 1970 only a few years after being opened. But the damage was done. No enemy of the United States has ever succeeded in wreaking as much pure destruction on American cities as urban renewal. Across the country, vibrant ethnic neighborhoods had been flattened, low-rent housing destroyed, and the complex web of urban life disrupted for a century to come. City living in much of America became harder, more expensive, and more inhuman. As long as the boom years of the 1960s continued, the full consequences were less than evident. But booms don't last forever.

DEINSTITUTIONALIZATION

Mental illness is one of those problems for which no satisfactory answer exists. In earlier eras, the insane were cared for at home or left to wander the streets and highways. Beginning in the 1850s, reformer Dorothea Dix introduced state-supported mental hospitals in which the insane could be treated en masse. For a century, such institutions prevailed, for both good and ill. Then it was time for the afflicted to take to the streets once again.

In 1955, under the sponsorship of the National Institute of Mental Health (NIMH), the Joint Commission on Mental Illness and Health embarked on a study to "evaluate the needs of the mentally ill and to make recommendations to Congress for future programs." Such a study was long overdue. American mental hospitals had developed a foul reputation as institutions where little in the way of meaningful treatment took place, where the mentally ill were subject to neglect or brutality from incompetent, untrained, or criminal staff members, and where troublemakers or recalcitrant members of well-connected families could be stored somewhere out of sight. The country's mental health system needed the kind of improvement that the commission promised.

But such commissions can be dangerous, often triggering precipitate action based on misunderstood or ill-considered conclusions. When the commission reported to Congress in 1961, it recommended that the existing hospital network be upgraded, that admissions to state hospitals be limited to a thousand per facility, that general wards become the standard, and that a nationwide network of community-based treatment centers be established.

It was that final recommendation that caught the attention of legislators. Community-based treatment was attractive on a number of levels—it circumvented the problem of reforming the hospital system, could be easily sold to the public, and was relatively cheap, a factor no politician could be expected to overlook.

Recent breakthroughs in antipsychotic drugs provided reason to believe that such an approach could work. Chlorpromazine (Thorazine) had been introduced in 1954, bringing about a revolution in treatment—over 2 million patients were administered the drug in less than a year. It was soon joined by reserpine (Raudixin) and haloperidol (Haldol). While the new drugs had their drawbacks—some observers likened Thorazine to "chemical lobotomy"—they represented a definite step up from the straitjacket and electroshock.

President John F. Kennedy had a personal interest in the treatment of the mentally ill—his emotionally disturbed sister Rosemary was institutionalized following a lobotomy ordered by paterfamilias Joseph Kennedy. In February 1963, Kennedy gave a speech encouraging Congress to act on the findings of the Joint Commission. In October of that year, in one of his last official acts before his assassination, JFK signed the Community Mental Health Act (CMHA), authorizing the establishment of a network of mental health clinics, known as Community Mental Health

Centers (CMHCs), throughout the country. Deinstitutionalization had become official government policy.

The governmental push for deinstitutionalization dovetailed with changing public attitudes toward the insane. Influential figures were rethinking the nature of insanity and its relationship to society. Hungarian-American psychiatrist Thomas Szasz viewed the question purely as one of rights, a matter of individual freedom as opposed to state authority. Szasz did not believe that mental illness actually existed as such, seeing it instead as behavior that was unacceptable to the status quo. In this view, society had to adapt to the rights of the individual, not the other way around. The Scottish psychiatrist R. D. Laing went a step further, with the contention that insanity was a form of liberation, a method of overcoming the limitations of everyday reality. The mentally ill were the truly sane ones, their "dysfunction" a useful adaptation to an absurd world. These attitudes were widely reflected in popular culture through films, books, and popular music, the most notable example being Ken Kesey's novel *One Flew Over the Cuckoo's Nest* (1962), later made into a well-received film starring Jack Nicholson.

The critical year for deinstitutionalization was 1967. In California, the Lanterman-Petris-Short Act, which restricted the causes for involuntary commitment for mental illness, was passed with no opposition. It became the model for anticommitment laws throughout the country. The legal establishment made a belated entry in the person of federal court of appeals judge David L. Bazelon. In 1966, Bazelon had found in *Rouse v. Cameron* that the mentally ill had a right to appropriate treatment. A year later, he extended that decision in *Lake v. Cameron*, finding that "appropriate treatment" meant treatment in the least-restrictive setting. These two decisions by Judge Bazelon (who, perhaps not coincidentally, had also been active in the procedural revolution of the early 1960s) became the basis of jurisprudence involving the mentally ill from that point on. Bazelon was quite proud of his role as pioneer. Even twenty years later, long after the consequences of his decisions had become inescapable, he wrote in his memoirs, *Questioning Authority* (1988): " . . . few doubt that recognition of mental patients' legal rights has precipitated far-reaching changes in attitudes and in the mental health system."

The ACLU had long fought against involuntary commitment for the mentally ill, and beyond that for the dissolution of the national mental hospital network. The *Lake* decision provided grounds for overturning commitment laws across the country. To carry out this program, the organization founded the Mental Health Law Project, marking the beginning of an involvement with the rights of mental patients that continues to this day. (Two decades later, the ACLU mental health effort was spun off and renamed the David L. Bazelon Center for Mental Health Law.)

The stream of released patients soon turned into a flood. In 1955, the number of patients in the state hospital system numbered over 565,000. By 1970, this had diminished to 413,066. When first introduced, deinstitutionalization seemed to be an overwhelming success, with little in the way of problems or social repercussions. What was being overlooked was the fact that the first wave consisted of high-functioning patients capable of interacting with the outside world, requiring little medication, and in many cases with close family ties. But as time passed, the hardcore schizophrenics and bipolar cases began to come up for release. These people represented a different state of affairs. They were the "truly crazy," deeply disturbed individuals who had often been incarcerated in the hospital system for decades and had little experience of the outside world.

It was with this troubled group that serious problems began to arise. While second-generation antipsychotic medications, known as "atypicals," were an improvement on earlier varieties, they still had a number of annoying and potentially dangerous side effects that encouraged patients to skip their doses. Even more critical was the fact that many schizophrenics, who comprised the bulk of released patients, suffered from anosognosia—they lacked insight into their condition, believed that nothing was truly wrong, and that they could therefore dispense with medication. Without the pills, the symptoms returned: the hallucinations, the voices, the paranoia, and the isolation. And there were no nurses, doctors, or attendants to step in.

Yet another complication lay in the fact that the community mental health centers (CMHCs) had begun to fail. Although their supporters insisted that hundreds had been established nationwide, most city dwellers would have been hard put to name one. Often situated in out-of-the-way locations under misleading names, many lacked inpatient facilities or rooms in which a patient could be observed overnight. They also suffered from a shortage of competent staff. Unwilling to accept the implied demotion, most institutional psychiatrists decided against transferring to the new facilities. They were replaced in large part by unqualified social workers. Many CMHCs turned to foreign-trained personnel, who lacked knowledge of American society and had little sympathy for the mentally unbalanced. As time passed, large numbers of CMHCs began to phase out treatment of the mentally ill, becoming instead crisis centers for normal individuals.

The mentally ill continued to pour out into society. Hundreds of thousands of unbalanced, highly vulnerable individuals were set loose across the country with no support system, with medical assistance limited to a few pills a day, living off of welfare and federal disability payments. They had been promised aid from their government, promised help in facing an unfamiliar and often terrifying world, promised a better life. Instead they were shunted off into the worst areas of town and left to fend for themselves, to compete with the down-and-outers for a place in a rapidly shrinking reservoir of rooming houses, SROs, and cheap motels.

Very few places existed for the mentally ill to go. Soon there would be none at all.

THE GREAT INFLATION

Economically, the 1970s was the worst decade since the Depression. This was the direct result of government manipulation of the economy. In the summer of 1965, President Lyndon B. Johnson decided to finance both the Vietnam War and his Great Society welfare state without raising taxes. He accomplished this through the time-honored expedient of printing more money. It appears that a kind of cargo-cult Keynesianism provided the rationale, with the benefits of government spending taking on the aura of a basic principle of existence.

Johnson meant well. He intended to continue spending only for as long and as much as was necessary. But as rulers since the Caesars have had occasion to learn, once the monetary floodgates are opened, they are very difficult to close. In a few short years the Great Inflation had taken hold with a vengeance.

Richard M. Nixon attempted to curtail inflation through wage and price controls. It failed to work, as Diocletian could have told him. Jerry Ford unveiled an empty PR campaign titled Whip Inflation Now (WIN) with even more dismal results. As the decade wore on, a new economic phenomenon made its debut—stagflation. Economists had long considered inflation to be a feature of an expanding economy. The 1970s proved them wrong. While the recession that began in 1972–73 dragged on through the rest of the decade, inflation, in complete contradiction to contemporary economic theory, continued increasing, finally reaching 18 percent in 1978–79.

One problem with controlling inflation involved the fact that the money produced by the economy was not being saved or put into productive investments but was going into "hedges," investments in assets that held value against inflation. Certain commodities such as gold and silver could be depended on to maintain their value in the face of inflationary pressures. Other such investments included artworks for the rich, and for the middle class, real estate.

An effort was made to persuade homeowners that their homes represented a hedge against inflation. The theory was that real estate would continue rising in value, remaining one step ahead of inflation. A homeowner should therefore purchase a property at the very edge of his means, with the highest mortgage he could conceivably handle. In a short time, inflationary pressures would adjust the payments in the owner's favor, at which point he could refinance. Eventually, the homeowner would sell out, gaining a substantial profit.

Such schemes were nonsense, as many financial commentators pointed out at the time. An investment is something you can afford to lose. By that definition, a home is not and never can be an investment. The belief that home prices would continue rising in perpetuity was an assumption, and as events were to prove, not a particularly safe one. And even if things worked out according to plan, where would the homeowner go after he cashed out? It wasn't as if no one else had heard the news. Every other property in the world would have been inflating at the same rate. As even journeyman investors are aware, a strategy that is widely used tends to lose its efficacy in direct relation to the number of people involved.

But in the straitened financial environment of the 1970s, the home-as-investment scheme caught on quickly. The national housing market was soon overwhelmed by speculation, panic buying, and an unparalleled rate of rising prices. Even after inflation came under control in the early 1980s, the pitch simply shifted to using your home as something on the order of a bank, with continual refinancing to gain funds to spend on toys and luxuries. Sanctioned by Fannie Mae and Freddie Mac (not to mention figures such as Christopher Dodd, Barney Frank, and Charles Rangel), the real estate bubble continued expanding for thirty years, enriching banks, mortgage firms, and real estate agencies. It collapsed at last in September 2008, when . . . but we all know that story.

As housing prices rose, so did rents, doubling and quadrupling in step with the price of homes. I was working as an office manager for a real estate company—think Kevin Spacey in *Glengarry Glen Ross*—at the time. The formula for an affordable rent was, "Be prepared to spend a quarter of your income." I clearly recall the day when, without consultation or discussion, this was suddenly transformed into: "Be prepared to spend a third of your income on rent." Federal rent-subsidy programs such as Section 8 Housing, by which landlords were paid more or less what they demanded, also played a role in rent inflation. By the end of the 1970s, the cheap apartment rental was at rest with the buggy whip and the butter churn.

The burden cannot be said to have fallen equally. As much as they hurt working people, skyrocketing rents most adversely affected transients, down-and-outers, and the insane. By the dawn of the 1980s, their SROs were being converted to condominiums, their cheap motels torn down to build developments, their rooming houses gentrified into single homes. It was into this rapidly closing environment that the mentally ill were being led to fend for themselves.

The result was inevitable, and is best expressed by an ancient Irish proverb: When the rock hits the egg, alas for the egg. When the egg hits the rock, alas for the egg.

HOMELESSNESS SETTLES IN

Homelessness is generally considered to be a problem of the 1980s, a by-product of the "decade of greed." In fact, it was already widespread in the country's large cities by the mid-1970s. It was during those years that the streets began to fill up with strange, disturbing figures stalking aimlessly through the urban landscape, their eyes staring, their hair matted, their clothes ragged and filthy—if they were dressed at all. Shrieking, babbling, singing, arguing with opponents who weren't there, occasionally confronting or assaulting passersby, the insane homeless added yet another layer of apprehension, terror, and pure misery to urban life.

Homelessness began drawing major public attention in the early 1980s, when the election of a Republican administration gave it a useful political context. The scant uneasy references of previous years were replaced by the full glare of publicity, particularly after homeless numbers increased during the recession of 1981–82. Many of these new arrivals on the streets were young, hard-hit families, which made for powerful imagery amid the flood of reportage. Commentators had no difficulty in explaining the phenomenon: the cause of homelessness was Ronald Reagan, greedy landlords, Ronald Reagan, capitalism, and Ronald Reagan.

One aspect of the mythology of the period is a claim that no attempt was made to deal with the problem. In truth, no end of efforts to aid the homeless were carried out by government, businesses, churches, NGOs, and so on across the social spectrum. Many of these efforts were aimless and ill thought out, doing little or nothing to attack the core problems: getting people to take their medicine and putting roofs over their heads.

Early attempts to relieve mass homelessness were channeled through the traditional avenues of churches, the Salvation Army, and similar charities. Direct government support for such organizations began as early as 1980. In 1983, a task force was created to assist charities and local governments in obtaining surplus government property for use as housing.

Federal homeless programs were formalized in 1987 with the enactment of the Stewart B. McKinney Act. Originally titled the Urgent Relief for the Homeless Act, the legislation was renamed when its Republican sponsor died just before passage. The McKinney act added fifteen programs to the battle against homelessness, including the Supportive Housing Program, the Shelter Plus Care Program, the Single Room Occupancy Program, and the Emergency Shelter Grant Program. Over $11 billion was appropriated to carry out the provisions of the legislation.

These programs had beneficial effects, particularly as involved families and those who had become homeless through a run of bad luck. Eager to put the experience behind them, these people took advantage of the programs, got back on their feet, and were seen on the streets no more. Few became "chronic homeless," the hopeless hard core wandering the streets and mobbing the homeless shelters.

But almost all efforts against homelessness, whether directed by churches, charities, or government, suffered from serious conceptual failures. The greatest of these was the inability to grasp the magnitude of the problem represented by the mentally ill.

Estimates of how many of the homeless suffered from mental illness ranged from 20 to 50 percent, with the higher number probably being more accurate. They comprised an even larger percentage of the chronic homeless. These people required more than passing assistance; they needed treatment and custodial care.

It wasn't as if the mentally ill homeless had no one in their corner. They had plenty of allies, in the form of political activists, government bureaucrats, and public-interest lawyers. But as is often the case, those allies had their own agendas, agendas that tended to come before the interests of the homeless.

The activists were typified by the Community for Creative

Nonviolence (CCNV), a D.C.–based group with roots in the 1960s counterculture. The CCNV viewed the homeless as the oppressed and the problem as a battle against authority, to be met with marches, sit-ins, and takeovers of empty buildings. In hindsight it is clear that the agenda of the CCNV was not pro-homeless as much as it was anti-Reagan administration. It was the CCNV that, through its spokesman Mitch Snyder, made the single most damaging statement about the homeless ever in a claim that they numbered over 3 million. This figure, which was up to ten times the actual number, made the problem appear utterly insurmountable and cost as much support as it gained. Snyder, an ex–Madison Avenue adman, later admitted that he'd made the number up. Although the CCNV was imitated by groups in cities around the country, little was accomplished and eventually all of them faded to nullity.

The federal government scarcely needed outside harassment and disinformation, since an in-house department handled such matters quite nicely. In 1977, the NIMH created the Community Support Program in an attempt to make up for the failures of the Community Mental Health Centers in aiding the deinstitutionalized mentally ill. The mission of the Community Support Program was to provide assistance "for one particularly vulnerable population—adult psychiatric patients whose disabilities are severe and persistent." Unfortunately, like the CMHCs before it, the Community Support Program ended up as a social work organization dealing with the far easier challenge of crisis intervention.

When a bureaucracy fails, a sure solution can be found in changing its name. In 1992, the Community Support Program was transformed into the Center for Mental Health Services (CMHS), an essentially independent department with its own budget. The CMHS was intended to act as the federal government's main instrument for dealing with mental illness. Unfortunately, the staff of CMHS was top heavy with firm believers in the romantic view of insanity, in full agreement with Laing and Szasz that mental illness did not exist as such but was a "healthy transformation process that should be facilitated instead of treated." Although the CMHS was funded with over $782 million, much of that money was wasted on frivolous programs. The actual benefit to the derelict insane was minimal.

The public-interest lawyers consisted of the ACLU along with later single-issue groups such as the National Law Center on Homelessness and Poverty and the David L. Bazelon Center for Mental Health Law. All remained wed to the notion that homelessness was a matter of "rights." Numerous legal actions were filed for the purpose of introducing and expanding homeless rights. These included the overthrow of the vagrancy laws, establishing a right to panhandle, a right to sleep and set up camp in public places, a right to loiter in bus and train stations, and a right to loiter in libraries despite appearance, behavior, or odors (these last two were the work of Richard Kreimer, a homeless man who embarked on quite a lucrative career in suing New Jersey institutions with the aid of the ACLU).

A number of the "rights" established by these efforts cannot help but be seen as contradictory: a right to government-provided shelter and a right not to be forced into shelter, a right to medical treatment alongside a right to refuse to take medication.

On occasion, public-interest lawyers worked directly against the welfare of the homeless. In the winter of 1985, Philadelphia mayor Wilson Goode ordered his police force to bring homeless people in off the streets whenever the temperature dropped below freezing. The ACLU immediately leaped to the defense of homeless "rights," accusing the mayor of "cutting constitutional corners" and threatening legal action. While Wilson Goode might not top anyone's list of the world's competent mayors (Goode was one of the few mayors to have successfully bombed his own city, when a 1985 attempt to root out the radical group MOVE through a helicopter attack misfired and burned down an entire city block), he was certainly on the side of the angels in this instance.

The most characteristic case involving homeless rights was that of Joyce Patricia Brown, who adopted the name "Billie Boggs" in imitation of a New York TV personality. Brown suffered from paranoid schizophrenia. Refusing her medication, she colonized a warm-air grate at Sixty-fifth Street and Second Avenue, on Manhattan's Upper East Side, where she exposed herself, raced screaming through traffic, and covered herself with her own waste. On October 28, 1987, she was committed to Bellevue, the city's major mental hospital. The ACLU took up her case on the grounds that her sojourn on the grate amounted to "a fearless independent lifestyle." They found a state Supreme Court justice, Irving Kirshenbaum, who agreed, ruling that Brown could not be forced to take medication. A short time later she was freed by another justice, Robert Lippmann.

The ACLU arranged for Brown to appear on talk shows and give speeches concerning her way of life, which she carried off with no difficulties. She was almost certainly on medication at the time, which goes a long way toward undermining the ACLU's case. The organization gave her a job as a receptionist at one of their offices, but again she refused meds, her condition deteriorated, and she found her way back to her grate. Little is known of her later life beyond the fact that she died in 2005.

It is clear that the rights crusade did next to nothing to aid the homeless, particularly the derelict insane. At best, it complicated efforts to offer assistance. The intricate web of interlocking laws and regulations surrounding the state of homelessness was next to impossible to penetrate unless the individual, often confused and disoriented, expressly asked for help. This was a rare occurrence at best.

The public interest groups acted as if they truly believed that their interpretation of "rights" trumped everything else, including shelter and medical care, that the homeless on their grates and in their cardboard boxes were well taken care of as long as their "rights" were protected by lawyers and paralegals in the warmth of their suburban homes. Anatole France once wrote that "the law in its majestic equality forbids both rich and poor alike from sleeping beneath bridges." Today it's exactly the opposite—that's how far we've progressed.

While the advocates played, the situation of the homeless deteriorated still further. Police, city governments, and the public adjusted to the new urban phenomenon. Once viewed with sympathy, the homeless now aroused contempt, anger, or at best indifference. Activists and social workers spoke of "compassion fatigue," when in fact what was being seen was an active revulsion against the behavior and circumstances of the homeless. Up to 40 percent were addicted to illegal drugs. Many showed no hesitation in shooting up in plain sight of passersby, including small children. Encountering used drug paraphernalia such as needles and pipes in parks, playgrounds, and even on front doorsteps became simply another aspect of daily life. Disease was yet another factor. In poor health to begin with, many of the homeless weakened to a point where they were easy prey for serious illness, often, as in the cases of AIDS and tuberculosis, either communicable or contagious. Little in the way of public health measures was carried out to contain the spread of such illnesses.

Fear also played a role in the hardening of public attitudes. Many of the derelict insane were violent, and without the benefit of medication were apt to act out under little or no provocation. It became a commonplace of city life to witness or hear of confrontations, assaults, and even murders committed by the homeless. The most notorious case involved Larry Hogue, a Vietnam War veteran who had sustained brain damage in an aircraft accident. Hogue preferred smoking crack to taking his meds, and chose West Ninety-sixth Street as the place to do it. The Upper West Side is one of America's great liberal bastions, and at first the locals welcomed him with food and blankets. This largesse ceased when Hogue began terrorizing the neighborhood. Among many other exploits, Hogue threatened and attacked pedestrians, smashed car windows (and in at least one case set a car on fire), stalked neighborhood residents, threw a concrete block through the stained-glass window of a church, and tossed a sixteen-year-old girl in front of a truck (the truck braked in time). Hogue was hospitalized on more than thirty occasions and jailed more than once. Each time he was released in short order, thanks to a legal paradox created by the "homeless rights" laws. While in custody and under medication, Hogue behaved as civilly as could be desired, and so could not be held. But out in the street and on his own, he could not be forced to take his medication and was soon transformed into a menace unequaled in a New York liberal's worst nightmares.

Hogue's reign as mad king of the Upper West Side lasted four years, until he was at last committed to a long-term treatment program in 1992. It is unlikely that he would have endured that long in many other parts of the country, particularly once it was discovered that, far from indigent, he had a $36,000-a-year military disability pension, most of which he spent on drugs. (In June 2009, Hogue escaped from confinement at Creedmoor Psychiatric Center in Queens and made a beeline for West Ninety-sixth Street. A terrified populace cleared the streets until he was recaptured.)

Larry Hogue was far from the sole example of the violent mental derelict. On July 24, 1998, Russell Weston, Jr., in search of a time machine he was convinced was hidden in the U.S. Capitol, shot to death two veteran police officers assigned to the building. Weston had for years suffered from increasingly erratic and violent behavior. Less than six months later, on January 3, 1999, chronic schizophrenic Andrew Goldstein shoved screenwriter

Kendra Webdale in front of a moving subway train in Manhattan. This murder led to the passage of "Kendra's Law," which provides for supervision of mental patients living outside of institutions to ascertain that they are taking their medication. The ACLU, needless to say, fought the bill tooth and nail. (Goldstein's ensuing legal odyssey is yet another example of the convoluted state of law dealing with the mentally ill. A late-1999 trial ended in a hung jury. Though Goldstein was found guilty a year later, a state appeals court vacated the verdict and ordered a new trial. It was not until 2006, seven years after Kendra Webdale's murder, that the process ended with a guilty plea by Goldstein. He received a sentence of twenty-three years.)

According to a widely quoted study published in the early 1990s, as many as one thousand people a year are murdered by the derelict insane. These are deaths that simply should not have occurred. Considering the nature of mental illness and our knowledge of how it can manifest itself (neither of which can be said to lie in the realm of the theoretical) the fact that no one—no psychiatrist, psychologist, nurse, social worker, or any other interested party—saw fit to voice a warning or take any other action to curtail the inevitable violence stands as a clear indictment of this country's mental health establishment.

As sympathy faded and the homeless metamorphosed into figures of terror, they, too, became victims. Street gangs and foot-loose youths often targeted the homeless for attacks excused by any motive or none. It has become common to hear of homeless individuals being beaten, stomped, or—a favorite tactic of the lowlifes—doused with flammable liquid and set ablaze. According to a 2005 study by the Feinberg School of Medicine at Northwestern University, the derelict insane are eleven times more likely than the average citizen to suffer a violent assault. Perhaps a million crimes are committed against such people annually.

As for the number of deaths suffered in such incidents, we have no clear idea. We have no idea how many homeless die of all causes. These people are outcasts, suffering the fates of outcasts. No one ever looks very closely, or keeps much in the way of records when the discarded leave this world.

The odds are against the mentally ill from the first. A 2009 study headed by Dr. Joseph Parks of the Missouri Department of Mental Health revealed that the life span of a typical mental patient is twenty-five years less than that of the average American. The insane die of obesity, preventable diseases, and accidents, many of which would be avoidable under other circumstances. One extremely disturbing finding reveals that the life span of the insane has decreased by over ten years since the early 1990s. Suicide is also a serious risk for the mentally disturbed. The suicide rate for schizophrenics can approach 15 percent. That of sufferers of bipolar disorder must be nearly equivalent.

Homelessness in and of itself raises the risk of death by a factor of three. Add these constituents together and the risk level to the derelict insane reaches the appalling. A U.K. study carried out in 1992 followed forty-eight mentally ill homeless for eighteen months. At the end of that period, three had died of natural causes, one had died of an accident, and three had vanished, leaving their possessions behind—not a good sign in the world of the homeless. Counting only those known to have died, the mortality rate was 8 percent. Including the vanished three brings the rate up to 15 percent—nearly one-sixth of the sample.

They die of every cause conceivable and some well outside the imagination of the comfortable. They die of starvation, they die of neglect, they die of accidents, they die of drug overdoses. They die of diseases not commonly seen in the United States for generations. They die of deterioration, they die of exhaustion. They die of exposure, frozen to death on the streets and sidewalks laid down with such care and expense. They die of murder, they die of suicide.

They die alone, ignored and overlooked, in the dark corners and shadowy places of this country. They die for reasons that are preventable, and in ways that simply should not occur in a twenty-first-century society.

It is to avoid such fates that the mentally ill homeless have for years been reinstitutionalizing (or, as the official sociological term puts it, "transinstitutionalizing") themselves in the only way open to them: by getting themselves arrested. The U.S. prison system holds up to 300,000 mentally ill prisoners, making Rikers Island, the Los Angeles County jail, and Chicago's Cook County jail the largest mental institutions in the country. Close to 20 percent of the inmates in those jails are receiving some form of mental health care.

Most of these prisoners are serving sentences for actual crimes. But a large percentage have simply made certain that they got caught in order to have a roof over their heads, "three hots and a cot," and some semblance of security and order in their lives. Institutions, even of the most onerous and degrading variety, represent an answer for these people. Institutions, of one kind or another, represent the key solution to the ongoing social catastrophe of homelessness. Even the insane realize this. Only the intellectuals have yet to catch up.

The problem with the modern world is that
stupidity has begun to think.
—JEAN COCTEAU

SHORT TAKES

The Long Reach of Soft Lethality

Rationalism is not all it's cracked up to be.

For our purposes, rationalism can be defined as the thesis that the world at large operates according to a fixed set of rules, so that a particular series of events will always and forever lead to the same end result. Therefore, in dealing with the world as it is, following a simple set of procedures one step after the other should provide us with consistent outcomes.

The liberal interpretation holds that if the rational process outlined above is adhered to, the results will match liberal desires, that is, the continual improvement of the world and everything in it by means of human action. Given simple and clear instructions on how to process a particular problem, created by disinterested and objective experts, any organization made up of any offhand selection of personnel can produce useful consequences.

It doesn't quite work that way. The average human being, by the time of reaching adulthood, has come to terms with the fact that, as the quantum physicists have established over the past century, this is not a universe governed by logic, and that in such a universe, rationality has definite and easily established limitations; that there exist no step-by-step processes that can be used to address any given set of circumstances; that there are things best left alone for all kinds of reasons.

Liberals fail to grasp this truth. The result is a system that operates in direct conflict with the world as it exists in all its ramifications on a consistent basis. This leads to the kind of outcome that the average American dismisses as "insane" or "demented." It is no such thing. It is rationalism carried to its logical extreme.

We see the consequences daily—schoolchildren tormented, bullied, and even expelled for possessing a toy gun or a couple of aspirin. City governments brought to a standstill by a bureaucrat's use of the word "niggardly." Agricultural regions exposed to searing drought in order to secure the comfort of a species of smelt. Ninety-year-old Swedish grandmothers subjected to airport strip searches for the purpose of overawing terrorists.

But there is no lack of deadlier aspects as well. Liberal infatuation with kindergarten rationalism turns the world into a combination obstacle course, shooting gallery, and minefield. Publicly certified and bureaucratically sanctioned dangers arise constantly, haphazardly, and without warning. As a result, we all sit in the crosshairs of democide.

After a near-century of liberal dominance, such dangers can be found in all corners of American society. Many readers will have put together a list of their own by this time—enough, if they were all collated, for another volume of this size or longer. Few Americans have not been affected in some way by the democidal impulse—it touches us all, by one means or another. The threat is always there, embodied in crime, in our automobiles, all the way down to the humble lightbulb. Out of many other possible examples, here are several short takes, what might be called snapshots of democide.

FOR THE SAKE OF THE CHILDREN

Child protection services have a long and honorable history beginning in 1873, when the brutalized Mary Ellen McCormack was presented to the court by the New York City SPCA with the request that she be "declared an animal." While animals were protected from cruelty and harsh treatment, no such protection existed for children, and this stratagem was the only means of assuring that Mary Ellen got the help she so desperately needed.

Within months, the state of New York passed legislation leading to the establishment of Societies for the Protection of Children, an effort that soon spread nationwide. For the next century, these organizations, most of them nongovernmental and funded through private charities, dealt with problems of child abuse and neglect. Two approaches were commonly utilized: the "child rescue" method, in which children were removed from threatening family environments and their abusive parents punished, and the preventive approach, pioneered in Massachusetts, which emphasized keeping families together. Both approaches, when applied by professional, well-trained social workers, were effective at keeping the problem within bounds.

Then in 1974, the federal government became involved through the Child Abuse Prevention and Treatment Act, known as the Mondale Act after its chief sponsor, senator and future vice president Walter Mondale. The Mondale Act was yet another example of the messianic social engineering that we've grown used to in these pages. Providing $4.5 billion in funding through Medicaid, the act promoted centralization of child abuse prevention efforts in state agencies. Since its first passage, the act has been revised, rewritten, and supplemented on numerous occasions without being improved in any detectable sense. (Mondale himself later had serious second thoughts, far too late to do anything about it.)

A major flaw in the legislation was a requirement that all accusations of child abuse and neglect be fully investigated. This
provision guaranteed that state resources would be consistently
stretched to the limit, particularly after it became known in low-
income neighborhoods that the wrath of the state bureaucracy
could be brought down on personal enemies with a single anonymous phone tip. The intensity of neighborhood quarrels in such
areas can often be gauged by how many times the phrase "I'm
gonna call Family Services on you" is repeated.

The impact of these efforts on children's lives and well-being is
exemplified by the record of the state of New Jersey. For nearly
thirty years, the state government has been involved in a losing
effort to operate a child protection system that is not complicit in
the actual murder of children.

Social workers with New Jersey's DYFS, or Division of Youth
and Family Services (in other states known as Division of Family
Services, Child Protection Services, or simply Social Services), have
been implicated in the deaths of children under their supervision
on an uncertain but disturbingly frequent number of occasions.
Such episodes generally take two forms: either the caseworker
overlooks signs of ongoing abuse—at times for years on end—to
the point where a child is killed, or the caseworker places a child
in a foster home or other situation in which such a murder is committed. (My interest in these cases was aroused in the early 1980s,
when a DYFS worker dumped a twelve-year-old girl at an Edison,
New Jersey, motel notorious as a haven for prostitutes and junk-
ies. Within hours, the child was dead. DYFS responded by turning back all inquiries in the interests of "privacy.")

The typical pattern is that a particularly ghastly murder occurs
with DYFS personnel implicated. Amid media uproar, an investigation is initiated, speeches made, promises offered, and a "solution" discovered that without exception amounts to spending
more money and hiring more caseworkers. The system then stum-

bles onward until another murder of sufficient horror to draw the public eye occurs. (DYFS's adroit use of the "privacy" cloak was often sufficient to dampen interest in run-of-the-mill killings. The agency's abuse of privacy statutes became so blatant that in 1997 a law was passed requiring that information on such murders be made public.)

This pattern has repeated itself regularly over the past two decades. In March 1989, the body of five-year-old Dyneekah Johnson was discovered in Newark. She had been beaten to death by a foster couple selected by DYFS. The state responded by establishing the Child Death Review Board. After nearly three years, the board filed its first report, calling for "better training for child-welfare personnel."

The new program failed to help two-year-old Amara Wilkerson, beaten to death in New Brunswick in 1997 by her mother's boyfriend (an outcome so common that they are referred to as "paramour cases"). DYFS had been alerted by the child's grandparents months before. Governor Christie Whitman appointed a twenty-five-member Blue Ribbon Task Force. When finally released, the task force's report revealed to a waiting world that DYFS was dysfunctional and that changes were required. In the meantime, legislation was passed creating an additional training program and allocating $18 million to hire 369 new caseworkers.

Neither programs, funding, nor new staff appeared quickly enough to save Enedia Rodriguez, yet another paramour victim. The child had dropped out of sight weeks before her death in December 1998. DYFS workers made no serious effort to track her down.

Performance had not improved by April 2001, when Jeremiah Parker beat to death his girlfriend's four-year-old son. DYFS workers had ignored reports of previous injuries to the child. What made this case resonate was the fact that Parker played defensive end for the New York Giants. He later received the maximum sentence for a child murder in New Jersey—ten years. The following October, acting governor Donald DiFrancesco allocated $12 million to create 124 new caseworker positions.

New Jersey's child welfare problem came to a head in 2003. On January 5, Raheem Williams and Tyrone Hill were found starving and dehydrated in a Newark basement. Their brother's mummified body lay a short distance away. DYFS workers had been informed two years earlier that the boys were being tortured by a female relative.

In March, Amir Beeks was lured by an older boy from a library in Woodbridge, one of the state's prime suburban enclaves, and was sexually assaulted, beaten to death with a baseball bat, and then tossed into a ditch. The older boy was "under the supervision" of DYFS.

In October, a boy was found rooting through trash in Collingswood, a suburban town across the river from Philadelphia. Responding police believed him to be about nine years old. He was in fact eighteen. He and his three brothers had been systematically starved by their foster parents for nearly a decade. DYFS workers had been monitoring the home for the entire period but noticed nothing at all wrong.

Of course, it's unfair to judge a national social problem solely in light of a state widely regarded as the Louisiana of the Northeast, but valuable lessons can be learned through discovering exactly how bad a situation can get. Ideological blindness in New Jersey has taken the form of putting the means before the end. The programs—funding, personnel, bureaucratic procedure— became the critical elements, with the children coming in a far distant second. The goal was transformed from rescuing children to rescuing DYFS. That object alone preoccupied governors, administrations, officials, caseworkers, and the media, while small bodies piled high.

It's impossible to even estimate how many children across the country suffer from the inadequacy of state child-protective agencies. The DYFS fetish for "privacy" extends to most such organizations. States in which agency-related child homicides have recently occurred include Missouri, Florida, New York, Arizona, Pennsylvania, and Georgia. The testimony of Yvonne Elliotte, a caseworker who resigned from an Atlanta, Georgia, child welfare office after two of her wards were killed due to agency incompetence, suggests that the number may be shockingly high, perhaps exceeding several thousand in the decades since the Mondale Act was passed.*

On May 25, 2006, two children in suburban Millville, New Jersey, were killed by their father. It seems that DYFS had not yet implemented its "plan" to keep the estranged parent away from their home. Governor Jon Corzine's administration vowed that every effort would be made to strengthen the system. And the long Halloween goes on.

BONEBREAK AND THE BORDER

The growing opposition to illegal immigration in recent years has usually focused on ill effects involving jobs and the economy. Little attention has been paid to one of the most worrying by-products of illegal entry: the reintroduction of long-absent diseases into this country. This question gained urgency in early 2009 when a spring outbreak of swine flu threatened to attain pandemic status. There was little doubt that the epidemic originated in Mexico—investigators even claimed to have pinpointed the pig farm that acted as ground zero. In response, a number of public officials

---

*We can no more than mention the irony that many such murders occurred at the same time as the child-care "satanist" frenzy of the 1980s and nineties that destroyed dozens of lives and in which the child protection agencies played no small part.

asked that the border be closed for the duration of the epidemic, among them Senator Joe Lieberman and Democratic congressman Eric Massa. (Although the outbreak was concentrated in the border states, at least one victim resided in Massa's New York State district.)

President Barack Obama demurred: "It would be akin to closing the barn door after the horses are out, because we already have cases here in the United States." The border remained open. Luckily, the epidemic failed to take off, with the death rate remaining below the level of seasonal flu.

But swine flu (or, as the Obama White House preferred to call it, "H1N1") was far from the first disease to trickle across America's too-porous southern border. For the past decade dengue fever, which we met in Chapter 3 as "bonebreak fever," has been making a comeback in the Texas border area, entering from points south.

Dengue fever was at one time endemic in Texas. During the 1920s, as many as half a million Texans suffered from the disease. But modern hygiene, along with that chemical from Hell, DDT, eliminated the disease for nearly fifty years. Only a handful of cases were recorded during the latter half of the last century.

Then, in the late 1990s, dengue began to return in force. A few cases emerged in 1995, with others suspected. But 1999 marked the watershed year, with the biggest outbreak in decades. At least fourteen cases were discovered in the border town of Laredo, with another hundred identified just across the border.

From that point on, dengue began erupting at shorter and shorter intervals. More than 541 cases were reported in the five-year period following 1999. In 2005, another outbreak occurred in Brownsville, concurrent with a serious epidemic across the border in Matamoros. At least twenty-five cases were treated in Brownsville hospitals, while no less than 1,251 occurred in Mexico. Alarmingly, sixteen of the Texas cases and over 220 of those in Mexico were identified as the potentially fatal hemorrhagic variant.

By 2007 the disease was once again regarded as established in southern Texas. Random tests in Brownsville revealed that up to 38 percent of the city's population possessed dengue antibodies, suggesting that a large number of individuals had been exposed. What made this a matter for particular concern were medical research findings showing that individuals who had previously suffered from the disease were at extremely high risk for developing the hemorrhagic variety.

The outbreaks in Texas occurred almost simultaneously with those in Mexico. Dengue is a mosquito-borne disease, and mosquitoes will wander without regard for borders. All the same, there can be little doubt that border crossings contributed to the spread of the disease.

While it would seem to be the minimal level of wisdom to curtail border traffic, both legal and illegal, during an epidemic, the thought does not appear to have occurred to officials on either side of the border. Illegal immigration serves many interests. In Mexico, it acts as a safety valve for social problems such as poverty and joblessness. To American liberals, it provides a painless opportunity to wave the multiculturalism and solidarity-with-the-oppressed banner, along with furnishing a means of impressing Hispanic voters.

A decision to close the border might well have proved difficult to implement in any case. After considerable empty controversy, Congress in 2006 passed the Secure Fence Act, authorizing a border fence system reaching from the Gulf of Mexico to California. But work on the project has been lackluster at best. While over six hundred miles of fencing have been completed, half of that mileage consists of three-foot-high vehicle barriers easily overcome by any desperate immigrant. In the face of international terrorism, a drug-fueled border war, and now epidemic disease, the federal government remains unwilling to seriously address the border question. Legislation introduced by Representative Duncan Hunter ordering completion of the fencing project has been stalled in Congress for a considerable period.

The Texas dengue problem is a warning. There exists no shortage of other diseases that can be brought into the country by the same route. Greater numbers of illegal immigrants are coming from areas farther south, stretching from Central America to Brazil, where much worse things than dengue are endemic.

Outbreaks in Mexico should be responded to with all the aid and assistance we can provide. (A binational emergency response team, perhaps under the aegis of the Centers for Disease Control, would not be a bad idea.) At the same time, the border should be closed, both to legal and illegal traffic, during periods of epidemics. The current policy—if that's the word to define a habit of complete inertness—needs to be rethought in light of public health before the next bug decides to make its mark.

DANGER: GUN-FREE ZONE

February 12, 2010, was a very bad day for the Huntsville campus of the University of Alabama. Dr. Amy Bishop of the biology department, disappointed in hopes of overturning a negative tenure decision, set out to resolve the situation by killing as many of her colleagues as possible. Drawing an unlicensed 9mm pistol, she shot six of them, killing three on the spot before the other academics present rushed her and forced her from the room. Leaving the building, Bishop waited calmly for her husband to arrive, and was picked up by the police moments later.

Bishop had a lengthy, though unacknowledged, history of explosive violence, including the fatal shooting of her brother two decades previously. (Her family's claim that the shooting was "accidental" fell apart with the revelation that she had attempted two carjackings and confronted police with a loaded shotgun only minutes later.) Bishop was the last person in the world any competent authority would allow to possess a firearm. So it was a good thing that the Alabama university system was a "gun-free zone," an area in which firearm ownership or possession was banned. University policy stated, "No firearms, ammunition, or dangerous weapons are allowed in buildings or other facilities." Or it would have been a good thing, had Dr. Bishop proved willing to cooperate.

The campaign against guns is one of the least rational elements of the entire liberal program. It makes sense only if complete abolition of firearms on the European model is the actual goal. But liberals insist otherwise, claiming that their sole aim is "common-sense regulation."

A look at the legislative record suggests otherwise. The first modern federal gun control law, the National Firearms Act of 1934, banned automatic weapons, sawed-off shotguns and rifles, pistol silencers, and gimmick firearms such as walking-stick pistols, along with setting a tax levy and paperwork requirements. The Gun Control Act of 1968 banned mail-order sales of firearms, restricted interstate sales, and strictly defined the classes of individuals, such as drug abusers and the mentally ill, who were not allowed to own guns.

The 1986 Law Enforcement Officers Protection Act (such euphonious and misleading bill titles are a literary art form in their own right) banned certain classes of pistol ammunition believed capable of penetrating body armor. The Public Safety and Recreational Firearms Use Protection Act (actually a subsection of the Violent Crime Control and Law Enforcement Act of 1994) banned possession, sale, and manufacture of "assault rifles," in reality ordinary sporting guns jazzed up with pistol grips, laser sights, and the like.

While some of these laws were perfectly justifiable—sawed-off shotguns are a gangster's murder weapon and nothing else—the overall trend is clear: an incremental strategy in which particular classes of weapons ("assault rifles"), ammunition ("cop-killer" bullets), and points of sale (mail order or gun shows) are targeted for ever more stringent regulation, if not outright prohibition. Once these regulations are in place, liberals move on to the next target. The apparent aim of this campaign is that such piecemeal efforts will eventually coalesce into something approaching complete abolition.

Many of these regulatory efforts fail in the courts. But for whatever period they remain in effect, they often create situations that are outré, illogical, and at times extremely dangerous. Liberal efforts against firearm ownership have undoubtedly cost a considerable number of lives—the intensity of the late-century crime explosion can be explained in large part by the fact that citizens in many urban areas had been effectively disarmed. It is no coincidence that the most stratospheric crime rates were recorded in localities—Chicago, New York City, and the District of Columbia among them—with the most stringent gun laws.* Entire volumes have been written detailing the absurdities of liberal firearms policies. But for our argument we need present a single example: the recent "gun-free zone" campaign.

*Any doubts on this score may be settled by an examination of the British experience. One of the Blair Labour government's major domestic initiatives involved the complete abolition of handguns in the U.K. apart from the military and police. No exceptions were granted—the U.K.'s Olympic pistol team must fly to Switzerland to practice. The result, in a country with no tradition of criminal gun usage, has been skyrocketing gun-related crime rates along with the appearance of a "knife culture" in which young street thugs have turned to knives as the weapon of choice. In response, British leftists have seriously proposed banning knives.

Gun-free zones are yet another attempt at a ban by increment. Under such policies, possession of firearms is prohibited within an arbitrary distance (usually a thousand feet) of schools and related institutions. At first glance, this proposal seems sensible and even attractive. Who, after all, would be opposed to assuring the security of children and students in the schoolroom? But it escaped the notice of most observers that the concept was drawn along the lines of an identically worded ban of illegal drugs that has failed to have any measurable effect on the sale and consumption of drugs in schools.

The unstated purpose appears to be to effect a de facto ban on guns in communities throughout the country. With the dramatic expansion of the American educational establishment in recent decades, there are many towns and cities where no one lives more than a thousand feet from a school or annex. Although exemptions are offered for homeowners, police officers, and hunters, most are worded in such a way as to be utterly meaningless. Hunters must ask permission of school administrations in order to carry unloaded weapons through a school zone, even while traveling in a car. The school administrations are under no obligation to give such permission. A legal gun owner living within a school zone could retain his weapon, but would be in violation if he so much as set foot out of his house, even to place the gun in his car. These restrictions applied even to off-duty police officers carrying service weapons. (Such violations are far from theoretical. In Wisconsin shortly after the law's passage, a bicyclist openly carrying a pistol chased off four thugs attempting to rob him but was then arrested because, unknown to himself, he was within a thousand feet of a school.) The establishment of gun-free zones acted, intentionally or otherwise, to curtail firearm rights nationwide while avoiding a direct public confrontation with a well-organized pro-gun movement.

The Gun-Free School Zones Act became federal law in November

1990 as part of that year's Crime Control Act. It was overturned five years later by the Supreme Court in *United States v. Lopez*, a decision that aroused widespread controversy due to its being based on a finding of congressional abuse of the interstate commerce clause. *Lopez* marked the first time in half a century that Congress had been found in violation of that clause. In 1996, Congress reenacted the law with additional wordage intended to reconcile it with the Court's objections but which instead rendered it unenforceable.

Unfortunately, the seed had been planted. Across the country, schools, colleges, and even shopping malls declared themselves "gun-free zones," often putting up prominent signs announcing the fact and threatening dire penalties for violators. The "gun-free" fad appears to have been purely ritual behavior, along the lines of wearing a Che T-shirt or putting a rising "O" sticker on your car. But the responsible authorities failed to consider possible consequences, particularly those involving potential mass murderers. However unbalanced such individuals may be, few cases exist where they have not displayed a knack for rational planning. Shooters tend to strike sites with plenty of victims and small chance of resistance—"soft targets," in security parlance. They have seldom if ever attacked sportsmen's clubhouses or bars in the vicinity of police stations. What the "gun-free zone" advocates were doing was informing potential mass killers where the easiest targets could be found.

Prior to the passage of the gun-free zone acts, school shootings, while not unknown, were relatively rare. Normally such incidents were restricted to two or three per decade. (One of the worst of these until very recently was the "Texas Tower Massacre" of August 1, 1966, in which a gunman suffering from a brain tumor shot fifteen passersby on the University of Austin campus after killing his wife and mother-in-law.)

But following the establishment of gun-free sites, incidents of this type simply exploded. Over forty school shootings have oc-curred since 1991, with fatalities on the order of 130. A large proportion of these incidents occurred at explicitly demarked "gun-free" campuses, including the deadliest of them, the Virginia Tech massacre of September 21, 2007, in which an insanely em-bittered undergraduate shot two students in a dorm room before entering a classroom building (chaining the doors shut behind him) to methodically shoot up one classroom after another until he accounted for thirty more victims. Only months previously, the school had prosecuted another student for possessing a pistol for purposes of self-defense. (A late revelation concerning the Vir-ginia Tech massacre appeared in a state report released in Decem-ber 2009. It seems that certain administrators were notified of the first two killings shortly after they occurred and responded by securing the president's office and warning their own relatives of the danger. The campus at large was alerted only an hour and a half later, allowing the gunman plenty of time to carry out his plans. Individuals of this level of incompetence should not be ad-ministering anything, anywhere, under any circumstances.)

Nor have schools been the only locations victimized. A number of malls and shopping centers also jumped on the "gun-free" bandwagon, placing large "No Firearms" announcements at their entrances. Shooting incidents, to which such sites had previously been immune, followed in short order. Such shootings have oc-curred at Kingston, New York (February 13, 2005, two wounded), Tacoma, Washington (November 20, 2005, six injured), Kansas City, Missouri (April 29, 2007, three killed, two injured), and Omaha, Nebraska (December 5, 2007, nine dead, including the shooter).

The most notorious of these instances took place at Salt Lake City, where on February 12, 2007, a gunman opened fire at the Trolley Square mall, killing five shoppers and injuring four others. Luckily, Kenneth Hammond, an off-duty police officer, had also disobeyed the mall's prohibition of firearms and was able to hold the shooter at bay until responding officers ended the confrontation by killing the gunman.

A number of similar defensive incidents at supposedly "gun-free" sites have underlined the fatuity of the policy. In 1997, Joel Myrick, a high school vice principal in Pearl, Mississippi, was able to retrieve his personal handgun from his car and halt a gunman planning to shoot up a junior high school. A few days later, a similar attempt at a school in Edinboro, Pennsylvania, was brought to an end when a local merchant held a shooter at gunpoint until authorities arrived. In 2002, a murderous shooting at Appalachian Law School in West Virginia was ended when two deputies attending the college used their off-duty weapons to apprehend the gunman. (Ironically, Appalachian Law is less than a hundred miles from Virginia Tech.)

The most compelling of these defensive episodes occurred in Colorado shortly after the Westroads mall shooting in Omaha. Apparently inspired by that incident, a gunman impelled by hatred of Christians entered a youth mission training center in Arvada, a suburb of Denver, on December 9, 2007, and shot four young people, two of them fatally. Twelve hours later, he attacked a Colorado Springs megachurch, the New Life Church, as services were ending. Opening fire with seven thousand worshippers present, the gunman killed one and wounded four.

Most churches ban weapons as a matter of course. But the New Life Church had established a volunteer security detachment made up of parishioners with carrying permits. It was one of these, Jeanne Assam, who engaged the killer. While another parishioner, Larry Bourbonnais, distracted the gunman—suffering a serious wound in the process—Assam took the shooter under fire and though heavily outgunned (the killer was armed with a rifle) shot him down before he could claim further victims. A search revealed that the gunman had been carrying enough rounds for several dozen reloads. Senior Pastor Brady Boyd stated that "perhaps a hundred lives" had been saved by Assam's action.

Interestingly, national media focused on the fact that Ms. Assam had previously worked as a law-enforcement officer in Minneapolis, implying that she was a professional security officer and completely obscuring the voluntary aspect.

John R. Lott, Jr., stands as one of the nation's leading authorities on firearms use. In 1999, working with the economist William Landes, he authored a paper demonstrating that the largest number of multiple-victim shootings occurred in states with the most restrictive gun laws, particularly those prohibiting open or concealed carrying of weapons. Conversely, states with more rational carry laws suffer not only fewer such incidents, but fewer victims in the shootings that occur, apparently thanks to the fact that armed individuals are more apt to curtail these crimes while they are being carried out. The implications for gun-free zones need not be belabored. In recent years, Lott has repeatedly stated for the record that almost all recent mass killings have occurred in "gun-free" milieus.

Recent mass slayings have borne out this contention. On April 3, 2009, a disturbed Vietnamese immigrant attacked the explicitly gun-free American Civic Center, an institution catering to the needs of new immigrants, in Binghamton, New York.

Blocking the rear exit with his car, he shot every person he encountered inside the building, killing thirteen people within a matter of minutes. Although summoned immediately, it took the Binghamton police over forty minutes to enter the building, and nearly three hours to ascertain that the shooter had killed himself alongside his victims. (Delays in police response involving mass killings—the police at Columbine waited several hours to enter the school—are a factor that cannot be overlooked in evaluating these cases. It has been pointed out, by veteran police officers among others, that many current law enforcement personnel lack combat experience, which provides both the proficiency and the coolness required to confront criminals capable of mass murder.)

Following the Fort Hood massacre, many Americans were non-plussed to learn that personnel on military bases, presumed to be well-trained and familiar with all types of weaponry, were effectively disarmed. Personal weapons are forbidden on all American military bases, even among officers, who are traditionally armed while on duty. When he chose to strike on November 5, 2009, Major Nidal Malik Hasan, a disaffected officer obsessed with Islamist teachings, knew he would encounter little resistance. Attacking the Soldier Residence Processing Center, Hasan killed thirteen victims and wounded another thirty-two before being shot and disarmed by two civilian police officers, Sergeants Kimberly Munley and Mark Todd.

We await the inevitable shootings of 2010 with a sense of frustration. This is one of those problems where the solution is obvious and at the same time unlikely to be put into effect. "Gun-free" zones act as magnets for the vicious and the demented, who can only be warded off by legitimately armed individuals, either lawmen or private citizens. We are faced here with uncomfortable evidence that the mere expression of certain liberal dogmas can lead to fatalities.

THE FDA AND BUREAUCRATIZED COMPASSION

The Food and Drug Administration (FDA) is one of the few federal bureaucracies that has no need to justify its existence. The FDA fulfills a necessary role, protecting the public from dangerous or badly formulated, manufactured, or processed drugs and foodstuffs.

But even essential agencies are subject to the basic shortcomings of bureaucracy. Throughout its existence, the FDA has failed to maintain any consistent policy for carrying out its mission, instead seesawing from easygoing to uncompromising standards for testing and approving pharmaceuticals and related medical technology, and then back again.

During its early decades, the FDA relied in large part on industry testing and reportage from physicians. This casual methodology ended with the thalidomide tragedy of the early 1960s. Prior to its introduction in the U.S., thalidomide was marketed in forty-six countries and was widely used throughout Europe as a sedative and tranquilizer. When application for U.S. manufacture was made to the FDA, Dr. Frances Kelsey became suspicious over the lack of data on side effects despite the drug's widespread use. Although she came under heavy pressure from her superiors and industry representatives, Dr. Kelsey blocked licensing of the drug.

Only a few months later, a report was published in the *British Medical Journal* suggesting that thalidomide caused nerve damage. Before the end of 1961, evidence appeared implicating thalidomide in a growing number of birth defects. Then, in 1962, the floodgates opened as women who had used the drug while pregnant began giving birth to badly damaged children. Along with the characteristic "flipper" teratology (called "phocomelia" by specialists), thalidomide also caused malformations of the eyes, ears, heart, digestive tract, and nervous system. Over ten thousand children were affected, most of them in Europe. Thanks to Dr. Kelsey's stand, only a handful of cases occurred in this country.

The episode revealed serious weaknesses in FDA drug-approval policy. In 1962, the Kefauver Harris Amendment was passed to ensure higher standards in testing and analysis of all proposed pharmaceuticals. As the system evolved, it eventually required at least fourteen years from the point where a drug was discovered to the point where it received approval from the FDA: six and a half years for initial tests and data analysis, and another seven years spent on patient testing, divided into three separate phases. The cost for this process could amount to a billion dollars.

The FDA operated on that basis until the appearance of AIDS in the 1980s. AIDS activists attacked the agency as being too restrictive and slow in approving drugs intended for treating AIDS patients. The FDA responded with a policy of "compassionate use" to provide seriously ill patients with access to drugs currently being tested. The new doctrine may have saved thousands of lives. (Ironically, one of the drugs that proved most effective against AIDS lesions was thalidomide.)

The AIDS drug policy led in turn to a general loosening of standards under the Clinton administration. As part of Al Gore's effort to "reinvent government," the FDA was encouraged to cut both the length and complexity of the approval process. The goal was to reduce "by an average of one year the time required to bring important new drugs to the American public." Even as FDA chief David Kessler was tightening the screws on processors of frozen orange juice, drug manufacturers found themselves effectively unbound.

As a result, a number of drugs were approved only to be yanked off the market once subtle but dangerous side effects were demonstrated. The most notorious of these was rofecoxib, better known by its brand name, Vioxx, an anti-inflammatory drug withdrawn in 2004 after it was shown to increase the risk of strokes and heart attack. But as many as ten others, including Redux, a diet pill that caused heart-valve problems; Raxar, an antibiotic that disrupted heart rhythms; Duract, a painkiller with serious potential for liver toxicity; and Propulsid, a heartburn drug blamed for heart-rhythm problems, were also withdrawn after being implicated in as many as 950 deaths.

The FDA once again tightened standards. From a high of thirty-six drugs approved each year between 1994 and 1997, the average fell to twenty-three a year between 2001 and 2004. Unfortunately, the practice of compassionate use was also adversely affected.

This situation was brought to a point by the death of Abigail Burroughs, a young woman who developed an unusual (for her age) case of head and neck cancer. Her doctor suggested treatment with two drugs being tested at the time, AstraZeneca's Iressa and ImClone Systems' C225. But she was found ineligible for clinical trials, and no exception was made for compassionate use. After a lengthy struggle, Ms. Burroughs died at the age of twenty-one.

Within hours of her death, her father, Frank Burroughs, founded an advocacy group, the Abigail Alliance for Better Access to Developmental Drugs, to lobby for a broader interpretation of the compassionate use policy. Only weeks later, he testified before Congress, encouraging several politicians to sponsor a bill to formalize a less stringent interpretation. Burroughs also filed suit against the FDA over its dilatory response to his daughter's plight.

What the reformers wanted from the FDA was an abandonment of the customary practice of blind testing in which a percentage of the test subjects are given a placebo while the rest are provided with the active drug. Instead, testing would be open to all subjects suffering from the disease the candidate drug was meant to treat, with no use of placebos whatsoever. Sophisticated statistical techniques, such as Bayesian analysis, which has been utilized successfully in biomedical applications for several decades, could derive workable results with as much efficiency as the placebo method. Not only would such a program bring the FDA up to date as regards scientific practice, it would also resolve the moral conundrum involved in deliberately providing deathly ill individuals with placebos intended to have no effect.

At first the reformers made considerable progress. *Abigail Alliance v. von Eschenbach*, filed in 2003, was decided in May 2006 in favor of the Abigail Alliance by the District of Columbia federal appeals court. At the same time, Senators Sam Brownback and James Inhofe agreed to sponsor the ACCESS (Access, Compassion, Care, and Ethics for Seriously Ill Patients) Act, intended to open clinical trials while encouraging medical researchers to modify their data-collection techniques.

But all this marked a false dawn. The FDA appealed the case to the full bench of the D.C. appeals court, which reversed the earlier verdict in August 2007. Frank Burroughs appealed to the Supreme Court, which in January 2008 refused to hear the case. As for the ACCESS Act, it was introduced before the Senate in November 2005, where it failed to obtain a vote.

The courts and the FDA acted on procedural grounds. Both spoke of the FDA's duty to protect patients and the public from unsafe drugs, though in fact patient safety was the last thing being served by FDA policy. Provenge, a vaccine for use in treating terminal prostate cancer patients, can serve as an example. The FDA delayed introduction of the drug for three years while it mulled over certain minor statistical anomalies. Prostate cancer causes an average of 32,000 deaths a year. During that three-year delay, nearly 96,000 men died of the disease, an unknown number of whom might have been helped by the new drug. The same situation prevails with all varieties of cancer, not to mention the vast array of deadly diseases beyond that. The number of deaths from cancer each year exceeds 550,000. Contrast that to the number of patients allowed to take part in trials of new drugs: 650 a year. The FDA's stance on drug trials is a textbook example of a bureaucracy embracing process instead of real results.

Whether or not the Abigail Alliance proposal is accepted, it should be easily possible to work out a method of ensuring accurate test results while not depriving tens of thousands of disease victims of what might well be their final chance at survival. The FDA itself had a plan to institute an expanded form of compassionate use, but this was attempted only once, with the cancer drug Iressa, which in the end was not approved. That result seems to have put all such future plans on the back burner.

• •

But the story hasn't ended yet. On August 21, 2008, a federal judge, in apparent defiance of *Abigail Alliance v. von Eschenbach,* ordered the drug company PTD Therapeutics to provide a teenager suffering from the rare condition Duchenne muscular dystrophy with a supply of its experimental drug PTC124. This is one of those issues that is not going to go away until a workable solution is found.*

Further examples of democide's penetration into our lives can be easily uncovered: the Veterans Administration policy of ejecting "disturbed" veterans from its facilities, so that many die on the streets, the common denial of Second Amendment rights by government agencies and affiliates, placing unarmed citizens at the mercy of lunatics and criminals, along with policies involving the "War on Drugs," immigration, AIDS, and onward as far as anyone cares to look. Ideology is a universal solvent, one that touches everything and destroys everything that it touches. Not even the most vulnerable are immune; not even childhood or the deathbed offer protection. Democide is a process innate to contemporary liberalism, to be found wherever liberalism is found. It cannot be avoided, and there is a strong possibility that it will only get worse.

---

*In September 2009 the FDA announced its solution: new rules for drug access procedures. "Expanded Access to Investigational Drugs for Treatment Use" made investigational drugs more easily available to patients, while "Charging for Investigational Drugs Under an Investigational New Drug Application" set up a fee schedule for drugs under clinical trial. It remains to be seen how well these rules will work in practice.

It was naive of the 19th century optimists to expect paradise from technology—and it is equally naive of the 20th century pessimists to make technology the scapegoat for such old shortcomings as man's blindness, cruelty, immaturity, greed and sinful pride.
—PETER F. DRUCKER

8

KISS TOMORROW GOOD-BYE

Liberalism and the Future

L iberals have long claimed a unique relationship with the future, on the grounds that theirs is the sole truly forward-looking political doctrine, the only one that can be trusted to lead American society through all the pitfalls that lie ahead. There is, needless to say, no evidence whatsoever to support this assertion. During the early twentieth century, liberalism embraced a wide-eyed, childlike confidence that progress was eternal and things could only get better. When it didn't quite turn out that way, liberals reacted by rotating full circle to portray the future only in relentless shades of black, a wasteland of nuclear war, automation, conformity, or any of a hundred other threats. (Environmentalism is a lingering remnant of this attitude.) At no point have liberals ever accepted the mature view of a future full of challenges but by no means overwhelming.

This does not mean that we can dismiss liberal forecasts. There exists such a thing as the self-fulfilling prophecy. As we have seen, ideological errors even when unsuccessful leave their mark in the form of distortion of the political, intellectual, and social spheres. A close examination of liberal expectations will at the very least tell us what we need to guard against.

LIBERALISM AND TECH

When we speak of the future in third-millennial terms, we speak largely of technology. The late-modern period preceding our own was the first in history in which the basic elements of life could be transformed within a single generation. During the twentieth century the automobile, aircraft, and broadcast technology utterly changed the world within the span of a lifetime, as infotech and biotech are doing today, though not yet as profoundly.

The liberal relationship with technology is ambiguous at best. Liberals have a deep distrust of technology (which they commonly refer to as "science") and its products. This has not always been the case. Tech, in the form of electrification, sanitation, and new methods of communication and transport, was the progressive's friend early in the last century, the tool with which the world was to be remade on a more rational and consistent basis. Traces of that attitude survived into the postwar period, embodied in such figures as Robert Moses.

But tech is a power in and of itself, not easily tamed, and as such less than compatible with any form of ideology aimed at social control. The Internet and cable TV did much to destroy the liberal ascendancy of the late twentieth century, a turn of events they are unlikely to forget. Liberals also loathe the way the public drives the adaptation of new tech, going for whatever is entertaining, amusing, or interesting rather than what is good for it.

Technical and scientific advances gain liberal support on an ideological basis. It's not so much how useful, necessary, or even plausible an innovation might be as how well it fits the agenda, how closely it matches liberal conceptions, and how useful it is in promoting liberal interests. This is the flip side of the process by which certain advances such as nuclear power or "frankenfoods" become malignant evils, to be resisted at all costs.

Such efforts are often extensions of old crusades, such as abortion, redistribution, or, in the case of neurolaw, criminal justice.

NEUROLAW

For several decades, a revolution in neuroscience has been underway to little public notice. Utilizing MRI sensors, PET scans, and related techniques, researchers have been able to record activity in the brain while thinking is actually taking place—a feat impossible for previous generations of scientists. Among other things, neuroscientists have demonstrated that damage or hyperactivity in certain brain centers—for instance, the amygdala, which governs expression of anger and rage—can encourage criminal behavior. Research has also demonstrated, to the shocked surprise of millions of parents, that incomplete development of the frontal lobes leads to poor impulse control in teenagers. (At last the ancient parental question, "If your friends all jumped off a cliff, would you jump off, too?" can be answered on a firm scientific basis.)

Research involving the amygdala has already had some impact on the criminal justice system. Beginning in the 1990s, brain scans have been presented as evidence in criminal cases in jurisdictions across the country, on the grounds that certain types of brain damage can act as mitigating factors in verdicts and sentencing. This strategy's success remains limited—while it does not appear to have influenced any high-profile verdicts, it may have affected sentencing in some cases. A Florida court recently held that failure to admit such evidence in capital cases could be taken as grounds for reversal. In the case of *Roper v. Simmons* (2005), Supreme Court Justice Anthony Kennedy appears to have

utilized neuroscience findings concerning teenagers in overturning a death sentence in which a murderer was seventeen years
old. (Along with two other youths, Christopher Simmons had
abducted Shirley Crook from her home, bound her with duct tape
and electrical cable, and threw her off a bridge into the Meramec
River in the Missouri Highlands, at least in part because he had
been previously involved in an auto accident with Crook.)

Neuroscience advocates also suggest that the technique may
prove useful in jury selection and in judging the veracity of witnesses. (While not as widely known as it should be, jury selection
has become a critical element of legal strategy. Selecting a compatible jury is often half the battle in criminal legal proceedings.
Jury-selection consultants earn excellent livings shuttling from
courtroom to courtroom across the country.) Claims have been
made that MRI equipment will, with a little more research, be
able to serve as an infallible lie detector.

But there is a major flaw in the way that neurolaw is being
introduced: application is occurring at the level of practice, with
little or no oversight or guidance from experienced jurists, psy-
chologists, scientists, or ethicists. Nor do they seem at all eager to
take up the matter. The legal profession appears to be flying by
the seat of its pants, making up the rules as it goes along.

Defense attorneys have taken the point in this effort, with
the result that neurolaw displays a distinct bias—one that will
be familiar to us from Chapter 2. The findings of neuroscience
are being interpreted in such a way as to fit the paradigm of the
functionally innocent criminal. We are seeing the return of the
blameless perp of the 1950s and '60s, when criminal acts were
attributed to every other factor in the universe except the individual who committed them—only now with apparent scientific
backing. Neurolaw supporters make no secret of this. Two prominent professors of psychology, Joshua D. Greene of Harvard and
Jonathan D. Cohen of Princeton, have gone on record to call for a

"redefinition" of the concept of guilt, based on MRI findings. As Greene told the *New York Times*, "it radically changes the way we think about the law. The official line in the law is [that] all that matters is whether you're rational, but you can have someone who is totally rational but whose strings are being pulled by something beyond his control."

This means, as it did in the 1960s, that we should abandon the concept of punishment, and replace it with . . . Concerning this, neurolaw advocates are unclear. They cannot repeat the "rehabilitation" claim of earlier reformers; severe brain damage does not respond to such treatment. What specific alternatives the neurolegalists have in mind remains a matter of speculation. But one thing we can be sure of: neurolaw supporters will not concede that an individual with no sense of responsibility is a constant threat requiring permanent confinement.

We'll be hearing a lot more about neurolaw over the next few years. Vanderbilt University has recently opened a $27 million institute that it hopes will become the worldwide center for the discipline. Certain research with profound implications has not yet even begun. (Though we should not expect any inquiries into the basis of gay behavior.) The social commentator Tom Wolfe has suggested that neuroscience will lead to an intellectual revolution to match those instigated by Copernicus, Darwin, and Freud. Many neuroscientists believe that their research demonstrates that human beings are no more than robots, at the strict mercy of nerve impulses and brain chemistry states.

But the vast promises of the neuroscientists are unlikely to come to pass. Such promises seldom do, no matter what the discipline— nuclear power, behaviorism, and criminology can serve as easy examples. Biological scientists today are in much the same intellectual position as physicists in the last decades of the nineteenth century. The classical physicists were convinced that they were closing in on the final secrets of the universe, that they had almost all the answers, that a little more research would enshrine the doctrine of determinism and the concept of the mechanistic universe as the last word in the physical sciences. The parallels with contemporary biological sciences need not be emphasized. The determinist fallacy in physics was demolished by Planck and Einstein. Figures of similar stature are very likely at work in biology today. It will be interesting to see how it all develops.

In the meantime, a liberal legal system will not hesitate to utilize the findings of neuroscience as tools to promote its agenda. Liberals have played this game many times before—Darwinism being only one example. (The "-ism" suffix is a clear sign of ideologization—who ever heard of "Newtonism" or "Einsteinism"?) Whatever its merits as scientific theory, Darwinian natural selection has often been used as a club to beat back traditionalist opposition to liberal programs, not uncommonly in situations where its relevance is difficult to discern. Liberals will repeat this tactic as long as it continues to work for them. Like sociology and the behavioral sciences before it, neurolaw will eventually be implicated in freeing career criminals to continue preying on the public. Only then will the discipline come under close scrutiny. It may well be too late at that point to establish a rational legal protocol. We are in serious danger of seeing the judicial system damaged even more profoundly than it was in the 1960s.

EUTHANASIA

On August 7, 2009, former vice presidential candidate Sarah Palin left a message on her Facebook page dealing with an overlooked aspect of the health-care bill winding its way through Congress.

Governor Palin was concerned with the prospects of euthanasia embedded in certain passages of the bill, specifically Section 1233, a strange provision providing for Medicaid funding for "end-of-life sessions." "The America I know and love," she wrote, "is not one in which my parents or my baby with Down Syndrome will have to stand in front of Obama's 'death panel' so his bureaucrats can decide, based on a subjective judgment of their 'level of productivity in society,' whether they are worthy of health care. Such a system is downright evil."

Traditionally, statements by losing VP hopefuls were usually featured in newspaper back pages among the recipes and the daily chess problem if they appeared at all. But Palin was a special case. Palin is yet another beneficiary of the liberal tendency to create their own bêtes noires. Terrified at the prospect of an upcoming female Republican politician who was attractive, capable, and in possession of a substantial record of achievement (Palin had taken a fire hose to the Augean stables of Alaskan GOP politics and had overseen the signing of a stalled international agreement to construct a new natural gas pipeline), American liberals unleashed their entire media arsenal. Palin suffered an unprecedented level of personal attacks. No element of her life, including her person, her childhood, her marriage, and her young family, were out of bounds. Not even her disabled infant child remained immune.

The result was the direct opposite of what the nation's liberal elite was hoping for. Seeing something of themselves in this housewife who had bootstrapped her way up the political ladder, Americans from across the country rallied to Palin's defense, endowing an all but unknown politician from one of the country's most remote states with a cachet unseen since the era of Reagan. Liberals responded by redoubling their efforts against Palin.

The Facebook entry was seen as another opportunity to degrade the governor. Newspaper opinion pages, news anchors, television comics, and liberal politicians unloaded on Palin as one. Howard Dean asserted that Palin had "just made that up. . . . There's nothing like euthanasia in the bill." Andrew Sullivan, who had previously promoted a bizarre conspiracy theory claiming that the infant Trig was not the governor's child at all but that of her eldest daughter, dismissed Palin's comment as "fantasy." David Brooks, yet another architect of the Palin-as-Gorgon myth, labeled her as "crazy." A few months later, the editors of PolitiFact .com, a website associated with the *St. Petersburg Times*, selected Palin's statement as "Lie of the Year."

And yet, on August 13, less than a week after Palin's words appeared, and while the uproar was still building, the Senate quietly dropped Section 1233 without debate or public announcement.

Why had Congressional Democrats given in while enjoying the total support of the media and political establishments? Because Palin had put her finger on an undeniable truth: as regards euthanasia, mercy killing, or whatever euphemism might be preferred, liberalism's hands were not clean, its record far from unblemished. That in fact euthanasia had for decades been a major goal for American liberals.

Euthanasia is by no means uncommon. It occurs in hospitals on a regular basis. It is an extreme solution, resorted to only as a final option, when the patient has deteriorated to the point of no return, all hope is gone, and all that remains is suffering. Then a respirator is shut off, a thumb goes heavy on a morphine plunger. No questions are asked, no one looks further into it. This may be sheer cowardice, or the height of wisdom. Whatever the case, we know instinctively that to intervene would be madness.

Make way for American liberalism.

The liberal impulse toward rationalizing euthanasia is easily understood. It has nothing to do with the reasons publicly stated: that legalizing and regulating euthanasia would be a humane action, that it would prevent physicians from being prosecuted (no doctor has ever been successfully prosecuted for an act of euthanasia), that the public approves. As is true of everything having to do with politics, the reality involves power. Absolute power is not absolute unless it controls *every aspect of existence* within reach. Liberal bureaucrats and politicians to some extent already regulate who will enter this world (though nowhere near as much as they would like to). It remains for them to regulate who will leave it, and when, and under what circumstances. Only then can the circle be completed. Only then can liberal ideology be said to have circumscribed life in all its width and breadth.

This alone explains the steady, decades-long campaign in favor of legal euthanasia. It is discreet and low-key, carried out for the most part by nongovernmental organizations ranging from the Hemlock Society, solely dedicated to promoting the practice, to the ACLU, which has devoted considerable resources to acting as a friendly advocate. It is seldom mentioned by politicians, and then only through such euphemisms as "quality of life."

This unusual sense of discretion arises in large part from the fact that the sole successful euthanasia program of the type envisioned by American liberals was carried out in Nazi Germany between 1939 and 1941. Known as Aktion T-4 (for Tiergarten 4, the Berlin address which served as headquarters), the program was begun under Adolf Hitler's personal orders in October 1939. It was aimed at the deformed, mentally retarded, and chronically ill, who were labeled "Lebens unwertes Leben," life unworthy of life. Three doctors decided each case, without benefit of a physical examination or medical records. If all three marked a government-approved form, the victim was transported to a killing center and put to death. (Some were simply allowed to starve in place.) The program began with small children and worked its way up.

At first Aktion T-4 met with little public protest. Nearly 100,000 victims had been killed before, on August 3, 1941, Catholic bishop Clemens von Galen condemned the program from the pulpit as "plain murder," telling Catholics to refuse cooperation with the Nazis "so that we may not be contaminated by their thinking and their ungodly behavior." Though Galen himself was too prominent for the Nazis to punish, they executed three priests who distributed copies of his sermon.

While the program was publicly halted, it in fact went on in secret at a reduced level. Aktion T-4 provided an opportunity to investigate techniques of large-scale extermination, and served as a training program for many figures later involved in the Final Solution, including Christian Wirth, father of the gas chamber, Franz Stangl, commander of Treblinka, and Rudolf Höss, commander of Auschwitz.

Under the circumstances, it's easy to grasp why euthanasia has not been slipped into practice through a surreptitious court case or as a rider on an unrelated bill. There are more attractive ways to commit political suicide. Unlike abortion, euthanasia requires active persuasion, an effort to make the public willing collaborators. This presents a problem, since no serious figures are inclined to support any such program. What liberalism needed was a Gandhi of mercy killing—that or a John Cave, the charismatic protagonist of Gore Vidal's novel *Messiah*, who founds a religion in which euthanasia is a sacrament. What it got instead was Jack Kevorkian, the Doctor of Death.

KEVORKIAN'S DANCE

Kevorkian was the last person anyone would choose as the public representative for anything. A loner, irascible, obsessive, and unspeakably strange, Kevorkian spent an entire career in a frenetic tango with death, one that he at last attempted to draw the entire country into.

Kevorkian got his nickname thanks to an early project he carried out while serving his residency: photographing the corneas of dying individuals before, during, and after death. Another one of his experiments involved the use of transfused blood from corpses.

So disturbing were activities such as these that the University of Michigan asked him to complete his residency elsewhere.

Further proposals followed: that experiments be performed on condemned prisoners, or alternately that their organs be harvested for transplant, that the army adapt his blood-transfusion technique for use in Vietnam, that a chain of for-profit euthanasia centers, which he called "obitoriums," be opened for business around the country. Kevorkian's reputation grew more baroque as time passed, and he found it difficult to obtain work in his specialty of pathology.

He would likely have remained no more than a local oddity but for the events of June 4, 1990. That afternoon Kevorkian's sister, Flora, drove Janet Adkins, a victim of early-onset Alzheimer's, to Kevorkian's van, waiting at a curb in a public park. Kevorkian asked Adkins a few questions to assure himself that she was ready to go ahead. He then hooked her up to a machine of his own invention, the "Thanatron," a device that killed by injection after the victim flipped a switch. As his sister recited the Lord's Prayer (the involvement of Kevorkian's family in his activities has attracted surprisingly little attention), Adkins flipped the switch as instructed, Kevorkian wished her "a good trip," and within seconds she was dead.

Unlike other doctors involved in similar acts, Kevorkian had no intention of allowing the incident to be overlooked. He immediately notified the authorities, not omitting his own role. An investigation was begun, the media was contacted, and "physician-assisted suicide" became a major controversy of the new decade.

A local judge on June 8 issued an injunction forbidding Kevorkian from assisting in any further suicides. He was defiant: "What's the court got to do with medicine? . . . You know the court is dominated by religion. . . . 'Life is sanctity, this and that. . . .'"

Murder charges filed against Kevorkian were quashed on December 12, 1990. It seemed that no state law specifically criminalized the act of assisted suicide. Nevertheless, he waited nearly a year before his next act of euthanasia, dispatching Marjorie Wantz and Sherry Miller in a state park cabin on October 23, 1991. The instrument of Miller's death was yet another one of Kevorkian's killing machines, a face mask dispensing carbon monoxide.

Over the next year and a half he killed a dozen people. His medical license was revoked in November 1991 and another murder indictment was handed down, to no avail. The state of Michigan, never the best-governed commonwealth in the U.S., was extremely slow on the draw. The legislature didn't get around to outlawing euthanasia until December 1992, in an act so ill-written that it was struck down by an appeals court. Kevorkian continued his campaign, the number of victims slowly climbing toward one hundred.

One complication in dealing with Kevorkian involved his new-found status as a celebrity, a kind of James Dean of the gas chamber, with his activities noted as if he were a rock star or actor, his opinions sought on all topics. He was photographed shaking hands with a delighted Tom Cruise, as clear an indication of elite acceptance as could be desired. Kevorkian was portrayed as a hero-victim, an underdog taking on the authorities (always a potent depiction for an American audience), a humanitarian coming to the aid of individuals mistreated by the "System." Much of the related commentary made use of the "Uncle Leo" thesis: "Poor Uncle Leo—he was sick for so long and suffered so much before he died." According to media commentators, Kevorkian was simply trying to help the Uncle Leos of the world. Of course, it was convenient that Leo himself was not around to give his own opinion.

Rebel or not, Kevorkian received full support from all levels of the liberal establishment. His flamboyant attorney Geoffrey Fieger represented him gratis, at one point even putting Kevorkian up in one of his properties. Legal advisors and jury selection consultants flew to Michigan on their own dime. Ministers, academics, and members of his own profession offered their backing. A candidate for Michigan attorney general ran on a platform that if elected, he would cease all efforts at prosecution. It is evident that these people—many of whom were in positions requiring them to protect the sick and helpless—saw nothing at all wrong with Kevorkian's activities. Large elements of the American elite would have been in no way discomfited if Kevorkian had been completely successful and the highways of America were today dotted with obitoriums. ("Dr. Jack's—welfare and Social Security checks welcome.")

As is often the case, a clean disjuncture existed between the media Kevorkian and the real article. To Kevorkian, the euthanasia campaign was merely a step toward the fulfillment of a lifelong dream: the ability to carry out experiments on still-living human beings, experiments of a type forbidden in accepted medical practice. These included removing organs from still-living individuals, drug research on death-row prisoners and cancer victims, removal of organs from the disabled, and experimentation with surgical techniques on healthy individuals. None of this was any secret; Kevorkian had published proposals for these and other activities in journal articles and at least one book.* But the information was kept from the general public for the simple reason that had it appeared in any major media outlet, it would have shut down Doctor Death then and there. What Kevorkian was proposing was equivalent to the crimes of Mengele, himself

---

*Prescription Medicide: The Goodness of Planned Death, Prometheus, 1991. His other books include The Story of Dissection (1959), Beyond Any Kind of God (1966), and Slimmeriks and the Demi-diet (1978). Amazon.com, not an outfit to miss a trick, features a special "Jack Kevorkian Author Page."

known as the "Angel of Death" to his victims at Auschwitz. The "humanitarian" mask would have vanished in a flash once the reality was exposed.

Nevertheless, a more accurate picture began coming together in defiance of media self-censorship. It developed that several of Kevorkian's victims had not been fatally, or even seriously ill— supposedly a necessary prerequisite for euthanasia. Some had nothing physically wrong with them at all. Marjorie Wantz, his second victim, was suffering from an obscure pelvic pain that could not be diagnosed and may have been psychosomatic in origin. Another victim was afflicted with nothing more lethal than serious depression. It appeared that Doctor Death would gladly put to sleep anyone who came along, no matter what their problem. Kevorkian did his own case no good by boasting that he could talk a healthy teenager into strapping on one of his machines.

Kevorkian beat no less than four accusations of murder, being found not guilty on three occasions, with a mistrial declared in the fourth. But at last he succumbed to the temptations of celebrity, allowing the CBS news program *60 Minutes* to film him injecting a lethal solution into Thomas Youk, a man suffering from amyotrophic lateral sclerosis (Lou Gehrig's disease). With irrefutable visual evidence in hand, Michigan indicted him in November 1998. On April 13, 1999, he was found guilty of murder and sentenced to ten to twenty-five years in prison. He served eight years before being paroled in 2007.

It had taken nine years from the date of Kevorkian's first murder to finally put him behind bars. So impotent had government become, so inept its procedures, so alienated had it grown from its actual duties, that it proved utterly incapable of fulfilling its basic task of protecting its citizens. Aided by a debased media establishment, a serial killer carried out repeated slayings on the streets of a major state with virtual impunity. As many as 130 sick and depressed individuals met their deaths at the hands of a figure out of a child's nightmare, while frightened and incompetent authorities repeatedly fumbled the ball.

The Kevorkian saga was a clear debacle for euthanasia interests. No worse poster boy could have been found to promote the practice. It's one thing to hear of an individual undergoing euthanasia, something else entirely to watch it on a news show. Most people decided that they did not care for what they saw. The image of jackbooted Nazis putting children to death was joined by that of Doctor Death watching eagerly as a victim expired in the back of his rusty van.

But euthanasia supporters could look to one victory: in the midst of Kevorkian's campaign, the West Coast's Ninth Circuit Court, perhaps the most erratic bench in the country (out of sixteen Ninth Circuit decisions reviewed by the Supreme Court in the 2009 term, fifteen were overturned), found in March 1996 that individuals had a constitutional right to assistance from medical personnel in committing suicide. On November 5, 1997, Oregon voters approved an assisted suicide law that allowed doctors to prescribe lethal doses of drugs for dying patients. Despite everything, the euthanasia crowd had its foothold.

THE SOROS DEATH PROJECT

At the same time that Kevorkian was carrying out his campaign, yet another figure, infinitely more powerful, though just as eccentric, was embarking on a similar program, with the full cooperation of no small number of medical professionals.

Though not a recognized medical specialty, palliative care is a legitimate field of health-care activity, an attempt to correct deficiencies in treatment long overlooked by many medical practitioners. Doctors have traditionally paid too little attention to alleviating pain suffered by patients under their care. The heroic concept of medicine, which views medical procedure as a head-to-head contest between doctor and disorder, allows little consideration for the comfort and peace of mind of the battleground—which is to say, the patient.

Palliative care was an effort to improve this state of affairs through application of advances in pain research along with mitigation of the psychological consequences of illness and treatment. Particular consideration was given to the terminally ill, the "hopeless cases" frequently shunted aside in the past. Palliative care advocates attempted to ease the ordeal of confronting death for both the patients and their families through sophisticated pain management and alleviation of psychological stress. In this effort they had a natural ally in the budding hospice movement, which sought to assist dying patients by removing them from sterile, forbidding hospital environments into a more homelike setting for their final months.

Palliative care had begun in earnest in the 1970s. It made steady progress over the ensuing two decades, with interest growing and programs being established at hospitals and medical centers across the country. Then in the early 1990s it caught the attention of George Soros, yet another entry into the weirdest contemporary American sweepstakes.

At first glance, the Soros story appears to be an exemplary narrative of an immigrant boy who made it big. A survivor of the Holocaust, Soros emigrated to the U.S. from Hungary by way of Britain. Along the way he obtained an education at the London School of Economics and got his start in international finance. In 1969, he founded the Quantum Fund, a pioneer hedge fund and one whose success made Soros one of the world's richest men, with a fortune estimated at between $7 and $8.5 billion.

But a closer look at this shining façade reveals blemishes that soon grow into gaping craters. After WWII, Soros was accused of wartime collaboration with the Nazis, in the form of assisting the SS in selecting Jews to be sent to the death camps. Years later he admitted as much, adding that he felt no sense of shame or remorse over his actions. While it is unseemly to judge the record of any Jewish survivor of Hitler's Europe, it's impossible to contemplate these activities without feeling serious disquiet.

His career as an investor also had shadowy patches. The most notorious of these was his 1992 currency manipulations involving the British pound, which came close to wrecking the U.K.'s financial system while earning Soros nearly $2 billion. In 1997 he attempted the same trick with the Thai baht, triggering an economic crisis that rocked every nation in Southeast Asia. Soros today remains persona non grata in Thailand and Malaysia. In 2002, he was found guilty of insider trading in France and fined $2 million. He is suspected of comparable infractions in other cases, for instance the 2000 NASDAQ market crash that led to the bursting of the infotech bubble.

Having made "more money than I could use for my personal needs," as he put it, Soros turned to dabbling in political and social affairs. His tool was the Open Society Institute, founded in 1993. The institute's stated purpose was to foster the growth of "open societies," democracies based on individual freedom, free trade, and the rule of law, through funding political and policy initiatives around the globe. Soros claimed to be inspired by the work of Sir Karl Popper, one of the titans of twentieth-century philosophy.

Popper was almost alone among the era's Western intellectuals in dedicating himself unreservedly to the defense of democracy. No other thinker was more effective at attacking the intellectual pretensions of the totalitarian ideologies, particularly those of communism. His demolition of historicism, the Marxist contention that "history" is the overriding force in human affairs, with its own laws and purposes beyond those of individuals, states, and societies, has never been answered. A few dozen others like Popper and recent history would have been very different.

The Soros definition of "open society" appears to conflict in significant detail with that of Popper. He first attempted to apply it in the former Warsaw Pact states, and seems quite proud of his accomplishments in the region, despite the fact that Russia, Moldava, Byelorussia, Kazakhstan, and Uzbekistan have developed into the most closed societies imaginable. Only in his native Central Europe, where a kind of Soros cult has sprung up, can he be said to have had a substantial impact.

Following his eastern triumphs, Soros turned his attention to the United States, where he sought to "preserve the open society" in its American form. He went about this by coming to the rescue of the Clintons, at the time enmeshed in the controversy over Bill's misjudgments with Ms. Lewinsky. Soros took over the sponsorship and funding of MoveOn.org, an organization founded to distract attention from the Clintons' troubles. He was instrumental in turning MoveOn into a vehicle for long-term liberal political activism. In the process he became a bête noir for many conservatives, who see his hand behind every adverse political development—particularly as regards his relationship with Barack Obama. In truth, his effectiveness is as questionable here as it was in Eastern Europe. Soros is a victim of the ancient liberal delusion that throwing lots of money at things will bring about results. He also lacks any deep understanding of American politics and culture.

Many of Soros's activities involve standard adversary culture obsessions such as legalizing prostitution and narcotics. But he was also an early supporter of palliative care. As always, he had his own particular interpretation.

Soros announced his intentions through a November 1994 speech at Columbia University. At the podium he charmed the audience with his bewilderment at why they would want to invite

George Soros, a lowly investor, to speak in the presence of such godlike scholars, and then embarked on one of the more disturbing speeches in the recent public record.

Much of it dealt with the deaths of his parents, expressed in terms not often heard from a public speaker. Soros revealed things in this speech that are seldom discussed even among families, much less in the auditoriums of major universities. Just as surprising was his ignorance of basic human psychology—he mentions that he "wrote off" his father at the time of his death while remaining glued to his mother's bedside, yet failed utterly to recognize what that meant in terms of his own personality. The rich, it seems, are not that different from the rest of us after all.

What Soros learned from his experiences was that something needed to be done about death. The American take on death, so asserted this recent immigrant, was all wrong. Death was "the last taboo," never acknowledged or spoken of in American society. This unhealthy situation needed to be challenged, and he, George Soros, was throwing his hat in the ring. Using his institute and all his personal resources, Soros intended to "change the culture of death."

Only a complete secular could make such claims about death and American culture. American religious believers have always been comfortable dealing with the topic, treating it as another step in their spiritual journey. As for the culture as a whole, it would be more accurate to say that death attracts public attention at intervals. Lengthy periods of neglect are marked by flurries of intense interest, such as that which greeted the appearance of *The American Way of Death* by Jessica Mitford (another immigrant of left-wing proclivities) in the early 1960s.

Soros proved as good as his word. In 1994 he established the Project on Death in America (PDIA), with Dr. Kathleen Foley, active in promoting palliative care since the 1970s, as its founding director. Working closely with the Robert Wood Johnson Foundation (RWJF), a health-care advocacy organization established by the founders of the medical-supply giant Johnson & Johnson, the PDIA aimed to "change the culture" by influencing opinion leaders within the health-care professions (with a few million here and there tossed to filmmakers and photographers). Once their attitudes were modified, they would act as a hinge to move the rest of society.

Over the next decade, Soros spent $48 million and the RWJF $148 million on the program. Grants were provided to individuals already active in the palliative care field, along with organizations such as the National Hospice and Palliative Care Organization (NHPCO), the American Academy of Hospice and Palliative Medicine (AAHPM), and the American Board of Hospice and Palliative Medicine (ABHPM). Hospitals and institutions were encouraged to open palliative care departments. Within a few years over eight hundred of the nation's five thousand hospitals possessed such departments. Medical and nursing textbooks were revised to give greater emphasis to pain management. Medical protocols for pain control were reexamined. In one example, a paper produced by Dr. Foley, "Improving Palliative Care for Cancer," became the standard guide for cancer pain management.

But at the same time, a discordant note began to sound from within the Soros death campaign. While Soros had mentioned palliative care in passing in his Columbia University speech, his actual emphasis lay elsewhere. He repeated several times that his mother had been a member of the Hemlock Society, an early right-to-die organization (although she chose not to claim that right at the time of her death). He ended his speech with a personal endorsement of euthanasia, while stating that he was fully aware that many would not agree.

Many—perhaps most—of the medical figures involved with Soros did not agree. Dr. Foley was adamant in her insistence that adequate palliative care removed any necessity for physician-assisted suicide. Clinical results supported her: when patients were offered effective pain control rather than the customary stick-'em-with-a-needle-on-schedule routine, requests for assisted suicide fell to near zero.

All the same, the euthanasia message made its way into the program. One of the project's key organizations was the innocuously named Partnership for Caring, a more acceptable name than the original, Choice in Dying, when it had been an advocacy group supporting initiatives such as Oregon's assisted-suicide law. Little had actually changed apart from the name. Although presented as palliative care advocates, Partnership for Caring publicly supported something called "patient's choice." And what a choice it was—the two alternatives consisted of withholding food and water on the one hand and double-effect pain medication—that is, sedation from which the patient was not meant to wake up—on the other.

What Partnership for Caring termed "patient's choice" was more widely known as the "third path," an indirect form of euthanasia that had gained acceptance in some corners of the medical profession. The "third path" was to become familiar to the country as a whole in the case involving Terri Schiavo.

Clearly, the PDIA had become a Trojan horse for euthanasia. As the program rolled on, the "third path" influence began to be felt in the hospice movement. Families placing sick members in good faith with institutions that they were assured were humane, quiet settings for their loved ones to spend their final weeks and months were shocked to be told that the survival time was "6 to 10 days." Many discovered that their ailing relatives were being deprived of food, water, and even necessary medicines. No small number thereupon returned the patients to conventional hospitals. In some cases, these efforts came too late.

The campaign also extended to state legislatures. In 1996, the Johnson Foundation, supported by the Soros project, sat down with the National Conference of State Legislatures to create guidelines for end-of-life legislation following Supreme Court rulings that said that physician-assisted suicide was a matter for the states to decide. RWJF spent over a half-million dollars in grants in twenty-three states in an effort to encourage legislators to rewrite end-of-life laws. The point of this campaign appears to have been to establish the legality of "third path" methods such as starvation and "double-effect" euthanasia.

The Soros death program would make a rewarding subject for thorough investigation. Many questions remain unanswered. Was the euthanasia effort intended from the start or was the program hijacked? How deeply did it affect the nation's hospice network? What was its impact on medical education? How much have attitudes shifted within the medical community? How broad was the influence of Soros himself? Was there significant internal debate concerning the path the project was taking? What is the full story behind the project's sudden closure in 2003?

Late in that year, both Soros and the Robert Wood Johnson Foundation acted to shut down the program. Soros proclaimed success, the same as he had in Eastern Europe, stating that the PDIA had achieved its goals. The RWJF turned to other pressing health-care issues—childhood obesity and the nursing shortage. Though both organizations expressed a desire to see the "transformation" continue with other funding sources, no effort was made to locate alternate financing, and many projects simply shut down. The Open Society website was cleansed of all material dealing with the program. Only a few difficult-to-access PDF files remain available. Almost immediately, Soros recast his efforts to become the godfather of American politics by setting out to defeat George W. Bush in the 2004 election.*

---

*Strangely, Soros is still involved in promoting palliative care internationally, in such areas as Ukraine and Africa. It seems that the program's "closure" was simply for American consumption.

The Soros death program marked a setback for two useful medical innovations, palliative care and hospice care, innovations that might yet save considerable amounts of money, aid patients at a critical point in their lives, and inject a much-needed sense of humanity into the medical profession. Instead, both came close to becoming synonyms for a particularly devious form of euthanasia, one that would have made a remarkably close fit to Governor Palin's "death panels" accusation. The obsessions of a billionaire of troubling—not to say sinister—reputation subverted the national health-care system and upset the lives of ailing individuals and their families across the country. Sometimes the world works exactly like pulp fiction after all.

THE ORDEAL

In February 1990, at age twenty-six, Terri Schiavo suffered a seizure while in the grip of an eating disorder, causing massive brain damage requiring constant nursing care. Eight years later, her faithful husband, wishing to start a new family, reluctantly decided to pull the plug.

This is the Schiavo story as the media portrayed it, and the public understood it: simple, straightforward, and heartbreaking. But as is often the case in the real world, there were a number of complications, none of them adequately addressed by the media.

The husband was in no way reluctant. Having made his decision, he stuck to it with a fixity that might have been admirable under other circumstances. Terri Schiavo's parents, the Schindlers (the name is one of the minor ironies of the case), offered to take up the burden of her care, as did several third parties. The husband, for reasons difficult to grasp, refused all such offers.

The Schindlers were given short shrift throughout, exactly as if they had no interest in the fate of their own daughter. The media treated them as interlopers with no legitimate claims. The Schiavo case marked the return of an ancient and long-superseded concept of marriage: that once a woman leaves the bosom of her family, she is her husband's property, completely subject to his will and to be disposed of as he wishes. The feminist establishment, quick to find offense in ads for Barbie dolls, somehow missed this entirely.

But the most compelling complication lay in the fact that Terri Schiavo was not dying. She was perfectly stable, requiring no heroic efforts, only food and water. What her husband was proposing was not euthanasia by any accepted definition but something of a different order altogether. This factor became obscured early in the controversy and was allowed to remain obscured by officials, lawyers, judges, and the media, all of whom behaved as if there were some unsettled question involved. There was none. The difference between heroic measures, which may be curtailed, and the basic elements of life, which may not, is long established and well understood. By pretending this was not so, or that it did not apply to Terri Schiavo, the experts and authorities acted out a lie. For what possible reason? To extend the definition and practice of euthanasia as widely as possible. Unless we conclude that they didn't know their own fields of expertise, or were legally insane and not responsible for their actions, there is no other rational explanation.

Permission to discontinue feeding was first sought in 1998. The court had questions concerning the husband's interest in his wife's estate, the fact that there was no living will, and the vagueness of the patient's expressed wish to die under such circumstances. The petition was denied.

But persistence pays off in legal matters as in everything, and at last the petition was granted by Judge George Greer, who ordered the feeding tube removed. Greer remained on the case through the entire legal process, handing down both the first and last decisions.

The Schindler family immediately appealed. They disputed every aspect of the case, including the husband's guardianship, the diagnosis of persistent vegetative state, the contention that their daughter would not respond to treatment, and the claim that she had implied she would rather die than live on as disabled. It was a remarkable effort, one that bought time and focused attention on the case. It also served to antagonize Judge Greer, whose comments concerning the Schindlers were abrupt and lacking in sympathy. Whatever his legal skills, Greer was a man of certain limitations—when asked by his Baptist minister to leave the congregation over his handling of the case, Greer complained to the media that he could not understand why.

Although hearings produced disquieting testimony concerning the husband's behavior toward his disabled wife—including implications that he had actively interfered with her treatment—Greer rejected the Schindlers' appeal and ordered that feeding cease. Terri Schiavo's feeding tube was removed on October 15, 2003.

By this time the case had attracted attention throughout the state of Florida. Many onlookers, including those in the state's political establishment, were well aware that more was involved than simply a family dispute over an invalid's care. Moving considerably faster than their Michigan counterparts, the Florida legislature on October 21 passed "Terri's Law," effectively making Governor Jeb Bush her legal guardian. Bush ordered the feeding tube replaced.

National media had been covering the case on a sporadic basis, but with entry of Governor Bush it became a story of national import. It would be inaccurate to say that relations between the media and the Bush family were at any sort of low—the two had been at odds since the governor's father had served as head of the CIA three decades before. Bush involvement gave the media an extra motive to cover the story. In keeping with their standards of coverage in dealing with the president's family, the media constructed a narrative maintaining that religious busybodies in collaboration with the Republican Party were interfering in "a private family matter," overlooking the fact that it had been in the hands of the courts long before any outsiders began paying attention.

Sensing a political opportunity, American liberals piled on. Liberal spokesman Robert Scheer attacked Republicans for "egregious political opportunism and shameless trafficking in human misery." Barry Lynn, director of Americans United for Separation of Church and State, an antireligious advocacy group, insisted that "Religious Right zealots" had "intervened in a personal family matter . . . and turned a tragic situation into a political football." Al Sharpton was "saddened by the blatant attempt by right wing extremists to use her condition and family disagreements to galvanize an anti-choice fervor in this country."

Much was made of an alleged "talking points" memo issued by "Republican leaders" asserting that the controversy would be useful in manipulating Evangelical voters. It turned out that the memo had been written by a junior staffer and distributed to no one.

But several religious figures did choose to "interfere." Among them was Pope John Paul II, who took the opportunity to remind all concerned of pertinent Catholic doctrine: "Water and food, even when provided by artificial means, always represents a natural means of preserving life, not a medical act . . . and as such [is] morally obligatory." Another religious interloper was Reverend Jesse Jackson, who in one of his finer moments traveled to Florida to counsel the Schindler family.

Opposed to these men were such representatives of humane liberalism as Democratic national chairman Howard Dean, who suggested that GOP interest in Schiavo was prompted by the fact that both were "brain dead." Liberal bloggers also took the opportunity to exercise their wit. Left-wing websites such as Daily Kos and Democratic Underground held informal contests to see who could come up with the coarsest joke about Schiavo's condition.

Amid all the political uproar, the reality of the woman lying silent in Florida was lost. People began to respond politically rather than in light of the facts. The polls turned relentlessly against Terri Schiavo. In an ABC News–Washington Post poll, 87 percent of respondents said they would not want to be kept alive in her condition; 63 percent supported the removal of Schiavo's feeding tube. Only 28 percent favored its reinsertion.

In May 2004, a Florida circuit court found Terri's Law unconstitutional, a decision ratified by the Florida Supreme Court, one of the most liberal in the country, in September of that year. The U.S. Supreme Court refused to hear the case. Though the Schindlers filed several more motions, the fight was effectively over. They had pled before state appeals courts, the Florida Supreme Court, Federal Circuit Courts, and the U.S. Supreme Court. The effort gained their daughter seven years of life. Few could have done as well. No one could have done better.

On March 18, Greer ordered Terri Schiavo's tube removed for the final time. She began to deteriorate from dehydration within hours. As the days passed, a sense of sobriety settled over the country. This was not what people had expected. They had been told that she was on the very edge of death, that it was simply a matter of flipping a switch. But Terri Schiavo was not ready to go. She held on day after day, dying by inches. Protestors picketed the facility and were ignored. Some attempted to break in with the simple glass of water that was all she required to survive. They were arrested. Last-minute appeals for relief were made to the Florida State Senate and the U.S. Congress but got nowhere. On March 30, the Eleventh Circuit Court in Atlanta, Georgia, denied the Schindlers' final appeal.

On March 31, Terri Schiavo died. She had lasted almost two

full weeks. Her brother and sister were present until nearly the final moments, when, in a gesture that speaks volumes about the motivations driving the affair, the husband ordered them out. Her parents were not even allowed into the room.

In pre-Christian times, it was common to take the old, the sick, the unwanted, lead them to a bleak spot far away from the habitations of men, and leave them there for the elements, starvation, or the wild beasts. In March 2005, in the mightiest of civilizations, in the name of the most humane, virtuous, and moral political creed ever devised, that epoch returned.

Liberal response was openly gleeful. Another round of jokes traveled the Internet. "We're going to use Terri Schiavo later on," Howard Dean promised, looking forward to the 2006 and 2008 campaigns. Nancy Pelosi, soon to be Speaker of the House, issued a statement that was one sentence condolence and three paragraphs diatribe against her Republican colleagues. All commentators agreed that there would be consequences.

But there were no consequences. Rather than remaining an issue, the Schiavo case faded away immediately, put aside, like a lynching in a small town, as something not open to discussion. The American people had been made to act as accessories, and now had to come to terms with the fact.

The euthanasists had won their battle but lost the campaign. To the odious gallery of mercy-killing imagery was added that of a helpless woman dying of thirst while suffering the mockery of the elite. The Schiavo case exposed the euthanasia movement for what it was. Euthanasia advocates continually speak of "guidelines" and "safeguards" that guarantee that no one will ever be euthanized without cause. But where were these safeguards and guidelines in the Schiavo and Kevorkian cases? None of them worked because none was intended to work. Kevorkian gassed anyone who came within reach. Terri Schiavo was killed with the active collaboration of the courts. At no point did any barriers come into play. The decision remained in the hands of those who wished to kill, and that was the end of it. There is no "slippery slope," no difference between voluntary and involuntary euthanasia. Legalize one, and you legalize the other.

Further evidence of the fatuity of euthanasia came from the state of Oregon. In 1998, sixteen people took advantage of the state's "Death with Dignity" program (an improvement on the German slogan, admittedly). That number increased to only forty-six in 2006. Over the program's first eight years, the total of mercy killings was 292, out of 86,000 deaths from all causes. So much for the "public demand" argument—nobody is knocking down the obitorium doors in Oregon.

But neither, for that matter, was the obitorium's inventor. Though seriously ill with Hepatitis C, the newly released Doctor Death appeared to be in no hurry to utilize one of his own machines.

Euthanasia is unlikely to become legal practice by any evolutionary process. Which does not mean that the world's Uncle Leos are completely safe. Critical as it is to modern liberalism, euthanasia will remain on the agenda whether the public approves or not. We may yet see obitoriums in our own neighborhoods—down the street from the multiplex, just across from the Micky D's.

THE STEM-CELL CHALLENGE

The 1990s may well be looked back on as one of the heroic epochs of the biological sciences. The decade saw breakthroughs involving two of most widely sought prizes in the field: stem cells and mammalian cloning. Each marked a giant step in human understanding. Together, they shook Western morality to its foundations.

Embryonic stem cells (ESCs) were isolated by a team led by Dr. James Thomson at the University of Wisconsin in 1998. ESCs are derived from embryos created through in vitro fertilization. They are the basic form of the human cell, from which all other cells descend. Embryonic stem cells are "pluripotent," that is, they can transform themselves into any other type of cell: nerve cells, bone cells, skin cells. It's easy to grasp how valuable they could be in treating diseases, providing organs for transplant, and other uses that we can't even foresee.

The previous year, yet another breakthrough had been announced: the birth of the world's most famous sheep, Dolly, the first mammal cloned from an adult cell. Dolly was created at the Roslin Institute in Scotland by a group led by Dr. Ian Wilmut through a process called somatic cell nuclear transfer, in which a cell nucleus is transplanted into a fertilized egg. Dolly had actually been born on July 5, 1996, but researchers waited until late February 1997 to announce their success.

Each achievement was quite impressive on its own. But combining the two created a situation no one had anticipated, the researchers least of all.

The single greatest problem involving organ transplants is that of tissue rejection. The patient's immune system views the new organ's strange genetic material as a threat and mobilizes to destroy it. Organ recipients require a lifetime regimen of immune-response-suppression drugs to control the immune reaction, most of them with unwelcome side effects.

But suppose the new organ was of the same genetic material as the patient? No immune reaction, and no drugs required. Organ transplants would become both simpler and cheaper. Beyond that possibility beckoned an entire array of new techniques currently too difficult or dangerous to attempt.

That was what ESCs combined with cloning promised. After cloning a cell from the patient, stem cells could be harvested, grown into the necessary organ, one genetically identical to the donor, and then transplanted. Of course, nothing comes without cost. Such a procedure would mean the destruction of the cloned embryo. Many embryos, in fact, since a large number would be required to assure success. (More than 277 embryos were cultivated to produce Dolly.) Eventually, once the technique caught on, billions of embryos.

That was what attracted the notice of pro-abortion extremists. While they might not grasp the science, they did understand that ESCs could help sustain abortion. As we saw in Chapter 4, support for abortion had been waning for years, with little prospect of reversal. But embryonic stem cells could turn that around. Industrializing abortion would transform it into a medical necessity and, so it was hoped, end all objections to the procedure. In an act of monumental cynicism, liberals were attempting to rescue abortion by appealing to the health concerns of the average American.

Embryonic stem cells remained largely under the public radar until President George W. Bush became personally involved. At issue was the question of federal funding. While research required support, the government could not be seen as financing abortions on a massive scale. Bush devoted several months of close study to the problem, speaking to biologists, medical specialists, ethicists, and other informed parties. At last, on August 9, 2001, Bush announced his decision, a carefully wrought compromise in which government-funded laboratories would be allowed to work on ESCs, but only those derived from seventy-two "lines"—collections of cells—already in existence. No new lines, which would require destruction of more embryos, would be created. Bush also established a Council on Bioethics to look further into stem cells and related questions, chaired by University of Chicago ethicist Dr. Leon Kass and including such figures as James Q. Wilson and Charles Krauthammer.

Like many compromises, it solved the problem while satisfying no one. Pro-lifers were angered that any such experimentation was allowed at all. But that was nothing compared to the reaction from regions leftward. Liberals simply exploded, condemning the compromise as a deliberate attempt to deny the American people the benefits of a medical miracle. Bush's consultants were dismissed as a gaggle of backwoods louts waving snakes and speaking in tongues. Bush, so liberal commentators claimed, had "banned" stem-cell research throughout the United States, assuring that all further progress would come from foreign countries. Reputable scientists were aware that the cures promised by ESCs could take years if not decades. Research was only beginning, and considerable work would be required before any useful results appeared. Liberals ignored this, insisting that magic cures—cures beyond anything promised by serious researchers—were just around the corner, being held back by George Bush, "a moral ayatollah," in the words of Senator Tom Harkin, and his army of fundamentalists.

Stem cells became one of the grand controversies of the new millennium, right up there with "Who lost Osama bin Laden?" and "Where did the WMDs go?" Public personalities began lining up, mostly in opposition to the president, and the subject became a hot electoral issue. In 2004, vice presidential candidate John Edwards predicted that if the Democratic slate was elected, stem-cell research would assure that "Christopher Reeve would get up out of his wheelchair and walk!" Reeve, paralyzed in a riding accident, had the grace to remain on the sidelines. Not so fellow actor and Parkinson's disease victim Michael J. Fox, who in 2006 made a series of campaign commercials repeating the "banned research" claim and imploring the electorate to vote for the Democrats, the stem-cell party. Fox's efforts were said to have swayed the senatorial election in Missouri.

In June 2004, Ronald Reagan died after a lengthy battle with Alzheimer's. Someone convinced his widow, Nancy Reagan, that the disease could have been cured using ESCs. She proceeded to mount a campaign to persuade President Bush to lift the "ban" on research, which included a letter signed by fifty-eight senators, virtually all Democrats. In truth, Alzheimer's was a full-organ disease, not a cellular disorder. Stem-cell therapy would have had little, if any, effect.

At this point, ESCs needed all the support they could get. Early research was not producing acceptable results. One attempt that began even before President Bush's intervention involved using stem cells to combat Parkinson's disease. Neural-cell transplants not only did very little to relieve the subjects, in 15 percent of the cases they intensified the victim's uncontrollable movements to an extent that the patients had to be restrained. Though published in the *New England Journal of Medicine*, these study results were not widely reported.

Much harder to ignore were the frauds and hoaxes that sprang up in the wake of stem-cell hype. Hwang Woo-Suk was a leading South Korean biologist specializing in cloning and related research. Hwang had several times claimed to have cloned animals such as cows, while providing no evidence. In 2004 he announced the creation of a stem cell through cloning. A year later, he announced that he had used the technique to create eleven new stem-cell lines from different subjects, another long-sought breakthrough. In August 2005, he laid claim to the cloning of a dog.

Hwang was widely praised—he was named as "A Person Who Matters" by *Time* magazine in 2004—and held up as an example of the foolishness of the Bush policy, which enabled only foreign countries to take advantage of American breakthroughs. Hwang himself criticized the president in the wake of his cell-line announcement in 2005.

Then it all fell apart. Hwang's American partner (a fact that in itself undercut the chief anti-Bush argument) in November 2005 ended the collaboration, citing doubts about Hwang's claims. Within weeks, Hwang was forced to admit that his results had been faked. There was no somatic transfer, no new cell lines, no cloned Afghan hound. Early in 2006, Hwang was banned from further stem-cell work by the South Korean government. A short time later he was indicted for fraud and embezzlement.

The Hwang fallout had scarcely ceased before yet another pioneering stem-cell organization was caught cooking the books. In August 2006, the Massachusetts company (which later moved to Southern California) Advanced Cell Technology (ACT) claimed that it had perfected a technique of creating stem cells without destroying embryos. Uncritical reporters published the claim without checking it. The actual scientific paper revealed that the process destroyed all embryos used. It was at least the fourth time the company had made an announcement that turned out to be false. Though nothing could be proven, industry observers suspected stock manipulation. The company's chief scientist, Dr. Robert Lanza, was yet another fierce critic of the Bush policy: "There are 3,000 Americans dying every day from diseases I believe could be treated using stem cell technology." Though, evidently, not that developed by ACT.

On an even lower level, there was Advanced Cell Therapeutics (note the similar name, and the identical initials—coincidence or sincere imitation?). Based in South Africa, the other ACT bought up cord-blood stem cells not cleared for human use and charged people who had heard that stem cells were good for you thousands of dollars for injections. The two owners, Stephen van Rooyen and Laura Brown, were indicted by U.S. courts and sought by the FBI. No word on their opinion of the Bush stem-cell policy.

These three can stand in for a number of related scams (the most horrific being a series of unverified reports of Ukrainian infants being stolen from hospitals and then "processed" for stem cells). The hothouse atmosphere generated by media coverage and industry rhetoric created perfect conditions for con artistry. Even entire states were not immune.

On November 3, 2004, the California Stem Cells Research and Cures Initiative, more widely known as Proposition 71, passed with 59 percent of the vote. Prop 71 was a naked attempt to make an end run around federal restrictions against ESC research. It allocated $3 billion in state funds to be invested in stem-cell studies at the rate of $295 million a year for ten years. The program was intended to attract cell-biology talent stifled by the Bush policy, making California the world center for stem-cell research.

Prop 71 featured a number of peculiarities. It could have been passed in few other states—California was an Initiative and Referendum state in which voters or special interests (here the state biotech industry) could place proposals on the ballot. What raised many eyebrows was the fact that Prop 71 was proposed and passed as an amendment to the state constitution. Once it was voted in, it was in for good—any attempts to modify it would have to take the form of another amendment.

Biotech companies were pleased at the results. But another group was less than satisfied—California's voters. The *San Francisco Chronicle* reported shortly afterward that most voters believed that treatments were already available or at most a year or two away. They were nonplussed to learn that actual applications lay decades in the future.

Despite media coverage hailing the "stem cell gold rush" and the state "getting a jump on the federal government," California's contribution to stem-cell research has been minimal. In late 2009, after five years of wasted effort, the California Institute for Regenerative Medicine, the agency in charge of stem-cell research, dropped its emphasis on ESCs in favor of the adult variety. Only four out of fourteen grants awarded in October 2009 involved ESCs. No public announcement of the policy change was made, and publicity handouts no longer mentioned ESCs, instead referring neutrally to "stem cells."

At the national level, efforts to overturn the "ban" took on a new intensity. Bush showed no sign of backing down. In response, Congress attempted its own end run, crafting a series of bills designed as much to embarrass the president as to encourage scientific research. The first was the Stem Cell Research Enhancement Act of 2005. After passing the House, the bill meandered through the convoluted senatorial process, at last reaching the floor in July 2006. It passed by a vote of 63–37. Bush, who had revealed a mysterious aversion to using the veto over the previous six years, utilized it for the first time against the stem-cell bill. Public response was not unexpected—scientists moaned, politicians blustered, and the media acted as an echo chamber for both. Senator Dick Durbin of Illinois, who had earned himself eternal popularity a short time previously by comparing U.S. troops in Iraq to Gestapo and KGB thugs, acted as senatorial spokesman: "Those families who wake up every morning to face another day with a deadly disease or a disability will not forget this decision."

The Senate proceeded to recycle the bill, using the same title, voting again almost a year to the day later, and ending up with the same numbers. Bush, unwilling to break such a streak, responded in kind with only his third veto.

It was evident that Congress was going to reintroduce the bill as many times as it took to pass it. The prospects for Bush were not good. The most recent tally was only a few votes short of the override number of sixty-six, and he had already lost several prominent Republicans, including majority leader Bill Frist, who explained that he was "Pro-life . . . I also believe that embryonic stem cell research should be encouraged." It seemed only a matter of time before the magic cells would be unleashed to make the deaf walk and the blind hear.

Then, only a few months later, came a development that ended the stem-cell debate once and for all.

Overlooked in all the uproar over ESCs was the existence of another class of stem cells that lacked the drawbacks of embryonic cells, were in wide medical use, and appeared to have as much potential as ESCs, if not more. These were adult stem cells (ASCs). Present in all varieties of body tissues, adult stem cells had been isolated and used in treatments for forty years. Over seventy medical procedures utilized ASCs, with 1,500 clinical trials under way—which was 1,500 more than could be claimed by the embryonic variety. George W. Bush's own Council on Bioethics had suggested that more attention be paid to ASCs.

The sole problem with adult stem cells was that they were not pluripotent—they lacked ESCs' ability to develop into other types of cells. But if that capability could somehow be triggered in ASCs, there would be no necessity to clone embyros in order to kill them for stem cells. The moral argument against stem-cell use would be rendered moot.

In 2006, Dr. Shinya Yamanaka of Kyoto University reported that he had successfully "reprogrammed" adult mouse cells to act as stem cells. The announcement caused high excitement in scientific circles but was ignored in the general media.

It was understood that Yamanaka would attempt the same technique with human cells, but it's doubtful that anyone expected results so quickly. Little more than a year later, in November 2007, Yamanaka released a paper announcing success. In a process called "somatic cell dedifferentiation," Yamanaka used four genes (we may as well name them here, since they will play a large role in the lives of many now living: Oct3/4, Sox2, Klf4, and c-Myc) to transform adult stem cells into "induced pluripotent state cells" (iPSCs), with all the characteristics of ESCs.

Several other teams had also set out to test Dr. Yamanaka's technique on human cells. The leader of one such team—James Thomson, of the University of Wisconsin—published a paper concurrent with that of Yamanaka, also announcing success. The man who had triggered the stem-cell hurricane in the first place was also involved in bringing it to an end.

• •

As if to underline the almost novelistic aptness of the moment, a third figure was heard from. Ian Wilmut, for all practical purposes the father of Dolly, announced that he would not utilize the license granted him by the British government to carry out therapeutic cloning. He preferred Yamanaka's technique: "This approach represents the future for stem cell research." The moral implications of Wilmut's decision were clear, and were emphasized by a remark from Thomson: "If human embryonic stem cell research does not make you at least a little bit uncomfortable, you have not thought about it enough."

The media (not to mention the politicians) wasted little time on discussions of morality. Nor did they refer to the man who, more than any other, had been the architect of the moment. Without George W. Bush's stubbornness, his sense of purpose, his clarity of vision, the new technique would have appeared in a world in which wholesale destruction of embryos was already the norm. Yamanaka's somatic cell dedifferentiation would have been considered an ancillary technique at best. It was Bush who drew the line behind which the skill, intelligence, and wisdom of Yamanaka, Thomson, and Wilmut could operate.

Behaviorally certified criminals roaming the streets, death parlors on every other corner, the industrial slaughter of human embryos . . . It's not a very appealing future that America's liberals had mapped out for us. But it is of a piece with the liberal past— the immense powers of government arrayed in support of policies that would inevitably lead to excess mortality while living up to none of their advance billing. History has moved on. The root ideologies of democide are scarcely an evil memory. Yet American liberalism still attempts to convey the same practices and beliefs into a new era that has no room for them, to use the methods of the past to create a future that no one wants.

Power is evil in itself, no matter who exercises it.
—JACOB BURCKHARDT

9

"LET ME BE CLEAR"

Barack Obama and Soft Lethality

Little question remains concerning Barack Obama's status as one of the most liberal presidents of recent history—perhaps the most liberal president ever. While considerable effort was made during the 2008 campaign to portray him as a "moderate" or "centrist," all that evaporated following his inauguration. If Obama's policies since taking office, which include progressive taxation, economic dirigisme on an unprecedented scale, reliance on "renewable energy," acceptance of the global warming thesis, and appeasement in foreign relations, aren't liberalism, and liberalism of the most extreme variety, then the word has no meaning and we'll need to come up with something else.

But far from being simply one more liberal politician, Obama must be seen as liberalism's last chance. For the preceding half-century liberal presidents have been uniformly disastrous, both in their general impact and in terms of the liberal program itself. Setting aside the truncated presidency of John F. Kennedy, we have Lyndon B. Johnson, whose attempt to fight a medium-scale war while at the same time creating a universal nanny state guaranteed the collapse of both. Concerning Jimmy Carter, the less said the better. While Bill Clinton may have talked the talk, his two most impressive domestic achievements, NAFTA and welfare reform, were both Republican initiatives seized upon to save a floundering presidency.*

This record of failure has resulted in fifty years of deferred dreams, dreams that gained a new lease on life with Obama's election. All the visionary proposals, all the mothballed programs, all the once-tried ideas were dragged out, dusted off, and presented as essential components of the Hope and Change crusade. What Obama offered was a kind of fossil liberalism, an unreformed and unregenerate ideology comprised of all the ideas too shiny to let go, regardless of whether they worked or not. It was as if the previous five decades, with their lessons concerning liberalism and the realm of possibility, had never occurred. You could drop Obama back into 1964, if not 1936, and he could run on the exact same issues using identical rhetoric, with scarcely a single comma changed. With Obama as the remnant liberal archetype, combining the arrogance of LBJ, and the flakiness of Jimmy Carter, and the disingenuousness of Bill Clinton, American liberalism has at last become a complete caricature of itself.

If our premise is valid—that ideological liberalism acts as a trigger for mass mortality—then it follows that Obama's ascension will serve to increase the dangers of democide, the same as occurred during previous liberal administrations. But we will not have to go looking for evidence; as always in the case of democide, the evidence will come to us.

OBAMA AND ABORTION

Obama has the most pro-abortion record of any American politician. He has never once voted in favor of any restrictions on

---

*His sponsorship of these two bills put Clinton farther to the right than several self-styled "conservative" presidents, Richard Nixon and the elder George Bush among them.

abortion, and in fact, while serving as an Illinois representative, actually voted against a purely humanitarian bill intended to save infants who survived the procedure. It's generally the case that presidents mellow as regards their more ideological positions when they take office and realize that "president of all the people" actually means something. But not in this instance.

One of Obama's first acts on entering office was to overturn the "Mexico City Policy" and restore federal funding for organizations promoting abortion overseas. This policy was a Reagan administration initiative intended both to get the government completely out of the business of funding abortions, as had been the case domestically since the passage of the Hyde Amendment, and to remove the possibility of a diplomatic fiasco associated with such a policy. (The potential for this is in no way difficult to grasp. Merely turn the situation around and imagine that a foreign power—say, the Saudis—was promoting abortions on a large scale in the U.S.)

The policy had become something of a political football, having been rescinded by Bill Clinton in 1993 and then revived by George W. Bush in 2001. So it could be said that Obama was simply fulfilling an inaugural tradition were it not for the unmistakable impression that he was laying down a marker promising further action.

Confirmation followed soon after when Obama ordered a review of the Department of Health and Human Services' "right of conscience" clause, a late effort by the Bush administration to prevent professional discrimination against medical personnel who refused to take part in abortions and related procedures. Obama found the new regulation "too broad" in that it might even allow a pharmacist to "refuse to sell birth-control pills." (The correct response to this in a liberal democracy is, "So what?") The administration called for a thirty-day comment period "for advocates on both sides" ending in early March 2009, after which the rule would undoubtedly have been overturned.

Obama then settled on possibly the second most pro-abortion politician in the country as his nominee for health secretary. Kathleen Sebelius, governor of the state of Kansas, was a politician unique for being under interdiction by the Catholic Church. Sebelius was forbidden to receive communion, a weekly sacrament in Catholicism, by bishops in Kansas, Virginia, and Washington, D.C., due to her activities in support of abortion. Similar penalties had been mooted previously but never put into effect concerning such nominally Catholic politicians as Nancy Pelosi and John Kerry. But the actions of Sebelius, which included social engagements with an abortionist under investigation for abuses,* were impossible for even the most congenial bishop to ignore.

On March 9, 2009, Obama by executive order ended all restrictions on stem-cell research and directed the National Institute of Health to formulate protocols for the research use of embryonic stem cells. The administration framed the action as an effort to correct a dreadful wrong committed by the Bush administration, promising that policy would from that point on be made using "sound scientific practice, responsible practice of science and evidence, instead of dogma."

The action was largely symbolic. It was far too late to reinstate ESCs as the predominant element of stem-cell research. Even as the president's decision was announced, the Texas Medical Center in Houston announced that it had begun treating victims of serious strokes with adult stem cells derived from the patient's own bone marrow to regrow damaged brain tissue. Early results gave considerable promise. Over the ensuing year, ASC research pro-

---

*This was George Tiller, the abortionist murdered by Scott Roeder. Almost none of the stories dealing with Tiller's demise saw fit to mention his relationship with the governor.

gressed with almost reckless speed. In Australia, twenty-year-old Ben Leahy left behind his wheelchair after being cured of multiple sclerosis. His immune cells were killed en masse and then replaced with new cells grown from ASCs. (John Edwards was otherwise engaged.) At the University of Miami's Miller School of Medicine, a team led by Dr. Joshua Hare perfected a method of healing damaged hearts with an intravenous injection of mesenchymal ASCs, which naturally home in on heart lesions to replace muscle tissue damaged by heart attacks. By contrast, the sole scheduled trials of ESCs by the California biotech firm Geron, involving treatment of severe spinal cord injuries, were halted without explanation by the FDA in August.

More effort was put into abortion during the first two months of Obama's tenure than into any other issue apart from the economy. To some extent even economic matters took second place—as treasury secretary Timothy Geithner struggled to contain the recession with a skeleton staff, government resources were freely expended on the abortion crusade. And looming behind all these actions was the specter of the Freedom of Choice Act (FOCA), the "nuclear option" of the abortion conflict, a bill that abortion advocates believed would end the controversy once and for all and one that Obama had promised would be "the first thing I would sign."

FOCA was a bill designed to supersede all previous, not to mention possible future, legislation dealing with abortion. The bill enshrined abortion as a "fundamental right," the same as freedom of speech and religion, with an even more thoroughgoing level of protection. FOCA guaranteed abortion under virtually all circumstances and with no restrictions or limitations. In one swoop, every last law and regulation covering the procedure on the local, state, or federal level would be rendered void. FOCA would immediately negate the partial-birth abortion ban, the Hyde Amendment, waiting periods, parental consent regulations, health and safety rules, and even requirements that abortions be performed by licensed physicians.

The bill was first offered by Senators Alan Cranston and Bob Packwood in 1989, and reintroduced on a number of occasions, only to be voted down each time. Cosponsors of the 2007 attempt included Hillary Clinton and the Illinois freshman senator Barack Obama.

But Obama the president seemed less than eager to see the bill cross his Oval Office desk, possibly due to the fact that his abortion blitzkrieg had already generated the first serious opposition to his policies in the form of the Catholic Church.

Obama, who had won 54 percent of the Catholic vote, was first put on notice by the country's Catholic establishment within hours of his election. The United States Conference of Catholic Bishops (USCCB) admonished the president-elect to be wary of extending government support for abortion. The bishops were in large part concerned about FOCA, which if passed could be used to force Catholic hospitals to carry out abortion procedures. The USCCB went so far as to declare that if FOCA went into effect, the Church would close down its hospitals, which comprised a full third of America's primary health-care facilities.

Obama's apparent defiance on taking office was no doubt infuriating to the bishops. The threat to the conscience clause was a direct affront to Catholic concerns, and the selection of Governor Sebelius, already in deep conflict with the Church, amounted to a blow upon a bruise. Catholic outrage rose with each new pro-abortion initiative taken by the president, at last peaking with Notre Dame's invitation to Obama to speak at the university's 2009 commencement.

Notre Dame is arguably the premier American Catholic institution of higher learning, and certainly the most widely known. Its decision to honor a politician so completely and firmly at odds with Church policy could not help but attract attention. The invitation soon took on the status of a major scandal. The action violated established Church policy stating that no Catholic institution might honor an individual opposed to Catholic positions. Although Notre Dame president Reverend John Jenkins was informed of this by his own bishop, John D'Arcy of the South Bend diocese, he refused to rescind or even modify the invitation. (In keeping with policies of academic freedom, American Catholic universities are not under direct control of the Church hierarchy.)

The scandal heated up with the spring weather. A petition asking Notre Dame to reconsider the invitation circulated by the Cardinal Newman Society, the country's leading Catholic academic organization, obtained more than 360,000 signatures. Former U.S. ambassador to the Vatican Mary Ann Glendon was scheduled to be awarded American Catholicism's highest honor, the Laetare Medal, at the commencement. Discovering that she was being used as a foil to excuse the president's appearance ("See, the ambassador doesn't mind . . ."), Professor Glendon rejected the award and denounced the proceedings. Of at least equal concern to the university was the fact that alumni had canceled pledges amounting to over $8 million. While the speech went off without a hitch, the entire affair marked the first serious public embarrassment for the new administration.

Like all such, it had its effect. The administration's campaign to mainstream abortion faltered and ground to a halt. The deadline for overturning the conscience clause came and went with no discernible action. Talk of passing FOCA faded as well. In announcing its revised stem-cell guidelines in late April, the NIH, rather than follow Obama's lead in allowing complete freedom in exploiting fetal tissue, fell back instead on the pre-Bush status quo, allowing embryos that would otherwise be destroyed to be utilized for research, but forbidding cloning or in vitro fertilization for research purposes.

• •

There would be no industrialization of abortion, no market in human fetal material.*

As intent as Obama might be in pushing the United States into a brave new posthumanist world, it appeared that the country at large was willing to follow him only so far.

THE HEALTH-CARE MOSES

Health-care reform is a matter of destiny for Barack Obama. It comprises a major element—perhaps the keystone element—of his vision for a new society. Obamacare is to be cheap, accessible, universal, and under complete control of the federal government. A shining example to the world at large, and an everlasting monument to the wisdom, perspicacity, and political skills of Barack Obama.

The American health-care system has been in a state of "crisis" for the entire adult lives of most of the country's population. It's one of those peculiar crises that continually simmers from year to year and decade to decade without ever quite coming to a boil. When we strip away the verbiage and rhetoric, we discover that this "crisis" consists almost in toto of rising costs. Little else is wrong with the American health-care system. There exists no shortage of hospital beds, and no one is going without care (not likely, with the government spending 16 percent of its budget on health care). There does exist a shortage of doctors, particularly those devoted to general practice. Medical school costs are so high that med students devote themselves instead to lucrative spe-

---

*At least for the moment, and in the United States. In the U.K., a consortium consisting of the National Health Service, the Scottish National Transfusion Service, and the medical charity the Wellcome Trust has embarked on a program to utilize ESCs to produce red blood cells for transfusion. A more emblematic pro-abortion project is difficult to imagine.

cialties such as oncology and internal medicine. Which means that the doctor shortage is the product of yet another "crisis"—that afflicting higher education, one more field under government control and one which—surprise!—is also troubled with ballooning costs.

While there are a number of explanations for rising medical costs—novel technology, tort abuse, and incompetent management, among others—a major contributor lies in the amount of money (that 16 percent of the budget) poured into the system by the government through such welfare programs as Medicare and Medicaid. Undergraduate knowledge of economics tells us that this creates a state of inflation, simply defined as too much money chasing too few goods. The solution, we have been assured, is to pump vastly larger amounts of money into the system, which is precisely what Obama, his captive Congress, and his tame bureaucracy are doing, to an extent previously unknown to history.

An earlier effort at reforming health care was made in 1993 by the honorable Hillary Clinton and a cast of thousands. Hillarycare (it's a bad sign when a program incorporates the name of its progenitor) was ill-fated from the start. Development and planning were carried out under conditions of utmost secrecy, extending even to the names of those involved. When finally unveiled, the plan turned out to be a thousand-page-plus monstrosity that sought to cover every last single aspect of the American health-care system, no matter how trivial. (Critics pointed out that a mother Band-Aiding her child's scraped knee could be held to be in violation.) The fact that a full third of its wordage was devoted to penalties for violating the rest was enough to expose the plan as a blatant power grab. Neither public nor political support was in evidence and Hillarycare was put to sleep without ever coming to a vote. The American health-care system survived intact.

One curious aspect of both Hillarycare and Obamacare is that each was developed and presented without reference to similar government health-care plans active around the world. We are constantly reminded that the U.S. lags behind the rest of civilization in lacking government-sponsored health care. But that's as far as such comments go—no serious attempt is ever made to analyze foreign plans in relation to American requirements and experience. At best, we hear that the U.K. or France supplies health-care services at a fraction of the cost of America's system. But seldom do we hear what those services consist of, and what the results are—matters which would seem to be of some importance. After all, such states as Burma, Somalia, and Burundi also operate health-care "systems" at a fraction of our cost.

Any cursory examination of the governmental health-care programs of the three major Anglophone nations—the U.K., Canada, and Australia, the countries closest in culture, lifestyle, and ethnicity to the United States, with the greatest similarity in health-care issues—clearly reveal such systems to be abject failures. And not merely failures, but what we have come to recognize as catastrophic failures. Government-run health care has become one of the chief instruments of democide in the millennial epoch.

U.K.

"Envy of the world"—that's the phrase commonly used to describe the British National Health Service (NHS). It's been a long time since it was spoken with anything but irony.

The NHS represents the apogee of government health care, as an organization established to act as health-care provider for every subject of the United Kingdom. It owns and operates most of the country's hospitals, and employs the majority of health-care personnel, including doctors and nurses.

The system is divided administratively into a series of Trusts and Regional Authorities that oversee operations in different areas of the country. The NHS Pay Review Body handles staff compensation. Another important agency is the National Institute for Health and Clinical Excellence (NICE),* which evaluates treatments and medications.

Health-care services are free of charge, though a nominal fee exists for medications that is waived for the unemployed, students, and retired persons. Private health-care services and insurance are available for those willing to pay for it.

The U.K. claims a life expectancy of 78.7 years, slightly higher than America's 78.06 years. Its major boast is that it runs a national health-care system on expenditures of only 8.4 percent of gross domestic product (GDP), as compared to the U.S. total of 13.9 percent.

The NHS was the brainchild of Aneurin Bevan, one of the most doctrinaire of British Labour politicians. Bevan was appointed minister of health in 1944. Four years later, he nationalized the British health-care system, utilizing wartime regulations still in force. The Attlee government seized 3,118 hospitals and clinics, and informed the staffs that they were now government employees.

In leaflets sent to every address in England, Scotland, and Wales, Bevan promised that from that moment on, all the health-care needs of the British people would be provided for by the government, without limits or direct cost.

Within six months, that guarantee had to be scaled back considerably. The NHS had spent £400 million (close to 2 billion dollars in 1948 terms—an unheard-of amount at the time), over three times its original budget. Labour politicians believed that once basic health needs were addressed, further demand on the service would drop off dramatically, a utopian misreading of both economics and human nature.

---

*The acronym clearly reveals that British health professionals never read C. S. Lewis.

The crisis was momentarily overcome by rationing, closing facilities, and instituting charges for medication. Costs were held down for the next two decades by neglecting to build or refurbish hospitals, clinics, or other infrastructure. Numerous efforts have been made to streamline, remake, and revitalize the NHS, none of which need detain us since none of them worked. The agency grew into one of the world's monster bureaucracies. On its formation in 1948, there were 480,000 beds and 350,000 staff. In 2002, there were 186,000 beds and 882,000 staff. By 2008, there were 160,000 beds and 1,368,000 staff.* The NHS is today the world's third-largest employer, utmatched only by the Indian National Railway and the Russian army. To pay for all this, the budget has swollen to £92 billion ($150 billion) annually.

Increases in budget and personnel have failed to translate into improved services for the public. Adding funding or resources to an organization established on flawed premises succeeds only in making things worse. Every shilling added to the NHS budget, every new hire approved simply drives the organization's level of practice closer to that of the developing world, and in some cases even lower.

On average, the NHS has approximately one million people awaiting treatment at any given time. Some wait for months, some wait for years, and it is by no means unusual for some not to live long enough to receive treatment at all. As is often the case with government organizations, the situation is worse than it first appears. In a bureaucratic trick of ancient standing, the NHS several years ago redefined "waiting list" to mean only those patients already diagnosed. People who have not yet been referred

---

*Readers of C. Northcote Parkinson will recognize this as a textbook example of Parkinson's law: "Work expands so as to fill the time available for its completion," referring to how bureaucracies grow larger even as they accomplish less.

by doctors are not on the list. So the number actually awaiting treatment may be 400,000 higher than official figures.

On taking office, the Blair government pledged a reduction of waiting times as its chief health-care priority. Through concerted effort and by pumping billions into the NHS, the waiting period was brought down to four and a half months for most patients. But a recent directive from the European Union threatens to overturn even this miserable achievement. New regulations written in Brussels limit the working hours of doctors to forty-eight hours a week. The new limits went into effect in August 2009, acting as a body blow to an already tottering system. Two-thirds of nine hundred doctors surveyed by the Royal College of Surgeons stated that the new regulations caused increased risk for patients and threatened further deterioration of already stressed NHS hospitals.

Attempts to control burgeoning costs have centered on denial of services, particularly as involves drugs and medications. This is where the NICE comes in. Acting as evaluator of new treatments, the institute in recent years has often found new medications "ineffective" even when they were in wide use elsewhere. Public suspicions that expense was the actual criterion were confirmed when the institute revealed that it had developed a formula, the QALY ("Quality-Adjusted Life Year") scale, in which only £15,000, or roughly $22,750, would be spent to gain six months' time for each terminally ill patient. Any treatment that exceeded that amount would simply be cut off, no matter how necessary to a patient's well-being. Numerous lawsuits have been filed by patients who have gone over the limit. British courts have consistently decided in favor of the NHS.

Many cancer patients denied necessary drugs due to this policy have gone outside the system to procure their own supplies, either in Europe or over the Internet, often going into debt to do so. A common stratagem has been to utilize the NHS for approved treatments while spending personal funds for private treatments with disallowed medicines. That door was recently slammed shut by an NHS decision involving breast-cancer victim Debbie Hirst. Ms. Hirst raised $20,000 and made arrangements to sell her home in order to purchase the cancer drug Avastin, banned by the NHS though widely available in the U.S. and other countries. Just prior to her first treatment with the new drug, Ms. Hirst was informed that if she continued with her plans, she would be dropped from regular treatment and forced to pay for everything. It's difficult to detect any shred of logic in this decision, which leaves thousands of desperate patients out in the cold and could well end up costing more money in the long run.* When asked for an explanation, an NHS spokesman piously stated that "That way lies the end of the founding principles of the NHS."

Further savings have been found by jettisoning all standards of hygiene established since the close of the eighteenth century. Throughout the hospital system, janitorial, cleaning, laundering, and sterilization services have been cut to the bone, if not dropped entirely. One American who recently experienced the workings of a British hospital found a single harried immigrant responsible for maintaining the cleanliness of an entire wing. In another London hospital, a female patient was so disgusted with the filth that she rose from her sickbed and cleaned the room herself, trailing her IV drip behind her. The nurses, she said, "Let me get on with it." As well they might—it is no longer uncommon for NHS hospitals to feature foul, blood-encrusted floors, patients lying on filthy sheets, often stained with their own waste, and medical materials and instruments badly cleaned if at all. In the spring of 2009, the Royal Children's Hospital was discovered to be infested with maggots.

---

*As it did in the case of Ms. Hirst, who was at last permitted to undergo treatment with Avastin—but only after her cancer had metastasized to several other organs.

Infection inevitably follows filth—particularly as regards the antibiotic-resistant "superbugs," such as the vicious and persistent MRSA (methicillin-resistant *Staphylococcus aureus*, a potentially fatal strain of staph), that have arisen as serious health threats in recent decades. Britain today has the worst MRSA infection rates in the industrialized world, with up to 32,000 patients dying of MSRA-related causes each year. In October 2007, British health secretary Alan Johnson was forced to apologize to Parliament after revelations involving a superbug outbreak in Staffordshire. As many as 1,200 patients died of infections picked up solely due to neglect and incompetence. Hospital administration and staff had been warned repeatedly since 2002 that conditions were unacceptable but refused to acknowledge any problems or even meet with inspectors. The responsible officials were suspended with full pay. The relatives of the victims had to be content with photo shrines on the hospital walls.

With conditions so degraded, it's no surprise that recovery and survival rates have plummeted. A 2007 study published in *The Lancet*, Britain's leading medical journal, revealed that the five-year cancer survival rate in the U.K. had fallen to a point where it was one of the worst in Europe. (The best cancer survival rate in the world is that of the United States, pretty good for a country with such a lousy health-care system.) The U.K. female cancer survival rate was only 52.7 percent, a full 10 percent below that of the United States. But the women were far better off than the men, who suffered a 44.8 percent survival rate. The U.S. rate for males was a full 66.3 percent. The U.K. also lagged behind such countries as Spain, Ireland, and Italy, not to mention Malta and Slovenia. Survival rates in the U.K. for strokes and heart disease have begun a similar plunge.

Perhaps the most disturbing recent development in the NHS is the introduction of policies that amount to euthanasia in all but name. Under the provisions of the Mental Capacity Act of 2005, patients unable to make their wishes known to hospital personnel can be declared "due to die" and have all fluids withdrawn—the same treatment meted out to Terri Schiavo. Their families have no legal right to dispute these decisions.

A related medical protocol operates under the name "Liverpool Care Pathway" (LCP). Developed in a hospice located in the Beatles' hometown, the LCP was originally intended for use with cancer patients. In 2004 it was approved by the NICE for use in all end-of-life situations.

The Liverpool Care protocol was intended to reduce the suffering of patients in their final hours. But as applied by the NHS, it was in plain fact the Soros death plan in action. After a medical examination, a doctor could order all fluids, foods, and medicine (with the exception of sedatives) withdrawn from a patient. The result, needless to say, was death within a matter of days at best. Without public debate, or even a public announcement by the NHS, the LCP became standard practice in the NHS, adapted for use in 300 hospitals, 130 hospices, and 560 care homes. At least twenty thousand patients annually were dying under LCP treatment.

Families were typically misled as to the purpose of the treatment. But many saw through it. In 2008, Mrs. Ellen Westwood, aged eighty-eight, entered the hospital for a routine operation. While there, she contracted the hospital infection *Clostridium difficile* (a bacterium responsible for serious intestinal infections). In response, the attending physician ordered all foods and fluids withheld. When Mrs. Westwood's family defied medical advice and brought her food and water, the hospital threatened to report them to the authorities. With the aid of a second opinion from an independent physician, the family took their mother home, where she recovered nicely.

In late 2008, Hazel Fenton, an eighty-year-old East Sussex grandmother, was put on the plan without her daughter's knowledge. After discovering the truth, her daughter fought for weeks (while her mother starved) until treatment was at last resumed. Mrs. Fenton recovered and was still alive a year later.

Jack Jones was a Liverpool bricklayer who had survived stomach cancer. After being told that the cancer had returned, Jones was placed on the LCP protocol in the Marie Curie hospice, the very institution where the LCP had been developed. After two weeks of starvation and thirst he died, at which point an autopsy discovered that he had not been suffering from cancer at all, but a mild case of pneumonia easily treatable with antibiotics. His widow received a substantial settlement.

Such treatment is by no means limited to the aged. Many retarded or learning-disabled patients have been allowed to die due to "errors" and "misunderstandings." In 2007, a forty-three-year-old Down-syndrome patient recovering from a stroke in an NHS hospital was left unfed for a month before dying of starvation. The organization's explanation amounted to "breakdown in communications," a claim difficult to reconcile with the circumstances, particularly in light of similar cases in which a retarded man was left untreated for a broken leg for two months before dying of infection, and another in which a learning-disabled young woman was denied treatment for an easily controlled cancer. These incidents are of a certain class of events where we know exactly what it is we are seeing—while being told something completely different.

In September 2009, only weeks after Sarah Palin's denunciation of "death panels," a group of doctors contacted the *Daily Telegraph* to warn that abuse of the Liverpool Care protocol was causing numerous needless deaths of aging patients. The practice of withholding food and fluids could potentially mask signs of recovery—exactly as claimed by family members. "As a result a national wave of discontent is building up, as family and friends witness the denial of fluids and food to patients."

None of this may exactly match Palin's comments, but it's close enough.

Not even death ends the abuses of the NHS. In January 2009 it was reported that the organs of British donors, expressly intended for use in the U.K., were being peddled on the overseas market. Fifty livers donated by British patients were sold to Europeans at an average price of £75,000 even though 259 British patients were awaiting liver transplants. The NHS response was a near-silence born of the secure knowledge that there exist no regulations expressly forbidding such transactions. So an organization established sixty years ago on the highest socialist principles has found its level in engaging in organ piracy for profit. Ironies do not come thicker than this.*

We could continue dissecting the NHS as long as we cared to. The ambulance technicians arrested for negligent homicide, the patients dying after waiting for hours in emergency rooms, mistaken drug doses, mistaken diagnoses—the bucket of NHS ineptness and callousness goes deep and is filled to the brim. But we've seen more than enough to demonstrate that the largest health-care organization in history, the mother of all national health services, the envy of the world, has become functionally the worst health-care system in the West. A system with ten bureaucrats for each hospital bed, with a budget nearing a hundred billion but which can still justify organ piracy, one which rejects medical advances on transparently false grounds and then lies about them. A government agency that has thrown aside its responsibilities, undercut its own traditions, and rejected the basic axioms that have governed medicine since its foundation as a discipline. The NHS is a case study of how modernism—particularly political modernism—corrupts absolutely and completely.

The NHS is sliding toward a state of utter inutility. How a national health-care system can recover from such a state we have

---

*In July 2009, the NHS prohibited the sale of organs to foreign patients, but only by private vendors, which seems to slightly miss the point.

no idea, for the simple reason that it has never happened before. Even in the worst wartime defeats, during the death spasms of Nazi Germany and Imperial Japan, when almost every other function of civil society had come to a frozen halt, the medical profession in large part remained active, true to its oath, refusing to abandon its patients or its standards. The only guidance we can find concerning the situation facing the NHS comes from countries in areas such as Central Africa, where medical systems followed entire societies into collapse. The answer from there is clear: there is no recovery.

Numerous studies have been made of the U.K.'s levels of medical mortality. The most compelling, because the most complete, is that of Trevor Sheldon in the *British Medical Journal* in 2007. According to Professor Sheldon, the NHS injures as many as 910,303 patients and kills 91,030 each year. There were 9.1 million hospital stays in the U.K. in 2005–6, not counting maternity and mental patients. Between 8.7 and 10 percent resulted in medical errors that caused serious harm, up to and including death. Half of these errors were held to be preventable, not a particularly meaningful statement. Professor Sheldon claimed that such figures were common among health-care systems around the world, a less than accurate contention, at least as regards the United States. Equivalent mortality figures for U.S. health-care institutions are on the order of 48,000 to 98,000 annually, with an American population five times that of Great Britain. American hospital deaths would have to exceed 450,000 a year to match those of the U.K.

The NHS itself admits to much lower numbers, while acknowledging that reportage is incomplete. The U.K. advocacy group Taxpayers Alliance used NHS figures provided to the World Health Organization and came up with 17,157 unnecessary deaths for 2004. The Alliance points out that this figure is five time the number of annual traffic fatalities in the U.K., and higher than the medical mortality levels in either Spain, France, Germany, or Holland.

Whatever the case, these figures are appalling, and have terrifying implications for any country contemplating a government takeover of health care. It's a good thing for Obama they never came up during the health-care debate.

CANADA

The Canadian health-care system is widely known in the U.S. as the system whose managers—Canada's politicians—regularly find their way across the border for treatment in state-of-the-art American hospitals. Recently Belinda Stronach, friend of Bill Clinton and Liberal MP, came south for treatment of breast cancer. The husband of another prominent Canadian pol, Sharon Carstairs, also sought treatment in the Yankee Goliath, as did Newfoundland's premier Danny Williams, who in February 2010 crossed the border for a heart operation. In all three cases, the excuse was that a particular type of treatment "wasn't available in Canada."

The Canadian system is called Medicare—no relation to the U.S. program of the same name. It is a "single-payer" program, in which the government acts as insurer for everyone in the country. Coverage is funded by taxation, with payments dictated to doctors and other health-care providers. The separate provinces and territories handle administration.

The Canadian government likes to say that the program is based on five principles: universal coverage, comprehensive services, income equality, portability both in and outside the country, and public administration. There is also an unmentioned sixth principle—anti-Americanism. In the north-of-the-border Medicare system, "Canadian values" are inviolate, never to be tainted by profitability, privatization, competition, or any other such alien emanations from points south.

Thanks to this attitude, the Yankee heresy of private competition is illegal. No health services provided by the government, including insurance, hospital and doctor care, and outpatient services, can be duplicated by private vendors. At the same time, a number of services including drugs, dentistry, and home care are not covered by government.

Supporters of nationalized health care point out that Canada's life expectancy of 80.4 years exceeds the American figure of 78.06 years.* Much is also made of the fact that Canadian health care's share of GDP is 9.5 percent, as compared to the U.S. figure of 13.9 percent.

But the bare figures conceal the fact that Canada's economies have been achieved at a price. Canadian Medicare savings are explained by a system-wide (and sometimes deliberate) default of services. This was brought home to American onlookers in March 2009, when actress Natasha Richardson died following a skiing accident in Quebec. Not a single helicopter ambulance was operational anywhere in the province to airlift her to a reasonably equipped hospital. While a helicopter would have been of little help in Ms. Richardson's case—she had refused medical attention until fatal symptoms appeared—the lack of such a resource in a province over twice the size of Texas was a sobering revelation of a health system stalled at a point somewhere well short of technological sophistication.

These failings are not limited to transportation. Canadian facilities lack many types of technology readily available in American hospitals. MRI scanners, a cornerstone of contemporary diagnostics, are a rarity in Canada. Waiting times for scans can extend to eight months or more for a procedure that takes only minutes.

---

*Such statistical comparisons typically overlook American fatalities due to crime and auto accidents, both much higher in the U.S. than in other countries. Once these are factored out, U.S. life expectancy is competitive and even superior to that of most foreign countries.

Competent doctors often choose to send patients to American hospitals to have scans carried out immediately. Similar deficiencies exist with electrocardiograms and CAT scans. Little wonder that some Canadian hospitals close letters scheduling appointments with the line: "If the person named on this computer-generated letter is deceased, please accept our sincere apologies."

Bureaucratic regulations are largely to blame. MRI technicians, for example, are allowed to work strictly limited hours. When five o'clock rolls around, waiting patients are sent home and the machines are then dedicated to the needs of veterinarians. An ailing pet waits two weeks or less for an MRI scan, with the clinic making a nice side income. As for the human patients . . . the story goes that one man, rather than wait months for his turn, tried to book himself under the name "Spot."

Like the British NHS, Canadian Medicare neglected to construct or expand hospital facilities during its early years. Canadians are paying for that decision today.

Waiting times for surgical procedures start at fourteen weeks and go up from there. According to the Canadian Medical Association, more than one million Canadians—nearly 3 percent of the population—are on waiting lists for treatment. Noncritical treatments fare even worse—pain clinics have waiting lists of up to three years, and sleep clinics two years. Another common feature of Canadian hospitals is "hallway medicine," the Third World practice of putting bed patients in any spare hallway because of overcrowding.

Canada also suffers a doctor shortage, with something on the order of two hundred physicians a year heading south to get out from under the system. As a result, the country has slightly over two doctors per one thousand population, well below the international average. More than 1.5 million Ontarians can't find a family doctor.

On August 16, 2009, the system's incoming director, Dr. Anne Doig, publicly admitted that Medicare was near collapse. "We all agree that the system is imploding. . . . We know that there must be change. We're all running flat out, we're all just trying to stay ahead of the immediate day-to-day demands."

The price in mortality is difficult to ascertain. As one critic of the system has written, "Statistics on Canadian health care's weaknesses were hard to come by." There have been no commissions or studies following the U.K. example and no indication that any are planned. But between lengthy waiting times, antiquated equipment and facilities, and stressed personnel, the number is undoubtedly high. There's no lack of anecdotal evidence along the lines of the seventy-four-year-old Manitoba man who died after three hours of neglect in a hospital emergency room, or the twenty-three-year-old Alberta man who after spending most of the day between two emergency rooms without being examined, returned home only to die of a burst appendix.

It's in order to escape such fates that tens of thousands of Canadians head across the border to obtain the treatment they need. Not only politicians seek relief in the United States. Canada's situation would be far worse without the existence of its despised and envied neighbor to the south.

AUSTRALIA

Australia's system is *also* known as Medicare. (One thing that bureaucrats can't be accused of is originality.) Like the Canadian system, it is a single-payer program. Coverage is universal and is paid for by taxes. Both hospital treatment and doctor visits are covered. Doctors can either bill patients, who are reimbursed by the government, or bill the government directly.

One way in which the Aussie system differs from Canada's is in the absence of the fanatic Canadian opposition to private practice. While 70 percent of Australian hospital beds are in state-owned public hospitals, the rest are provided by for-profit private hospitals open to anyone who can afford them. Australia also covers medication expenses through a Pharmaceutical Benefit Scheme (PBS) that subsidizes drug costs.

If any government-run health-care system might have looked forward to success, it was Australia's. With a population of only 20 million (lower than that of California, Texas, or New York), a stable government, and a steady economy, Australia is untouched by the social maladies afflicting Great Britain, while its system avoided the ideological errors of Canada's. It should have been smooth sailing for the Aussies.

But it wasn't. Instead, Australia's health-care system is facing a collapse nearly as swift and thorough as that threatening the mother country.

Australia has been dogged for years by the same problems afflicting other nationalized health-care systems—spiraling costs, lengthening waiting lines, and a deteriorating infrastructure. A further unique complication involved Australia's own "Doctor Death," Queensland surgeon Jayant Patel, who was accused of responsibility for the deaths of as many as eighty-seven patients. Patel had earlier practiced medicine in the U.S., where his license was suspended following a series of irregularities. Evidently, no attempt was made by Australian authorities to check his record. The Doctor Death revelations rocked Queensland's Labour government and led to a nationwide loss of confidence in the health-care establishment.

Problems apparent in the first years of the new millennium included a sclerotic IT system still using 1980s technology, costs rising at 5 percent a year, and the bankruptcies of two major malpractice insurers in New South Wales and Queensland. Then, in 2008, for reasons still not clearly understood, the health-care system hit a brick wall. The entire New South Wales hospital network collapsed, with repercussions shaking the entire country. All of the state's 220 public hospitals ran out of cash, ran out of beds, and began shedding trained personnel. Spending was cut to the bone, with patients deprived of basic drugs, medical supplies, and even adequate food. Single-use equipment such as syringes and sponges were being reutilized, often without necessary sterilization. Fears of superbug outbreaks swiftly became reality with the appearance of antibiotic-resistant *Enterococcus* bacteria. Port Macquarie Hospital ran out of morphine, leaving surgical patients writhing in pain on their beds. Other hospitals were cut off by suppliers for failure to pay their bills. By the end of the year, Third World–style chaos was beginning to spread to Australia's other states. "The system," said Dr. Brian Morton, president of the NSW branch of the Australian Medical Association, "is basically broke and all the health services are in trouble."

While accurate mortality figures are impossible to obtain, there is no reason to doubt that they have soared in the past few years.

Three separate systems, three distinct failures. All the nationalized health systems in Anglophone countries have fallen short. The U.K., the mother of them all, is in a state of near-collapse, Australia close behind, with Canada limping along only because it has a big neighbor to take up the slack.

Other advanced industrial states seem no better. France, number one on the UN's list of national health systems, can look back on the great "heat wave" of 2003, in which nearly 15,000 seniors died, in large part because health professionals had taken off for the beaches, leaving emergency rooms unmanned. If any such thing had occurred in the backward U.S., doctors' homes would have been mobbed, investigations launched, and arrests for negligence made. From France, we did not hear a peep.

Japan, a country in which efficiency is a facet of national character, is facing a growing problem with patients dying after being turned away from multiple hospitals. In 2007, over 14,000 patients were refused by at least three hospitals before at last being admitted. One Tokyo woman, aged seventy, was turned away no less than forty-nine times.

Even Sweden, the pioneer social-welfare state (though not, as many assume, a socialist state—Sweden is a capitalist economy that pays for its large-scale programs through progressive taxation), has characteristic problems with rising costs, denial of care, and long waiting times. The Swedish government recently began privatizing nearly half its health-care operations, contracting out a number of services to private vendors.

Government health care presents us with a landscape of universal failure. The argument that the U.S. health system is in crisis can be dismissed—they're all in crisis, and the United States, with its antiquated, unfair, capitalistic, market-oriented system, is in far better shape than most.

An ontogeny of the government-run health-care system looks like this:

1. Idealistic origins
2. Limitations of some original promises and guarantees
3. Increasing bureaucratization . . .
4. . . . accompanied by slipping standards
5. Public controversy answered with fruitless "reforms"
6. Curtailment of services
7. The threat of system-wide collapse
8. Degeneration accompanied by mass fatalities

The U.S. has scarcely mounted that ladder. As for our Anglophone cousins, Canada has reached level 6 and is precariously maintaining itself there (what happens to Canada after the U.S. nationalizes health care is not worth thinking about). Australia and the U.K. are cruising past level 7 and approaching level 8—medical catastrophe on a nationwide scale, a disaster of a type that has not yet occurred in an advanced technological state. What comes after that, we simply don't know.

THE OBAMA PLAN

Obama prefers a single-payer plan on the Canadian model, but that turned out to be too radical a step. While it's impossible to say exactly what is contained in the 2,400 pages (more than twice as long as Hillarycare!) comprising the Affordable Health Care Act, in rough outline, Obamacare is structured as a private insurance-based plan in which all U.S. citizens would be required to carry medical insurance or face substantial fines, with payments aided by subsidies from their employers. Types and levels of coverage would be mandated, and policies could be obtained either from private insurers or from a government-run insurance plan yet to be established. The full program is budgeted at between $1.5 and $2 trillion for the first ten years (rather more than Britain's NHS in the same period), to be paid for by taxes, debt issuance, and financial juggling involving Medicare and other programs.

The interesting thing about Obamacare as it stands is that it's a near-copy of the Massachusetts health-care plan introduced in 2006. While not an unmitigated disaster, Commonwealth Care can in no way be termed a success, and has been drifting closer to outright failure with every month that passes.

Commonwealth Care was intended as a showcase program for Mitt Romney, something designed to make him look presidential in time for 2008. That was only the first of its failures. Suffice it to say, Romney is not leaping up to take credit for it now. (In 2009, Romney admitted to the GOP Voters Summit that the results had not been quite what he'd hoped.)

The program was completely ineffective in achieving its chief object of halting the inflation of health-care costs. Medical expenses in Massachusetts continue to rise, outpacing national cost increases by as much as 33 percent. While the state claims to have halved the level of uninsured from 13 to 7 percent, these figures are disputed. The program may even have increased the number of uninsured, with many individuals choosing to pay the penalty—roughly half the price of a health-care policy—rather than burden themselves with a skyrocketing insurance bill.

In May 2009 the *Boston Globe* reported that waiting periods had grown to fifty days to see a specialist, sixty-three days to see a family doctor, and over three months for an ob/gyn visit, despite the fact that Massachusetts has the largest number of doctors in the United States.

Many businesses have taken the subsidy provision, which acts as a business tax, as the last straw and have closed their doors and fled "Taxachusetts." But perhaps the program's greatest flaw lies in the state's entry into the health-insurance business as a direct competitor to private insurance companies.

As we saw with Fannie Mae and Freddie Mac, government inevitably distorts, and often wrecks, any market it enters into. Against governments, private companies operate at a complete disadvantage. A government agency has more resources, better access to potential customers, and can change the rules anytime it wants. Private business simply can't compete. The end result is either a corrupted market, private companies forced to flee, or some combination of the two.

The Massachusetts insurance industry was hobbled with the customary set of regulations, prominent among them one that required that both sick and healthy clients be charged the same rates. As a result, rates skyrocketed for everyone. This in turn increased public clamor for admission into the state-run indigent program. Corruption being not unheard of in Massachusetts, many thousands too well-off for eligibility were signed up anyway. The cost for Commonwealth Care for 2008–9 exceeded $1.3 billion. If the process continues in line with basic economics—as it always does—we will see private insurance companies dumping their business and running for the state line, state government passing laws to prevent this (as the state of New Jersey attempted to do with auto insurers after trashing that branch of the industry), followed by a series of bankruptcies, reorganizations, and state takeovers, with Massachusetts at last becoming the sole proprietor of its very own single-payer health-care plan.

Precisely the same process occurred in Hawaii in 2008 with its Keiki (child) Care program, an attempt to provide health-care coverage for every child in the islands not covered by a private plan. Parents all over the state began dropping private plans and signing their children up for the far cheaper state plan. Within weeks, Keiki Care, originally budgeted at $50,000 a month, had doubled and then tripled that figure. Governor Linda Lingle, displaying more sense than the average politician, shut the program down after only seven months, transferring needy children to available federal programs.

Commonwealth Care has not been operating long enough for the full implications to work themselves out (most of its provisions didn't go into effect until 2009, a bit of insurance for someone running for president in 2008). But the endgame, even now being played out in the U.K., in Canada, and in Australia, is certain. There's only one direction for state-run health-care systems, and that is down. Costs will continue to soar, coverage and services will be cut, hospitals will close, doctors and other trained personnel will head for greener pastures. The sick and desperate will flee to other states for treatment. People will start to die.

Obamacare diverged only slightly from the Massachusetts model. Among the major differences (along with fines for possessing too privileged a private health plan and free coverage for illegal aliens) was an annual penalty on individuals for noncompliance, as opposed to fines on employers. While far from trivial, these fines were also far from draconian, and provide little incentive to comply, undercutting the financial logic behind the Obama bill, in which a flood of new insurance clients would provide at least part of the financing for expanded coverage. Lacking this private financial component, government will have to take up more of the burden. As the federal share grows, private insurance will become increasingly vestigial, to be absorbed at last through nationalization. Eventually all payments will be channeled through the state bureaucracy, and Obama will have created his single-payer plan.

Obama will also have created a duplicate of the Canadian and Australian health-care systems, with all their flaws and failings. Former senator Tom Daschle, Obama's first choice for health secretary (until he encountered a feature of American life previously unfamiliar to him known as "taxes" and was forced to withdraw) is currently involved in establishing a regulatory board to work out "standards for public health care," supposedly based on the Federal Reserve Board and the Securities and Exchange Commission. But the direct inspiration for this board is the British National Health Service's NICE, and it is clearly intended to fill the same role—evaluating treatment and medication for the purpose of withholding services and containing costs. The Obama administration is already foreseeing shortfalls and is taking steps to create a basis for rationing and denial of services.

What we have to look forward to is a program that will combine the worst qualities of the failed U.K., Canadian, and Australian health systems. A single-payer system, government controlled and operated, with a board set up for the sole purpose of dictating treatments, and not a single check or balance to protect the interests of the public.

It doesn't have to be this way. We have the example of Singapore, which utilizes a system of health savings accounts to pay for health care. These accounts remain in the hands of individuals, who decide how to utilize them. Singapore has a thriving, almost problem-free health-care establishment, operating on only 4 percent of GDP, along with one of the highest life-expectancy rates in the world. (To those who dismiss Singapore as a mere city-state with a population of a quarter-million and nothing to say to a populous, continent-spanning nation—why, then, are we imitating Australia and Canada?) In early 2009, the GOP offered a plan utilizing exactly such health savings accounts. But far from being considered, it was never even mentioned.

American medicine is already adjusting to new medical challenges. Most large cities now have private centers—some of them in drugstores and shopping malls—acting in the role of emergency rooms. These perform a diagnosis for a flat fee, offer treatment for minor injuries and ailments, and refer more serious cases to hospitals. Such centers show considerable promise in easing pressure on hospitals. Will there be room for them in Obama's new world?

Americans doubted that there would be room for anything at all other than the state and its interests, and watched with a sense of relief as the Affordable Health Care Act crashed and burned at the last possible moment in January 2010, thanks to the loss of the Democratic supermajority in the Senate. Democratic members of Congress, already unsettled by the backlash the bill had aroused (public opposition stood at 64 percent, nearly two-thirds of voters), began jumping ship within hours of the election of Scott Brown in Massachusetts. To the relief of the country at large, the bill appeared to be dead on arrival.

But its demise was only apparent. Obama had pegged his presidency, and his status as the new FDR, on health-care reform, and could not be expected to merely throw up his hands and walk away. Even as Scott Brown took his seat, an end run was being made around the obstacle he represented, by means of ramming the already approved Senate version of the bill through the House. In the face of massive public hostility, in defiance of customary procedure, with the help of political muscle flexing unseen since the days of Czar Reed, the president got his bill. Barring repeal, intervention by the courts, or widespread civil defiance (Arizona has already acted to prevent the bill's mandates from being enforced. At least twenty other states are considering similar actions.), U.S. health care is now doomed to the same downward trajectory being followed by the rest of the industrialized world.

But the U.S. will go faster and more thoroughly. The United States is a different proposition from other nations. It has a larger and vastly more varied population. It has more interests to serve, more stakeholders to please, more problems to confront. In health care as in any other aspect of modern experience, the United States is sui generis, with a set of unique challenges unmatched by those of any other nation-state of its era.

When it cracks, as the U.K. and Australia are starting to crack today, it will crack completely. The system painstakingly built up over generations will fall in on itself.

Hospitals will fold, technicians and practitioners will flee, and communities will be left with no medical resources whatsoever. Medicines will vanish, new drugs will become a legend, cutting-edge technology will consist of broken-down machines shoved into the back of a storage room. Horrors we believed confined to the Third World or left behind in the medieval epoch will return. Diseases unknown in advanced states will first stalk the corridors of government wellness centers before bursting out into communities at large. (Since 2001, the U.K. has seen a dramatic increase in diseases once thought conquered, including a quadrupling of whooping cough cases, an increase of 153 percent in scarlet fever cases, and near tripling of typhoid cases from 45 to 127.) Hospitals will again become what they once were to the ignorant and unschooled—places of terror where one is sent only to die. And the bureaucracy will keep very, very good records of it all.

Americans are not the cowed Britons of the postwar period. They are not easygoing Strines. They are not obedient and patient Canadians. They will not willingly accept state control of their personal health. Alternate methods of obtaining necessary medical care will be created (and are probably being created now). A black market, one that operates the same as all black markets under similar conditions. And don't forget the Canadian example. Mexico will experience a vast boom in health tourism, perhaps large enough to solve its long-term economic woes. Americans will cross the border for necessary treatment in clinics likely owned by expatriate U.S. doctors. They will return home thanking God that they had the cash to spare, while shaking their heads at the endless, hopeless lines in front of the local U.S. Health Department facility.

But they will not be content, and they will not tolerate it for long. Eventually, some form of status quo will be restored. But before then, we may well achieve that figure of 450,000 dead per annum. And Obama will have his monument.

SERVANT OF GAIA

During the 2008 campaign Obama placed considerable emphasis on his qualifications for the role of environmental messiah ("the moment the seas stopped rising," and so forth). On taking office he lost no time in pulling on the green robes.

Less than a week after his inauguration, Obama struck the first blow in his save-the-earth campaign by ordering the Department of Transportation to issue regulations mandating a 40 percent increase in gas mileage for cars and light trucks by 2020. As we saw in Chapter 7, there are few things more conclusively demonstrated than the dangers to life and safety posed by such attempts at manipulating automobile design. The message seems to have gotten lost before reaching the Oval Office. (No surprise there—Carol M. Browner, Obama's select representative to the auto companies, went to great pains to assure that those involved in the CAFE discussions "Put nothing in writing, ever.")

As always, the heavy lifting was to be done by the auto industry, at that point in a state of near-total collapse, with GM and Chrysler sliding into receivership and only Ford showing any signs of life. The Obama "plan" mandated—but made no provisions to pay for—enormous amounts for research and development. Under those circumstances, the auto companies would have little choice but to take the cheapest way out: to make cars smaller and flimsier yet, with the inevitable accompanying rise in mortality. The scheme was a perfect illustration of the Obama policy method: come up with a fantasy plan, hand out orders, and then move on before disaster can hit.

Next on Obama's Green agenda came the Waxman-Markey cap-and-trade bill, intended to deal with the menace of global warming, a threat so malignant that it has vast effects even when it isn't happening. (No climatic warming has been recorded since 1998—in fact, global temperatures dropped a fraction of a degree during the period. All the same, hundreds of honest, objective, and well-trained scientists such as Michael Mann and Phil Jones have discovered no end of dire climatic effects, including collapsing ice sheets, vanishing glaciers, dying coral reefs, animal migrations, droughts, and so forth exactly as if something like warming was actually taking place.)

Cap and trade is a scheme in which an artificial carbon market would be established under government supervision, with a ceiling for greenhouse emissions put in place and companies issued "carbon credits" representing the amount of emissions each would be allowed in the course of operations. These credits could be traded between companies—if one company beat its quota, it could sell the remaining credits to others not quite so fortunate. The aim of the program is to reduce greenhouse-gas emissions by 14 percent in 2020 and 83 percent in 2050—the same level as in 1875, before any heavy modern industry had been established on the North American continent. The interesting thing about Waxman-Markey is that even if the bill's projections worked out to the last decimal point, it would have next to no effect on the level of greenhouse gases, which would drop only a fraction of one percent. The largest sources of these emissions lie in South Asian cookfires, Amazonian burnoffs, and Chinese coal mines accidentally set ablaze and left to burn themselves out (more than three hundred such fires are known to exist). Cap and trade, like most environmental efforts, is a ritual gesture at best.

The bill was so unpopular that its chief sponsor, Representative Henry Waxman (Democrat of California), attempted to sneak it out of committee without a vote. Congressmen and senators from the industrial states opposed the bill on the grounds of the damage that the "emissions market" would have on industry. The public, after a series of unusually cold winters, was growing skeptical of the warming thesis. A January 2009 poll revealed that only 30 percent considered global warming to be an "urgent priority." Throughout the ensuing year, repeated revelations of fraud battered the warming fraternity. A whistleblower's disclosure of thousands of incriminating e-mails demonstrated that the staff of East Anglia University's Climate Research Unit (CRU), the leading such institution in the U.K., had systematically cooked data and undermined the peer-review process. Temperature data in New Zealand's weather database had been deliberately manipulated to raise the figures by a degree or more. The Russian meteorological service complained that the U.K.'s Met Office, acting as a clearinghouse for international meteorological records, had been cherry-picking readings to show only high figures. The UN's climate watchdog body, the International Panel on Climate Change (IPCC), was revealed to have taken a crucial finding on glacier retreat from a fanciful pop-science article and data on the increasing frequency of weather-related disasters from an unreviewed and errant scientific paper. This train of events played a large role in the collapse of the consensus in favor of an international anti-warming regime at the December 2009 Copenhagen conference.

By the end of 2009 it was clear that the entire corpus of climatological data needed to be reviewed and if necessary corrected before any conclusions concerning prospective warming could be drawn. Despite this, Obama remained adamant that his cap-and-trade bill be passed.

Waxman-Markey might not directly threaten any lives. But its economic impact is the equivalent of a major war—and a defeat at that. The bill would cost a typical American household up to $3,900 a year. It would reduce GDP by $7.4 trillion, destroy up to 844,000 jobs per year, raise electricity rates, gasoline prices, and natural gas prices by up to 90 percent, and increase the federal debt by 29 percent, or $33,400 per person. All of which is not to overlook the ancillary costs created by the destruction and diversion of resources and funds.

These two efforts offer ample proof that Obama is willing to implement the Green agenda in defiance of all doubts concerning its validity. With an economic panic unfolding, two wars in progress, and sinister doings in North Korea, Iran, Pakistan, and elsewhere, the president found the time and energy to devote himself in the first critical weeks of his administration to enacting an environmentalist wish list.

And what is the environmentalist agenda? Most Americans have a vague image of environmentalism as a movement whose adherents glory in defending spotted owls, harp seals, polar bears, and other warm and fuzzies against the depredations of various corporate and industrial baddies, when not conducting stream walks or handcuffing themselves to various objects. This cheery picture fails in every regard to match the record, which includes deliberate attempts to instill panic concerning pollution, nuclear energy, and climate change, open fraud in the cases of Alar, "acid rain," electromagnetic fields, and "secondhand smoke," and terror campaigns waged by "Hard Green" and animal-rights groups. Environmentalism is an iceberg ideology, with the bulk of its activities, program, and purpose unknown to the public. Very few—Obama certainly not among them—have bothered to look past the surface pretense to discover the actual nature of one of the ruling ideologies of the new millennium.

Environmentalism is divided into two distinct and competing systems of thought ("philosophies" is probably too grand a term to use here). "Social ecology" holds that abuse of the environment is similar in nature and causation to other social ills such as racism and sexism, and can be combated in much the same way. "Deep ecology" contends that nature exists totally separate from human interests, possessing its own innate value that transcends all human values. Humanity, in this view, is an interloper in the natural world, and its activities and effects must be controlled and minimized to the greatest extent possible.

Deep ecology was formulated by the Norwegian environmentalist Arne Naess in 1970 and refined by numerous other writers in the decades since. Its influence was originally limited to the extremist fringes of the environmental movement. Direct-action groups such as Earth First! and the Earth Liberation Front utilized deep ecology as the theoretical basis for their "monkeywrench" sabotage campaigns. Elsewhere, social ecology continued to hold the stage. But environmentalism could serve as a textbook example of the tendency for liberal movements lacking guiding principles to shift steadily toward radicalism. Deep ecology, and the rigid antihumanist ideology it embodies, has displaced the more rational forms of environmental activism. Organizations such as Greenpeace and the Sierra Club and figures such as James Hansen, Al Gore, and James Lovelock all accept the Hard Green worldview. In today's world, "deep ecology" and "Green" have become synonyms.

One of the basic tenets of deep ecology is depopulation. Humanity, in the words of the Gaian prophet James Lovelock, is the cause of "Earth's disease, the fever brought on by a plague of people." The human race has exceeded the earth's "carrying capacity" and has begun degrading the ecosphere. Therefore, the human race must be reduced to a level—two billion, according to some, a half-billion to others, on down to a figure as low as 100 million—where it is no longer a menace. And this must occur quickly, before Gaia acts to remove the human tumor from the natural world through a massive, universal "die-off," which will leave only a handful of wretched survivors living a Neolithic existence.

The concept of depopulation was first introduced in 1796 by Thomas Malthus, whose *Essay on the Principle of Population* raised the possibility that "natural increase" could end only in mass starvation. Malthus viewed this eventuality as catastrophic. Two centuries later, depopulation, transformed into a desirable outcome, has become a consistent strain in environmentalist thinking. Paul Ehrlich, one of the fathers of modern environmentalism, believed that famine, pollution, and disease would kill billions before the end of the twentieth century. In the 1970s, Garrett Hardin preached "lifeboat ethics," encouraging rich countries to isolate themselves and allow the underdeveloped world to go under. In the 1980s and nineties, groups such as Earth First! hoped that AIDS would destroy vast numbers of human beings. Today ecofascists such as Pentti Linkola contend that all except a small human elite are expendable.

Numerous suggestions have been made as to how such a program should be carried out. Alan Weisman, author of *The World Without Us*, a volume portraying an earth without human tenants, proposes that we "limit every human female on Earth capable of bearing children to one." The British government's chief environmental official, Jonathon Porritt, is slightly more generous in allowing two, though any more would be "irresponsible."

Lester Brown of the Worldwatch Institute looks to the Iranian Islamic theocracy for guidance—the ayatollahs in the late 1990s established a forced birth-control program to "encourage smaller families," an effort Brown views with admiration. Nowhere does he mention that as a result Iran is in the midst of a demographic crash that will by 2050 leave it with too few inhabitants to maintain a working society.

Academic John Reid cuts to the chase with his suggestion that we "put something in the water, a virus that would be specific to the human reproductive system and would make a substantial proportion of the population infertile." We have already mentioned Earth First!, whose founder, Dave Foreman, has called for a complete collapse of industrial civilization that would kill a majority of living human beings. Operating in the same ballpark is the Voluntary Human Extinction Movement, which believes that the extinction of humanity by any means necessary is the only way to save the planet. But the ecofascist demagogue Pentti Linkola outdoes them all: "Who misses all those who died in the Second World War? Who misses the twenty million executed by Stalin? Who misses Hitler's six million Jews?"

These examples make it apparent that Hard Green environmentalism is no well-intentioned, meliorist humanitarian movement but a true heir of the killer ideologies of the last century. Its attitudes, rhetoric, and methods are little different, its aims virtually identical: to obtain and wield power not for personal satisfaction or aggrandizement—which, however contemptible, are at least understandable—but in the service of an ideology. An ideology based on premises so divorced from the human norm as to arouse incredulity when they are first encountered. To the old collectivist formula we must add one more element: that of nihilism, the rejection of that which exists solely because it does exist. Granted that the Green ideology is a refined form of nihilism, rejecting only the human elements of the world, rather than the world as a whole. But it remains nihilism all the same. Only in those terms can we understand the phenomenon of environmentalism. (Any doubts as to how seriously we need to take this, or whether it may not be a pose after all, can be laid to rest by the actions of Toni Vernelli, an official of People for the Ethical Treatment of Animals [PETA], who aborted her child because of its potential effect on the environment: "It would have been immoral to give birth to a child that I felt strongly would only be a burden to the world." It doesn't get more serious than that.)

What place does such an ideology have in a democracy? Absolutely none. The Green ideology denies concepts basic to not only our society but our civilization. The value of tradition, hopes for material progress, and the primacy of the human individual all become meaningless when the human race itself has been downgraded to the status of universal pest. In the Green utopia to come, not only our political but our very existential rights will be tossed aside. The most intimate and private human activities will become the business of vast bureaucracies. Normal life will be transformed into a variety of criminal behavior. All for the purpose of meeting an emergency whose nature is undefined, whose actuality is doubtful, and whose duration is effectively eternal. Such a stance takes the ideologies of the past century not only a step forward, but into an entirely new dimension, one in which not only individuals, nations, and societies are open to manipulation and control, but the entire human species.

How much does Barack Obama buy into this? Is he simply another badly informed devotee of the happy snail darter façade, or does he accept the Hard Green ideology in all its antihuman ugliness?

In July 2009, a mild controversy arose concerning the fact that John P. Holdren had collaborated with pioneer ecocatastrophe prophets Paul and Anne Ehrlich on a book titled *Ecoscience: Population, Resources, Environment*. In that volume, Holdren (in collaborations of this type, it can be taken for granted that the junior partner did most of the work) contended that "neither the Declaration of Independence nor the Constitution mentions a right to reproduce," opening the door for total government control of reproduction. That could be accomplished by "sterilizing women after their second or third child" or otherwise "adding a sterilant to drinking water." Holdren also called for a "Planetary Regime," a global benevolent dictatorship based on environmentalist principles that would " . . . control the development, administration and distribution of all natural resources."

And who is John Holdren? The Obama administration's science "czar," the assistant to the president for science and technology, a post that also includes directorship of the Office of Science and Technology Policy. John Holdren, a man who believes that the Constitution allows forced sterilization, today oversees this country's science policy.

When interviewed by the BBC in early 2009, Dr. Nina Fedoroff stated that "There are probably already too many people on the planet." Humans had gone beyond earth's "limits of sustainability," she asserted. "We need to continue to decrease the growth rate of the global population; the planet can't support many more people."

And who is Nina Fedoroff? A leading official of the U.S. State Department, no less than the science and technology advisor to the secretary of state. Dr. Fedoroff was first appointed during the secretaryship of Condoleezza Rice. She retained the post in the Obama administration, and today works with Hillary Clinton.

The advent of Obama also marked the return of Carol M. Browner, whom we last saw adding to the torments of America's asthma sufferers on behalf of the ozone layer. Browner was appointed the presidential advisor on energy and climate change, making her perhaps the country's leading official on environmental issues. There's a bitter irony insofar as her decree concerning asthma inhalers went into effect at the precise moment that she was taking up her new position. As millions of lives were disrupted and countless ailing individuals unnecessarily endangered, Browner ascended the next step on the bureaucratic ladder.

There we have it: Hard Green advocates in control of every major government office dealing with American scientific and environmental policy. People who believe that nature is beleaguered, that too many human beings are crowding the planet, and that it is government's job to take corrective action. What can we anticipate from an environmentalist cadre so deeply embedded in the bureaucracy and enjoying the full support of the president? One thing is certain: it will not end with smaller cars, carbon caps, renewables, and all the rest. Those are merely the prelude. The Hard Green agenda is clear: deindustrialization, depopulation, an eventual return to an ecological never-never land in which the polar bear lies down with the spotted owl and human beings are simply a kind of talking animal.

It will not occur at once, but will be put in place through small increments, a series of trivial, irritating changes that will build up over time. A recent decision in Australia—often the bellwether of Green initiatives—can serve as an example. The states of Victoria and South Australia have announced plans to cut off air conditioning at times of peak use—that is, whenever it grows hottest. Along with placing a surcharge on electrical rates during hot periods, a proposal has been made to place remote-control switches in homes to cut off power to air conditioners whenever a bureaucrat decides that it's appropriate.

In a climate like that of Australia, such a program amounts to a death sentence for many elderly and ailing people. Over 450 people died of heat complications in Victoria and South Australia in January 2009. Curtailing air conditioning under such circumstances would be, as one paper put it, "murder by remote control."

Our own domestic variants of this policy are easy to imagine (it has been reported that the Minnesota power authority also put such a policy in effect as of the summer of 2009), particularly after power becomes more costly and more restricted as "renewable energy" programs collapse of their own weight. Critics who make the sensible objection that solar and wind power cannot possibly replace current power sources are missing the point—they're not *supposed* to. American citizens are supposed to accept the far lower energy usage—along with the restricted standard of living—that is all that renewable sources will allow.

Despite the CRU e-mail revelations, which represent a knock-out blow to the Anthropogenic Global Warming Thesis, and the not-unrelated Copenhagen fiasco, the legacy of Rachel Carson goes on. The level of mortality contingent upon Hard Green plans being carried out would be utterly unprecedented in human experience. These plans are nearly impossible to grasp, and probably impossible to execute, depending as they do on Americans playing the part of willing victims. But the cost is likely to be very high before environmentalism is seen for what it is—the last gasp of the rationalist ideologies, a direct challenge to both democracy and the Western way of life. We are still at the beginning of this battle, and the precise outcome remains hidden. Suffice it to say that if democide ever achieves numbers in the United States similar to those recorded in Europe and Asia, environmentalism will be intimately involved.

OBAMA'S APOTHEOSIS

At least in his own estimation, Barack Obama is a man of destiny. Obama sees himself as a world-historical figure, a man who embodies his epoch, a man for whom the age will be named, for whom the very nations will mourn as his bier passes. He has a task, a task set him by history, a task too great for anyone else to handle. But he sees his way clearly where others cannot. The plans are concrete in his mind. He will carry them out in detail, against all obstacles, bringing along with him his nation and the world.

He will fail. He will fail despite his unmatched self-assurance. Despite his control of the Congress and the bureaucracy. Despite the support of elites in this country and elsewhere. Despite an almost frightening level of adulation among his followers. He will fail because every program he has embarked on has been attempted previously, and has failed.

Government control of industry was attempted in the U.S. under the New Deal with the same results as everywhere else on earth: debilitation, stagnation, and collapse. Lyndon B. Johnson preceded Obama in an effort to create a universal nanny state though his Great Society, which did nothing more than add to the humiliation of its progenitor and inflict enormous social damage that required decades to overcome. Hail-fellow-well-met foreign policy has been practiced by every liberal president since Franklin D. Roosevelt (Harry Truman excepted), resulting in support for dictators, catastrophe for American interests, and endless trouble for our friends. Obama reveals no awareness of this record, or inclination to learn from it. He is committing the same errors as his predecessors, and will harvest the same results.

And what happens when a man of destiny fails? He doesn't give in. He doesn't even pause. He tries again. He finds other avenues, employs different tactics, discovers new methods. That's where the final danger lies regarding Barack Obama.

The storeroom of democide has been in no way depleted, any more than those of other forms of human iniquity and error. The methods and techniques of democide may seem blessedly restricted. But they are products of stupidity and evil, two of the ground states of the human animal, for which no known boundaries exist. So there will be no end to it. Democide will prove to be as infinitely fertile as any other brand of human corruption. The centuries to come will produce new forms without limit.

The danger for Obama is that, after his policies collapse and his plans have proven empty, rather than accept failure, he will choose to rummage through that dark space, desperate to find anything at all to throw into the hole that is devouring his vision. That he will discover something that seems to fit—that must fit— and emerge, in complete innocence, beyond guilt or accountability, with yet another method of killing human beings in large numbers.

He will do this for the same reason that others have done it before him. The same reason as FDR, and Rexford Tugwell, and Harry Hopkins, and Lyndon Johnson, and William Ruckelshaus, and Harry Blackmun. Because he is a liberal, an adherent of an ideology that long ago severed any connections with the world as it exists. An ideology that encompasses all answers, that contains everything within itself, an ideology to which results and consequences are completely irrelevant. An ideology divorced from its own principles and ideals, and those of the country in which it operates. An ideology that has become a machine for the creation of human misery, one that will continue accelerating its operations until the plug is at last pulled.

A good government implies two things; first, fidelity to the objects of the government; secondly, a knowledge of the means, by which those objects can be best attained.
—*JOSEPH STORY*, COMMENTARIES ON THE CONSTITUTION OF THE UNITED STATES, *1833*

10

ON A COLD, DARK CORNER OF HISTORY

How Do We End Democide?

Killing is among the most strictly regulated of human activities, for good reason. Many of the higher animals are hardwired to cease attacking a member of their own species if certain submissive actions or gestures are made. A bird beaten in a confrontation lowers its head to reveal a colored spot, a dog rolls over and whines. The attacker then pulls back and performs a victory display while the defeated animal flees unharmed.

That is not the case with human beings. There is no specific action or sign that would flip a switch to create an armistice, no particular switch to flip, as far as anyone has ever been able to discover. So to prevent a constant war of all against all, societies of all types and on all levels of development have taken steps to circumscribe the killing of humans by other humans. In primitive cultures, taboos exist against killing relatives, killing on certain days, and killing in certain areas. More advanced societies established institutions such as the wergeld, or blood money, outlawry for repeat offenders, chivalry as a channel for aggressive impulses, and complex religious prohibitions against murder. In modern societies, we have completed the process by reserving the power of killing to the state. Except in instances of self-defense and defending one's family or an innocent victim in extremis, the state retains a monopoly on killing in wartime, as punishment, and as a means of protecting the public peace. Even these instances have been deeply compromised in recent years.

In general, the restriction to the state of the right to kill has served the West well. Such crimes as revenge killings, ethnic or religious massacres, and mass murder for gain are common today only in pestholes such as the Balkans, Sudan, or America's urban slums. Otherwise, within the confines of the civilized world, we are the beneficiaries of a historically rare level of social peace. It cannot be argued that the unspoken pact relegating lethality to the state has been anything but a blessing. We see the possible alternatives in failed states across the world.

But, clearly, the state monopoly on violence can also go horribly wrong. Democide is so characteristic a disorder of advanced nation-states that it would almost appear to be an unavoidable part of their historical development. The practice of democide truly seems to be a universal—when states achieve the technical and managerial capability to commit this type of crime, commit it they do.

So what's the solution in such cases? Simply put: overthrow. The offending government must be brought down, its murderous policies ended, and those responsible taken into custody and punished. In light of contemporary levels of state power, this commonly requires overthrow by external forces—normal states that have not submitted to the democidal temptation. The chief historical examples of this type of action include Fascist Italy, Nazi Germany, and State Shinto Japan, all defeated by the Allies in WWII and their criminal leadership put on trial and in many cases executed. Communist Russia, for its part, was slowly worn down over the decades of the Cold War until it was finally nudged into its grave in the early 1990s. Overthrow appears to be the only viable method of curtailing the crime of democide. There is no known instance of a democidal state reforming itself back to normalcy.

Which brings us to American liberalism.

THE LIBERAL RECORD

In the final half of the twentieth century, up to 262,000 Americans died of crimes that would not have been committed but for liberal interference with the criminal justice system. Up to 121,000 died in automobile accidents directly attributable to the CAFE standards. Unknown thousands have perished due to the failure of other forms of government activity. (It would be a surprise if the numbers weren't somewhat murky— it's not as if we can find this information on a USA.gov website.) A large number of children have died under the "protection" of DYFS and similar agencies. Many of the "homeless"—the chronic mentally ill thrust out into the streets—have died in miserable circumstances. Individuals from all social levels have died due to various forms of environmental legislation. Others have been killed by rogue illegal immigrants. Many sick individuals have suffered premature death from being denied necessary medical drugs thanks to the FDA's convoluted certification process. We could go on as long as we had the stomach to do so. There is scarcely a single agency of government that is not hiding its own roster of the slain.

To avoid losing our focus amid other controversies, we will omit the numbers taken by abortion. We will also set aside the victims of the DDT ban and the millions destroyed by overambitious and overidealistic foreign policy. For our purposes, we will remain within our borders, never forgetting that there are many reasons why people across the world loathe and fear the United States.

We scarcely know enough to even estimate the total. The best we can say is that between 400,000 and 500,000 Americans have in the past half century died prematurely thanks to government policies, victims of the American democide.

That number is a match for all our fatalities in the past century's wars. It is greater than all American deaths from epidemic disease. It places government near the top of the list for causes of death in this country, accounting for a minimum of twenty-two deaths each day, every day, for fifty years.

That 400,000 to 500,000 doesn't amount to much, in the bloodsoaked history of the Age of Massacre. It scarcely compares to the numbers achieved by Nazi Germany, the U.S.S.R., Red China, or any of the other champions of extermination. It has required half a century for the U.S. to achieve that figure. The Hutu mobs of Rwanda, using only machetes, surpassed it within weeks. It scarcely rates an asterisk in the past century's long record of atrocity.

But it happened in our country. It happened in America.

SOLUTIONS

No one is going to rescue us, as occupied Europe and Asia were rescued in the 1940s. The U.S. is the great power of the millennial era. There is no possibility of a foreign state or coalition overthrowing the government of the United States. The idea of the UN intervening is laughable on any number of counts. We cannot count on an advanced galactic civilization swooping in to set things right. So it is going to be up to us.

As always, the U.S. will have to take on the role of pioneer, to become the first state to overcome democide by its own unaided efforts. This is not a hopeless task. Several factors will serve to ease the taming of the democidal impulse. First, the U.S. is not a monster state, a state based on mass murder, such as the U.S.S.R.

or Nazi Germany. It is more of a halfwit state engaged in negligent homicide due to stupidity, inattention, and runaway idealism. It also remains a democracy, which means that high levels of public pressure can be brought to bear on the political and bureaucratic classes. In the millennial era, technology has created a state of transparency in regard to information unknown in previous epochs. No longer is it possible to restrict information in the manner of the ideological dictatorships of the twentieth century. Gateways exist across the country on every desk that bears a PC. Once the concept is grasped, information concerning democide is freely available.

The single most urgent action is to immediately drop all democidal policies: fuel standards, criminal justice experimentation, environmental antihumanism, any and all activities that create even the most minimal chance that American citizens might die unnecessarily due to the actions of their government. There is no excuse for lethal governmental policies anywhere, at any time, under any circumstances.

A government's basic responsibility, its chief reason for existence, is to protect the lives and safety of its citizenry. This is the other side of the lethality coin—in exchange for restricting its own right to kill, a nation's populace demands the state's protection from threats of any sort. A government that fails in that obligation—much less one that deliberately violates it as a matter of policy—has lost legitimacy, and with it any claim on the people's loyalty. That, and no less, is the situation we now face. The implications of this fact are obvious and do not require belaboring, which doesn't mean that our political leadership will grasp them until forced to.

There is a distinct possibility that democidal policies unmentioned in these pages may also be active. (This approaches near-certainty when we consider that any federal bureaucrat can place a proposal in the *Federal Register* that will, if not challenged within a certain period, attain the force of law. That's how far we've departed from our original governmental blueprint.) Such policies need to be identified and uprooted. The best method of addressing the problem would be an independent commission convened to examine suspect policies and give recommendations. This commission should be insulated from control or influence by the executive and legislative branches. Appointments would best be made by members of the judiciary, specifically the Supreme Court. No one who may have had a hand in creating such policies—politicians and bureaucrats certainly, but also academics, consultants, and media figures—would be allowed to serve. Such a commission would require subpoena powers, an investigative staff, and the ability to enforce its recommendations. It would need to call upon members of all governmental branches for testimony, including sitting senators and congressmen. Any citizen would be allowed (not to say encouraged) to alert the commission to potential abuses.

New policies and proposals will need to be examined in light of the same type of error. This calls for yet another commission, separate and distinct from the first, though operating on similar principles. This commission would have full access to every individual and all paperwork and data involved in planning or proposing a government program. Anyone attempting to pull the Carol Browner "nothing in writing" trick would open themselves up for further investigation right then and there. This commission would have the power to demand modifications to a program or alternatively simply to shut down planning or execution for any project that failed to meet minimal standards of public safety. Private individuals, corporations, and nongovernmental organizations are all required to operate on a basis of due diligence where harm or damage is possible. Why should government be immune? Government activities subject to consideration would range from minor regulatory changes at the departmental level up to Obama's health-care extravaganza. While this commission's deliberations might well slow down the workings of government, there are many who would not view this as a drawback.

Finally, we require what in the former Iron Curtain countries is called a "lustration." We need full public exposure of historical governmental democide in all its aspects. An exhaustive study by independent scholars and researchers must be made of this country's democidal record. This would include a detailed analysis of all democidal programs, to establish who called for them, who formulated them, who promoted them, and who put them into effect. We need to learn everything we can about their aims, their cost, their results, and above all, how many victims they accounted for. It is necessary to know as much about these events as possible to assure that they are not repeated.

This series of actions would bring the American democide to an abrupt halt. Excess mortality through government action would simply cease. Few situations exist in which such beneficial results could be gained with so little effort.

THE WORLD AS IT IS

That's how it would work in a rational world. Unfortunately, we do not live in a rational world. In our world, Saddam Hussein, among the most murderous of modern tyrants, received the firmest support during his final confrontation with the West from none other than humane, life-affirming liberals. In our world, the political party responsible for the direst economic slump since the Depression was rewarded by the voters with even greater political power. In our world, the fuel-economy standards that have already killed tens of thousands of Americans were not abolished but expanded by act of Congress.

The world being what it is, there will be no commissions, no investigations, no lustration. The policies of democide, by which our government ensures the deaths of its own citizens, will continue unabated. The problem lies with social inertia. It's a simple, horrifying, yet undeniable fact that every society tolerates a certain level of human wastage. Ours is now set just a little higher than it was before our government embraced ideology. Somewhat higher than in much of Europe, but still lower than in most of Africa or Asia. A society that has adapted to such a situation tends to remain in that state. There will be no mass reaction until an as-yet-unknown threshold of mortality is breached. As long as that threshold remains uncrossed, liberalism, and its policies of democide, will go on as it has.

That being the case, we will require a longer period, more complex tactics, and considerable effort to end the plague of democide in this country. Democracy does have drawbacks, and this is one of them. (Of course, the simplest solution would be effective democracy—a voting public that sees through all the rhetoric, all the promises, all the vain dreams, and votes responsibly and with a sober view of its own interests. But that may be the most utopian vision of them all.)

A major stumbling block in confronting democide lies in the question of belief. Accepting that the government is engaged in such activities is similar to awakening to the fact that your friendly, outgoing next-door neighbors actually comprise a tribe of vampires. There are few things more terrifying than the realization that your own government is involved in the murder of its citizens, which is a major reason why the question has never yet arisen as an issue. (We see the same phenomenon at work in the general reluctance to grasp the reality of such horrors as the Holocaust, the Cambodian Year Zero, the Darfur massacres, and so on, endlessly.) A concept of such enormity can only be put across by continuous reiteration and repetition, constant exposure of the butcher's bill combined with a relentless undermining of the dogma responsible.

The legacy media will not be part of the solution. An inevitable Pulitzer awaits the journalist who exposes the true nature of government child-protective agencies. Yet after nearly forty years, that journalist has yet to appear. Instead, during the late 1980s we were treated to a wild-eyed witch hunt for imaginary "Satanists" active within the nation's child-care industry, a campaign that occupied a large fraction of the American media sphere for the better part of a decade. Similarly, the human cost of environmentalist regulations goes essentially unmentioned, while the mass media trumpet every Green crusade, from protection of snail darters to the menace of global warming.

But we need no longer depend on the legacy media, staggering into twilight as they are. The new media, primarily the Internet and talk radio, have made vast strides in changing the country's political culture. This has been accomplished in large part through distribution of information and coverage of stories ignored by conventional media sources. Democide, overlooked for decades, is the mother of all such stories. We must look to the new media to put the story of democide across.

Education will be a key element of this campaign, a concerted and continuing effort to inform the public of the reality they face, of the threat to their loved ones, their neighbors, and themselves. As it stands, people "know" that crime has effectively been institutionalized. They "know" that the CAFE standards kill. They "know" that child protective agencies act as a serious threat to the welfare of children. But they fall short of making the connection that these efforts are interrelated, arising from the same source and exhibiting the same morphology. Such connections must be established—lines must be drawn, interactions mapped, the point reiterated that certain events don't just happen but have been made to happen. That an undeniable percentage of seemingly random misfortunes—fatalities, accidents, misadventures—are not simply bad luck but by-products of policy. In the conspiratorial atmosphere fostered by the rhetoric of the left over the past forty years, this shouldn't be at all difficult.

Once a substantial percentage of Americans are convinced, the next step will involve the traditional national method of overcoming entrenched, nearly unassailable, authorities—the method of the abolitionists, of the civil rights movement, and of the pro-life movement. The slow, systematic grinding-down of offending interests over a period of years and decades, however long is required to end malignant practices and behavior and scatter the elements that made them a part of American life.

This method is often the sole means of attacking such an establishment. Without the abolitionists raising public awareness and generating disgust over slavery, the practice might well have stumbled on for generations before it died out from sheer vileness. Similarly, the civil rights movement assured the collapse of segregation within a decade after nearly a century of empty promises. Without the constant pressure exerted by the pro-life movement, abortion might have attained the status of an accepted facet of the American scene that its proponents hoped for it.

Defeating democide will require the full gamut of public resistance: protests against attempts to implement lethal policies, civil disobedience in defiance of democidal laws and regulations, and the boycotting of companies and organizations that bow to governmental fiat in such matters (automobile manufacturers are an obvious target). Constant effort, continuous pressure, and total commitment will be required. We must demand an answer for every democidal decision, an explanation for every life wasted.

A major effort must be made to prevent the expansion of existing policies, such as we recently witnessed with the CAFE standards. Senator John F. Kerry sponsored the bill, the House and Senate voted it into effect, President George W. Bush signed it, and President Barack Obama toughened its provisions, each of them acting in full knowledge of the program's role in increasing highway mortality. Nothing underlines the necessity of a dedicated opposition movement more clearly than this chain of events. The watchdog media, tribune-of-the-people activists, and rebel congressmen were nowhere to be found while that bill was being debated and passed. All that's required for democide to prevail is to leave current programs in place and allow the natural expansionary tendencies of government to have their play. Democidal programs will metastasize on the grounds of necessity and completeness with no limit and at the cost of tens of thousands of further lives. Curtailing this process will be a crucial element of an antidemocide campaign.

The third step will be to roll back the policies already in operation. This will be the most difficult phase of the entire effort. It will involve direct confrontations with program sponsors—many of them powerful politicians—and the agencies in charge of execution. A long-term battle against both career politicians and professional bureaucrats is not something to be entered into lightly. Bureaucracies have been defined as "the only immortal organisms known to nature." They are almost impossible to control and very difficult to kill. In the 1980s, the Reagan administration shut down the Legal Services Corporation, established two decades earlier to provide free legal assistance to the poor but which instead became notorious for frivolous lawsuits, harassment of private interests, and protection of criminals. The corporation's leadership succeeded in preserving it by placing the "crown jewels," the agency's critical departments, under the protection of other sections of the bureaucracy. When the Democrats returned to power, Legal Services was revived, almost intact.

A campaign to defeat democide will also require direct attacks on the liberal ideology itself. Many democidal policies, such as environmentalism and abortion, have become central elements of the liberal creed. All ideologies operate in terms of a "ratchet" effect—once a social or political objective is achieved, there is no going back. So liberals attempt to "solve" the homeless problem while dismissing as off-limits any suggestions favoring institution-alization, at the same time that the mentally ill are rapidly rein-stitutionalizing themselves within the country's jails and prisons. The same attitude is apparent as regards abortion, education, wel-fare, health-care reform, and any number of other liberal policies. As we saw in regards to DDT, we cannot expect liberal "gains" to be given up without a lengthy and bitter confrontation.

But eventually, politicians will begin to sense votes in the an-tidemocidal stance. The media (or whatever remnants may exist) will take note, and will begin to cover the story in their thorough, honest, and evenhanded fashion. The general mass of the public who pay no serious attention to politics will discover the reason why they have for many years been dogged by a sense of forebod-ing, a conviction that something has gone terribly wrong, that in some indefinable way their own government, in all its power and mastery, has turned against them. At that point, we will be able to begin contemplating a world without democide.

But what about the liberals? What becomes of them after a major prop is knocked out from under their worldview? Liberalism is powerfully delusive—any dogma based on the premise of pro-viding its adherents with complete moral certainty has a nearly irresistible appeal. Many liberals are true believers, and will go to their graves convinced that liberalism is the ultimate goal toward which humanity has been striving since the days of the Serengeti. But the majority adhere to it for reasons of political sentimental-ity. They are not storm troopers, Red Guards, or Weathermen. They believe because it is the path of least resistance, and because it makes them feel good about themselves. Apart from the politi-cians, they bear no direct responsibility for the crimes and errors of liberalism. They are gentle, well-meaning, kind, and misguided people. They truly believe in the ancient rationalist dreams of total liberty, perfect equality, and managed brotherhood, of the new man who with his unparalleled freedoms would remake the world as it should have been. They are our neighbors and friends, standing proudly behind their rising doughnut signs, convinced that this time it will work, that the promise will come to pass at last. The revelations concerning democide will hit them very hard. And what will these good people think? How will they react?

They will react with shame. Shame that they were taken in. Shame that they were used. Shame that they gave their allegiance and support to such a repellent system.

Shame is a powerful and often underrated social force. It played a large role in the collapse of legal segregation in the Old South. The Southern middle class became ashamed of the way that blacks had been treated, ashamed of the lengths that fringe elements were willing to go to preserve the doctrine of white supremacy, ashamed of their own timidity and cowardice. That is why in the end the system collapsed far more quickly and with less disruption and bloodshed than anyone thought possible. That story could be repeated in our time. It may well turn out that democide will at last be ended by the liberals themselves.

It will end. It will end because it is unjustifiable—a violation of every aspect of the social contract, all the traditions we maintain, all the concepts we hold about what our society is and could become, the very ideas upon which our civilization is founded.

It will end because it is undemocratic. A self-styled elite has surreptitiously implemented policies that kill their fellow citizens without discussion, without debate, with no agreement or even awareness on the part of the public at large, without any consideration of alternatives or options. Modern liberalism is a total negation of the idea of democracy, a standing insult to the American concept of government.

It will end because it is unnecessary. None of the democidal policies ever achieved their goals. Nothing was gained from any of it. Crime was not meliorated. The insane were not healed. The environment was not transformed. The multitudes killed by these policies died for no reason. The plans of modern liberalism proved to be worthless, as stupid and vicious a waste of lives as can be found in the historical record.

William James asked a haunting question that, once heard, is impossible to forget. Would it be just, he wondered, if the perfect happiness of all was guaranteed by one single act: the relentless and endless torture of a small, innocent child? There is but a single answer, the one that rises without a thought in every normal individual who contemplates the question. And yet, in this country, the closest yet reached to a working utopia, we kill dozens each week, hundreds each month, thousands each year, children and adults both. Not for the purpose of guaranteeing the happiness of anyone. For nothing. For no reason. Simply to meet the requirements of a secular religion that should have died out decades ago.

Liberalism as it exists today is a mockery of our history, our heritage, of everything this country has endured and accomplished. A liberalism that reigns over ruined cities nationwide, that continues to turn its back on the victims of crime, on the derelict insane, on forsaken children, and on the victims of deadly disease. A liberalism that makes us collaborators, all unknowing, in the deaths of the helpless. A liberalism that found its inspiration in the foulest ideologies of the modern era. A liberalism that kills.

"Protect us, and you may govern." That is the foundation of the relationship between ruler and ruled. All government, no matter what its outward form, operates on that basis. Every ruler, whether king, emperor, dictator, or president, must fulfill that bargain. Nothing can take its place or render it inoperative, not majesty, not terror, not duress. A ruler can commit any other crime, ignore every other responsibility, as long as that obligation is fulfilled. If it is not, then all other efforts are futile. Not even Alexander or Caesar could, in the end, overcome that.

In a democracy, that compact is all there is. Nothing else exists—no divine right, no mandate of heaven, no historical dialectic, no almighty State. Merely the bargain between governors and governed, and nothing more. Once that is gone, there is no haven for an errant ruling elite.

Liberals were once the heirs to such a compact, as pure and golden a contract between government and people as has ever existed. But they threw it away. For the illusion of omnipotence, the illusion of absolute certitude, the illusion that liberalism is something greater than it actually is.

Any governing entity that denies the compact must go, and will go, as surely as the British went in 1781, as the imperial states went after WWI, as the U.S.S.R. went in 1991.

American liberals, with their policies that kill, have repudiated the compact as clearly and completely as any governing power in history. They have lost the trust and the worthiness without which they cannot endure. It is time for them to go.

BIBLIOGRAPHY

CHAPTER 1: PROMETHEUS IN GRAY FLANNEL

Books

Billington, James, *Fire in the Minds of Men: Origins of the Revolutionary Tradition* (London, 1980).

Bork, Robert H., *Slouching Toward Gomorrah: Modern Liberalism and American Decline* (New York, 1996).

Flynn, John T., *The Roosevelt Myth* (New York, 1948).

Gellately, Robert, *Lenin, Stalin, and Hitler: The Age of Social Catastrophe* (New York, 2008).

Goldberg, Jonah, *Liberal Fascism: The Secret History of the American Left* (New York, 2008).

Jacobs, Jane, *The Death and Life of Great American Cities* (New York, 1961).

Johnson, Paul, *Modern Times: The World from the Twenties to the Nineties* (New York, 1991).

Laqueur, Walter, *Fascism: Past, Present, Future* (Oxford, 1997).

Minogue, Kenneth, *Alien Powers: The Pure Theory of Ideology* (New York, 1985).

Namoroto, Michael V., *Rexford G. Tugwell: A Biography* (Westport, Connecticut, 1988).

Powell, Jim, *FDR's Folly: How Roosevelt and His New Deal Prolonged the Great Depression* (New York, 2003).

Rummel, R. J., *Death by Government* (New Brunswick, New Jersey, 1997).

———, *Power Kills: Democracy as a Method of Nonviolence* (New Brunswick, New Jersey, 1994).

Schivelbusch, Wolfgang, *Three New Deals: Reflections on Roosevelt's America, Mussolini's Italy, and Hitler's Germany, 1933–1939* (New York, 2006).

Shlaes, Amity, *The Forgotten Man: A New History of the Great Depression* (New York, 2007).

Sowell, Thomas, *A Conflict of Visions: Ideological Origins of Political Struggles* (New York, 1987).

————, *The Vision of the Anointed: Self-Congratulation as a Basis for Social Policy* (New York, 1995).

Articles

Cole, Harold L., and Lee E. Ohanian, "How Government Prolonged the Depression," *Wall Street Journal*, February 2, 2009.

Shlaes, Amity, "Cheering for Obama Stimulus Buys Into 1930s Myth," Bloomberg, February 18, 2009.

Sullivan, Meg, "FDR's Policies Prolonged Depression by 7 Years, UCLA Economists Calculate," UCLA Newsroom, August 10, 2004.

CHAPTER 2: AMERICAN NOIR

Books

Chessman, Caryl, and Joseph Longstreth, *Cell 2455 Death Row: A Convicted Man's Own Story* (Westwood, Connecticut, 1969).

Dunbar, Ian, and Anthony Langdon, *Tough Justice: Sentencing and Penal Policies in the 1990s* (Oxford, 1998).

Fletcher, George P., *A Crime of Self Defense: Bernhard Goetz and the Law on Trial* (New York, 1988).

Garland, David, *The Culture of Control: Crime and Social Order in Contemporary Society* (Chicago, 2002).

Jackson, Bruce, *Law and Disorder: Criminal Justice in America* (Champaign, Illinois, 1984).

Kaminsky, Alice R., *The Victim's Song* (Buffalo, New York, 1985).

Kelling, George L., and Catherine Coles, *Fixing Broken Windows: Restoring Order and Reducing Crime in Our Communities* (New York, 1996).

Menninger, Karl, *The Crime of Punishment* (New York, 1968).

Posner, Richard A., *The Federal Courts: Challenge and Reform* (Cambridge, Massachusetts, 1996).

Rosenthal, A. M., *Thirty-Eight Witnesses: The Kitty Genovese Case* (New York, 1964).

Rothwax, Harold J., *Guilty: The Collapse of Criminal Justice* (New York, 1996).

Seedman, Albert A., and Peter Hellman, *Chief!* (New York, 1971).

Walker, Samuel, *Popular Justice: A History of American Criminal Justice* (Oxford, 1980).

Wilson, James Q., *Thinking about Crime* (New York, 1983).

Wilson, James Q., and Richard J. Herrnstein, *Crime and Human Nature* (New York, 1985).

Wilson, James Q., and Joan Petersilia, eds., *Crime: Public Policies for Crime Control* (Richmond, California, 2002).

Articles

Bork, Robert H., "Travesty Time, Again," *National Review*, March 23, 2005.

Bratton, William, and George Kelling, "There Are No Cracks in the Broken

Windows. Ideological Academics Are Trying to Undermine a Perfectly Good Idea," *National Review*, February 28, 2006.

Butterfield, Fox, "U.S. Crime Figures Were Stable in '00 After 8-Year Drop," *New York Times*, May 31, 2001.

———, "Rate of Serious Crime Held Largely Steady Last Year, Report by F.B.I. Says," *New York Times*, October 28, 2003.

———, "Study Tracks Boom in Prisons and Notes Impact on Counties," *New York Times*, April 30, 2004.

Cassell, Paul G., "Miranda's Social Costs: An Empirical Reassessment," *Northwestern University Law Review* (1996).

Daley, Suzanne, "Man Tells Police He Shot Youths in Subway Train," *New York Times*, January 1, 1985.

Dalrymple, Theodore, "How Criminologists Foster Crime," *City Journal*, Autumn 1999.

DeParle, Jason, "The American Prison Nightmare," *New York Review of Books*, April 12, 2007.

Dewan, Shaila, "The Real Murder Mystery? It's the Low Crime Rate," *New York Times*, August 1, 2009.

"FBI: Crime Declines for Eighth Straight Year; 21-Year Low. Murder Rate Also Is at a 33-Year Low," Associated Press, October 16, 2000.

Fein, Esther B., "Angry Citizens in Many Cities Supporting Goetz," *New York Times*, January 7, 1985.

Gansberg, Martin, "37 Who Saw Murder Didn't Call the Police," *New York Times*, March 27, 1964.

Johnson, Carolyn Y., "Breakthrough on 'Broken Windows.' In Lowell Experiment, Crime Linked to Conditions," *Boston Globe*, February 8, 2009.

Johnson, Kirk, "Goetz Is Cleared in Subway Attack; Gun Count Upheld; Acquittal Won in Shooting of 4 Youths—Prison Term Possible on Weapon Charge," *New York Times*, June 17, 1987.

Keizer, Kees, et al., "The Spreading of Disorder," *Science*, November 20, 2008.

Kelling, George L., "Measuring What Matters: A New Way of Thinking about Crime and Public Order," *City Journal*, Spring 1992.

LeDuff, Charlie, "Getting Away With Murder Is the Norm in Detroit," *Detroit News*, September 10, 2009.

MacDonald, Heather, "Time for the Truth About Black Crime Rates: The Lessons of the Sean Bell Case," *City Journal*, April 2007.

Martinson, Robert, "What Works? Questions and Answers about Prison Reform" *The Public Interest*, Spring 1974.

Moore, Solomon, "California Prisons Must Cut Inmate Population," *New York Times*, August 4, 2009.

National Center for Policy Analysis, "Crime Decreases for Ninth Straight Year," October 23, 2001.

Reuters, "U.S. Violent Crimes Drop for Second Straight Year," June 1, 2009.

Rust, Amy, "Chicago Economist Links Abortion to Falling Crime Rates," *University of Chicago Chronicle*, August 12, 1999.

Sahm, Charles Upton, "Broken Windows Turns 25," *City Journal*, Spring 2007.

"Serious Crime Declines for Fourth Straight Year," Associated Press, May 5, 1996.

Sousa, William H., and George L. Kelling, "Policing Does Matter," *City Journal*, Winter 2002.

Tomasky, Michael, "The Day Everything Changed: How Rudi Giuliani Made Modern New York," *New York Magazine*, September 28, 2008.

Wilson, James Q., "What Works? Revisited: New Findings on Criminal Rehabilitation," *The Public Interest*, Fall 1980.

———, "Crime and American Culture," *The Public Interest*, Winter 1983.

Wilson, James Q., and George L. Kelling, "Broken Windows," *The Atlantic*, March, 1982.

Wood, Daniel B., "State Rethinks Three-Strikes Law: Proposed Initiatives in California Would Give Judges More Leeway in Sentencing," *Christian Science Monitor*, February 28, 2006.

Studies and Reports

Brown, Brian, and Greg Jolivette, "A Primer: Three Strikes—The Impact after More Than a Decade," State of California Legislative Analysts Office, October 2005.

Cassell, Paul G., Bret S. Hayman, "Police Interrogation: An Empirical Study of the Effects of Miranda," *UCLA Law Review* (1996).

Mocan, Naci H., and R. Kaj Gittings, "Pardons, Executions and Homicide," National Bureau of Economic Research, Inc., 2001.

———, "The Impact of Incentives on Human Behavior: Can We Make It Disappear? The Case of the Death Penalty," National Bureau of Economic Research, Inc. (2006).

President's Commission on Law Enforcement and Administration of Justice, "The Challenge of Crime in a Free Society," February 1967.

Reynolds, Morgan O., "Crime and Punishment in America: 1999," National Center for Policy Analysis, October 1, 1999.

Subcommittee on Criminal Laws and Procedure of the Senate Committee on the Judiciary, 90th Congress, "Controlling Crime through More Effective Law Enforcement," 1967.

Supreme Court Decisions

Mapp v. Ohio, 367 U.S. 643 (1961).

Gideon v. Wainwright, 372 U.S. 335 (1962).

Escobedo v. Illinois, 378 U.S. 478 (1964).

Miranda v. Arizona, 384 U.S. 436 (1965).

Furman v. Georgia, 408 U.S. 238 (1976).

Roper v. Simmons, 543 U.S. 551 (2005).

Websites

Bureau of Prisons: http://www.bop.gov/

Department of Justice: http://www.usdoj.gov/

Department of Justice, Prison Statistics: http://www.ojp.usdoj.gov/bjs/prisons. htm

FBI Uniform Crime Statistics: http://www.fbi.gov/ucr/ucr.htm

U.S. Crime Statistics, Total and by State: http://www.disastercenter.com/crime

CHAPTER 3: THE DARKER SIDE OF GREEN

Books

Armfield, Blanche B., et al., *Medical Department of the United States Army in World War II: Organization and Administration in World War II* (Washington, D.C., 1963).

Carson, Rachel, *Silent Spring* (New York, 1962).

Whelan, Elizabeth, *Toxic Terror: The Truth behind the Cancer Scares* (Buffalo, New York, 1993).

Articles

Attaran, Amir, and Rajendra Maharaj, "DDT for Malaria Control Should Not Be Banned," *British Medical Journal*, December 2, 2000.

Bailey, Ronald, "DDT, Eggshells, and Me," *Reason*, January 7, 2004.

Carter, Tom, "Use of DDT Urged in Malaria Fight," *Washington Times*, September 15, 2004.

Dugger, Celia W., "W.H.O. Supports Wider Use of DDT vs. Malaria," *New York Times*, September 16, 2006.

Kristof, Nicholas D., "It's Time to Spray DDT," *New York Times*, January 8, 2005.

Mangu-Ward, Katherine, "Suffering in Silence: Rachel Carson's Ideas Are Still Popular, with Deadly Effect," *Wall Street Journal*, April 20, 2007.

McNeil, Donald G., Jr., "A $10 Mosquito Net Is Making Charity Cool," *New York Times*, June 2, 2008.

Rosenberg, Tina, "What the World Needs Now Is DDT," *New York Times*, April 11, 2004.

Tierney, John, "Fateful Voice of a Generation Still Drowns Out Real Science," *New York Times*, June 5, 2007.

Tren, Richard, and Philip Coticelli, "How DDT Can Stop Millions of Malaria Deaths," *Toronto Globe and Observer*, November 9, 2005.

Zuckerman, Laura, "Worries for Bald Eagles Leaving Endangered List," *Reuters*, April 13, 2007.

Press Releases

Environmental Protection Agency, "DDT Ban Takes Effect," December 31, 1972.

World Health Organization, "WHO Gives Indoor Use of DDT a Clean Bill of Health for Controlling Malaria," September 15, 2006.

Websites

Centers for Disease Control, Malaria Page: http://www.cdc.gov/malaria/facts.htm

Centers for Disease Control, Malaria Statistics: http://www.cdc.gov/malaria/impact/statistics.htm

DDT (dichlorodiphenyltrichloroethane), http://extoxnet.orst.edu/pips/ddt.htm

Environmental Protection Agency, DDT Page: http://www.epa.gov/pbt/pubs/ddt.html

Malaria Foundation International: http://www.malaria.org

World Health Organization, Malaria Page: http://www.who.int/malaria/docs/FAQonDDT.pdf

Speech Transcript

Nobel Prize Presentation, Professor G. Fischer to Dr. Paul Müller (1948).

Papers

Anderson, Daniel, and Joseph Hickey, "Chlorinated Hydrocarbons and Eggshell Changes in Raptorial and Fish-Eating Birds," *Science*, October 1968.

Ratliffe, D. A., "Decrease in Eggshell Weight in Certain Birds of Prey," *Nature* (July 8, 1967).

Tren, Richard, and Roger Bate, "When Politics Kills: Malaria and the DDT Story," Competitive Enterprise Institute, January 2001.

CHAPTER 4: *ROE* V. THE PEOPLE

Books

Balkin, Jack, *What* Roe v. Wade *Should Have Said: The Nation's Top Legal Experts Rewrite America's Most Controversial Decision* (New York, 2005).

Greenhouse, Linda, *Becoming Justice Blackmun: Harry Blackmun's Supreme Court Journey* (New York, 2005).

Solinger, Rickie, *Abortion Wars: A Half Century of Struggle, 1950–2000* (Berkeley, California, 1998).

Terry, Randall, *Operation Rescue* (Springdale, Pennsylvania, 1988).

Tribe, Laurence H., *Abortion: The Clash of Absolutes* (New York, 1990).

Articles

Corpus, Leilani, "Operation Rescue and Civil Rights Movement of the 1960s," *Forerunner*, September 1988.

Doyle, Michael, "Partial-Birth Abortion Ruling Could Lead to More Restrictions," *McClatchy-Tribune*, May 27, 2007.

Eastland, Terry, "Blackmun's Constitution," *Weekly Standard*, March 11, 2004.

Feldmann, Linda, "The Abortion Wars 30 Years After *Roe v. Wade*," *Christian Science Monitor*, January 22, 2003.

Goldberg, Michelle, "Abortion Under Siege in Mississippi," *Salon*, August 1, 2006.

Harmon, Amy, "Prenatal Test Puts Down Syndrome in Hard Focus," *New York Times*, May 9, 2007.

Hendershott, Anne, "How Support for Abortion Became Kennedy Dogma," *Wall Street Journal*, January 1, 2009.

Hentoff, Nat "The Democrats and Abortion," September 12, 2008.

Kissling, Frances, "Can We Ever Say a Woman Can't Choose?" *Salon*, June 21, 2009.

Lott, John R., Jr., "It's Not Enough to Be 'Wanted'; Illegitimacy Has Risen Despite—Indeed, Because of—Legal Abortion," *Wall Street Journal*, June 19, 2007.

Mauro, Tonay, "Blackmun Clerks Had Too Much Power, Says Historian," *Legal Times*, April 18, 2005.

Page, Susan, " *Roe v. Wade:* The Divided States of America," *USA Today*, April 17, 2006.

Ryckman, Lisa, "Ground Zero on Abortion: Four Decades Ago, Colorado Became First State in the Nation to Liberalize Law," *Rocky Mountain News*, April 24, 2007.

Saletan, William, "Fatal Vision: The Suicidal Idealism of Abortion Activists," *Slate*, October 3, 2003.

Stafford, Terry, "The Abortion Wars: What Most Christians Don't Know About the History of Prolife Struggles," *Christianity Today*, January 1, 2003.

Townsend, Tim, "Could St. Louis Lose Its Catholic Hospitals Under New Federal Abortion Legislation?" *St. Louis Post-Dispatch,* March 6, 2009.

Wolf, Naomi, "Our Bodies, Our Souls," *The New Republic*, October 16, 1995.

Supreme Court Decisions

Poe v. Ullman, 367 U.S. 497 (1961).

Griswold et al. v. Connecticut, 381 U.S. 479 (1965).

Roe v. Wade, 410 U.S. 113 (1973).

Doe v. Bolton, 410 U.S. 179 (1973).

Harris v. McRae, 448 U.S. 297 (1980).

Webster v. Reproductive Health Services, 492 U.S. 490 (1989).

Planned Parenthood of Southern Pennsylvania v. Casey, 505 U.S. 833 (1992).

Ayotte v. Planned Parenthood of Northern New England, 546 U.S. 320 (2006).

Legal Memoranda

Tribe, Laurence H., "Memorandum Addressing the Constitutionality of a Partial-Birth Abortion Ban," March 6, 1997.

Legislation

Freedom of Access to Clinic Entrances Act: http://www.usdoj.gov/crt/split/facestat.php

CHAPTER 5: GAIA'S CHILDREN

CAFE STANDARDS

Articles

Adelman, Ken, "Road Regs: Wrongs That Don't Make Rights," *National Review*, January 17, 2002.

Balis, Ryan, "CAFE Standards Kill: Congress' Regulatory Solution to Foreign Oil Dependence Comes at a Steep Price," National Center for Public Policy Analysis, July 2006.

Burnett, H. Sterling, "CAFE's Three Strikes—It Should Be Out," National Center for Policy Analysis, February 13, 2002.

Caterinicchia, Dan, "Fuel Standards Will Force Lighter Autos," Associated Press, December 23, 2008.

DeFalco, June, "The Deadly Effects of Fuel Economy Standards: CAFE's Lethal Impact on Auto Safety," The Competitive Enterprise Institute's Automobility and Freedom Project, June 1999.

Grady, Robert E., "Light Cars Are Dangerous Cars," *Wall Street Journal*, May 22, 2009.

Kazman, Sam, "Regulated to Death: Obama's CAFE Standards Will Prove Bad for Business and Lethal for Consumers," *National Review*, June 22, 2009.

———, "Small Cars Are Dangerous Cars," *Wall Street Journal*, April 17, 2009.

Koppelman, Alex, "Are the New Fuel Standards Worth the Cost?" *Salon*, May 19, 2009.

Laffer William G., "Auto CAFE Standards: Unsafe and Unwise at Any Level," Heritage Foundation, April 19, 1991.

Schmidt, Charles W., "Debate Percolates over CAFE Standards—Spheres of Influence," *Environmental Health Perspectives*, August, 2002.

Studies

Crandall, Robert W., and John D. Graham, "The Effect of Fuel Economy Standards on Automobile Safety," *Journal of Law and Economics*, April 1989.

Healey James R., "Death by the Gallon," *USA Today*, July 2, 1999.

National Research Council, "Effectiveness and Impact of Corporate Average Fuel Economy (CAFE) Standards," National Research Council (U.S.) Committee on the Effectiveness and Impact of Corporate Average Fuel Economy (CAFE) Standards, Washington, 2002.

Portney, Paul R., et al., "Effectiveness and Impact of Corporate Average Fuel Economy (CAFE) Standards," National Academy of Sciences, 2002.

ASBESTOS

Articles

Alleman, James E., and Brooke T. Mossman, "Asbestos Revisited," *Scientific American*, July 1997.

Hooper, Joseph, "The Asbestos Mess," *New York Times Magazine*, November 25, 1990.

Lange, J. H., "Emergence of a New Policy for Asbestos: A Result of the World Trade Center Tragedy," *Indoor and Built Environment*, 2004.

Lemonick, Michael D., and Andrea Dorfman, "Environment: An Overblown Asbestos Scare?" *Time*, January 29, 1990.

Mossman, Brooke T., and J. Bernard Gee, "Asbestos-Related Diseases," *New England Journal of Medicine*, July 29, 1989.

Mossman, Brooke T., et al., "Asbestos: Scientific Developments and Implications for Public Policy," *Science*, 1990.

Stevens, William K., "Despite Asbestos Risk, Experts See No Cause for 'Fiber Phobia,'" *New York Times*, September 5, 1989.

————, "Risk Is Seen in Needless Removal of Asbestos," *New York Times*, January 19, 1990.

Warrick, Joby, "Study Questions Cancer Threat from Asbestos: Moderate Levels of Exposure Didn't Increase Rate for Quebec Women, Team Finds," *Washington Post*, May 28, 1998.

Studies

Banks, D. E., et al., "American College of Chest Physicians Consensus Statement on the Respiratory Health Effects of Asbestos: Results of a Delphi Study," *Chest*, 2009.

Camus, Michel, "Nonoccupational Exposure to Chrysotile Asbestos and the Risk of Lung Cancer," *New England Journal of Medicine*, May 28, 1998.

Guthrie, George D., Jr., "Biological Effects of Inhaled Minerals," *American Mineralogist*, April 1992.

Brochures and Handbooks

United States Environmental Protection Agency, Control Action Division, "School Asbestos Program. Questions and Answers," April 1979.

United States Environmental Protection Agency, "Asbestos Fact Book," August 1995.

Websites

http://www.epa.gov/asbestos/

Asbestos Exposure and Cancer Risk—National Cancer Institute: http://www.cancer.gov/cancertopics/factsheet/Risk/asbestos

The Asbestos and Mesothelioma Center: http://www.asbestos.com/

Safety and Health Topics, Asbestos: http://www.osha.gov/SLTC/asbestos/

ASTHMA

Articles

Fishman, Henry J., "Patients Balk at New Asthma Inhalers: HFA Inhalers Are Better for the Environment but How about the Patients?" *Consumer Affairs*, December 7, 2007.

McCormick, Lisa Wade, "Victims of Government: Asthma Patients' Lives Shattered by 'Green' Inhalers," *Consumer Affairs*, September 8, 2009.

McGuire, Kim, "Asthma Sufferers Must Go 'Green' on Inhalers This Week," *St. Louis Post-Dispatch*, December 28, 2008.

Payne, January W. "So Long, 2008—and Farewell, Cheap Asthma Inhalers," *U.S. News & World Report*, December 31, 2008.

Schroeder, Michael, "Ozone Fears Put Inhalers at Issue," *Fort Wayne Journal Gazette*, March 29, 2009.

———, "Ozone-Friendly Inhalers Could Face Early Demise," *Fort Wayne Journal Gazette*, March 30, 2009.

"Switch to 'Green' Inhalers Costly," *Detroit News*, December 2, 2008.

Tarkan, Laurie, "Rough Transition to a New Asthma Inhaler," *New York Times*, May 13, 2008.

Wade, Lisa, "Asthma Sufferers Live in Fear of New Inhalers: Do New Rules Pit Human Life against the Ozone Layer?" *Consumer Affairs*, February 16, 2009.

UNITED NATIONS AGREEMENT

The 1987 Montreal Protocol on Substances That Deplete the Ozone Layer—United Nations Environment Programme.

BEARS, COUGARS, ETC.

Articles

Alford, Roger, "The Three Bears? Try 163,000 . . . and Counting," Associated Press, June 13, 2009.

Brown, Matthew, "Grizzly Attacks Evoke Response," Associated Press, December 4, 2007.

Correll, DeeDee, "To Shoot Coyotes or Shoo Them?" *Los Angeles Times*, May 11, 2009.

"Cougar Attacks Increasing in West," Associated Press, August 8, 1998.

Latshaw, Greg, and Marty Roney, "Coyote Migration Worries Urban East," *USA Today*, August 12, 2009.

Vallis, Mary, "Toronto Musician Dies After Coyote Attack in Cape Breton," *National Post*, October 28, 2009.

Studies

Timm, Robert M., et al., "Coyote Attacks: An Increasing Suburban Problem," Hopland Research and Extension Center, University of California, 2004.

BULBS

Articles

Carney, Brian M. "Bye Bye, Light Bulb," *Wall Street Journal*, January 2, 2008.

Deutsch, Claudia H., "No Joke, Bulb Change Is Challenge for U.S.," *New York Times* December 22, 2007.

Gray, Richard, and Julia McWatt, "Energy Saving Light Bulbs Offer Dim Future," *Daily Telegraph*, August 29, 2009.

Hamilton, Tyler, "Future Is Dim for Light Bulb: Province to Ban Wasteful Incandescents by 2012 to Cut Electricity Consumption," *Toronto Star*, April 19, 2007.

Lavelle, Marianne, "FAQ: The End of the Light Bulb As We Know It," *U.S. News & World Report*, December 19, 2007.

Lott, John R., Jr., "Looking at Fluorescent Bulbs in Different Light," June 3, 2008.

HALONS

Articles

Browne, Malcolm W., "As Halon Ban Nears, Researchers Seek a New Miracle Firefighter," *New York Times*, December 15, 1992.

Butler, James H., et al., "Growth and Distribution of Halons in the Atmosphere," *Journal of Geophysical Research*, October 1998.

Keafer, Yvonne M., "Protection without Halon: What Are the Alternatives?" *Disaster Recovery Journal*, July 29, 1998.

Websites

EPA Halon Final Rule Summary: http://www.epa.gov/spdpublc/title6/608/halons/halsumm.pdf

Halons and Halon Blends: http://www.epa.gov/ozone/title6/608/halons/halsumm.html

Protection of Stratospheric Ozone: Manufacture of Halon Blends, Intentional Release of Halon, Technician Training and Disposal of Halon and Halon-Containing Equipment: http://www.epa.gov/EPA-AIR/1998/March/Day–05/a5720.htm

CHAPTER 6: DEATH'S PAVEMENT

Books

Bosco, Dominick, *Bedlam. A Year in the Life of a Mental Hospital* (New York, 1992).

Caro, Robert A., *The Power Broker. Robert Moses and the Fall of New York* (New York, 1970).

Foley, H. A., and S. S. Sharfstein, *Madness and Government: Who Cares for the Mentally Ill?"* (Washington, D.C., 1983).

Isaac, Rael Jean, and Virginia C. Armat, *Madness in the Streets: How Psychiatry and the Law Abandoned the Mentally Ill* (New York, 1990).

Laing, R. D., *The Divided Self* (New York, 1969).

Powers, Stephen P., and Stanley Rothman, *The Least Dangerous Branch? Consequences of Judicial Activism* (Westport, Connecticut, 2002).

Szasz, Thomas, *The Myth of Mental Illness: Foundation of a Theory of Personal Conduct* (New York, 1961).

———, *The Manufacture of Madness: A Comparative Study of the Inquisition and the Mental Health Movement* (New York, 1970).

Torrey, E. Fuller, *Nowhere to Go: The Tragic Odyssey of the Homeless Mentally Ill* (New York, 1988).

Articles

Allen, Charlotte, "The ACLU Against the Cities," *City Journal*, Spring 1994.

Barbanel, Josh, "Joyce Brown Obtains a Ban on Medicine," *New York Times*, January 16, 1988.

Burden, Amanda, "Jane Jacobs, Robert Moses and City Planning Today," *Gotham Gazette*, November 6, 2006.

Campbell, Duncan, "300,000 Mentally Ill in US Prisons," *Guardian*, March 3, 2003.

Constans, Gabriel, "This Is Madness. Our Failure to Provide Adequate Care for the Mentally Ill," *USA Today*, November 1991.

Dowdall, George, "Mental Hospitals and Deinstitutionalization," in C. Aneshensel and J. Phelan, eds, *Handbook of the Sociology of Mental Health*, (New York, 1999).

Elias, Marilyn, "Mentally Ill Die 25 Years Earlier, on Average," *USA Today*, May 3, 2007.

Lamb, H. Richard, "Will We Save the Homeless Mentally Ill?" *American Journal of Psychiatry*, May 1990.

MacDonald, Heather, "The Reclamation of Skid Row," *City Journal*, November 9, 2007.

O'Donnell, Eugene, "Cops and the Mentally Ill: How Police Can Better Handle Emotionally Disturbed Citizens," *Newsweek*, July 31, 2008.

Pearson, Erica, "The Power Broker Revisited," *Gotham Gazette*, August 18, 2003.

Reich, R., "Care of the Chronically Mentally Ill: A National Disgrace," *American Journal of Psychiatry*, August 1973.

Rochefort , D. A., "Origins of the 'Third Psychiatric Revolution': The Community Mental Health Centers Act of 1963," *Journal of Health Politics, Policy and Law*, Spring 1984.

Talbott, John A., "Deinstitutionalization: Avoiding the Disasters of the Past," *Psychiatric Services*, October 2004.

Torrey, E. Fuller, "Hippie Healthcare Policy," *Washington Monthly*, April 2002.

Torrey, E. Fuller, and Mary Zdanowicz, "Deinstitutionalization Hasn't Worked," *Washington Post*, July 9, 1999.

———, "Why Deinstitutionalization Turned Deadly," *Wall Street Journal*, August 4, 1998.

Trujillo, Manuel, et al., "Deinstitutionalizing the Mentally Ill," *City Journal*, Spring 1993.

Surveys, Studies, and Reports

Burt, Martha R., et al., "Homelessness. Programs and the People They Serve: Findings of the National Survey of Homeless Assistance Providers and Clients," December 1999.

Department of Housing and Urban Development, "Review of Stewart B. McKinney Homeless Assistance Programs Administered by HUD," January 1995.

Kondratas, S. Anna, "A Strategy for Helping America's Homeless," Heritage Foundation, May 6, 1985.

Lamb, H. Richard, "The Homeless Mentally Ill: A Task Force Report of the American Psychiatric Association," 1985.

Leshner, Alan I., et al., "Outcasts on Main Street: Report of the Federal Task Force on Homelessness and Severe Mental Illness," U.S. Department of Health and Human Services (1992).

Legislation
Stewart B. McKinney Homeless Assistance Act of 1987 P.L. 100–77; 101 STAT. 482; 42 U.S.C. 11301 et seq.

Websites
National Coalition for the Homeless: http://www.nationalhomeless.org
National Law Center on Homelessness and Poverty: http://www.nlchp.org
The Bazelon Center for Mental Health Law: http://www.bazelon.org

CHAPTER 7: SHORT TAKES

DYFS

Articles
Aaron, Lawrence, "DYFS Reform Should Be First Priority for Corzine," *Bergen Record*, January 20, 2006.

Alaya, Ana M., "Taking a Young Life Often Means Lesser Sentence: A Review Finds the Average Prison Time Was 11 Years for Those Convicted in Child Homicide Cases," *Newark Star-Ledger*, August 24, 2003.

"Arizona's Child Protective Services Is Receiving Low Marks from a National Child Welfare Expert," Associated Press, November 2, 2007.

Chan, Sue, "N.J.'s 10-Year-Old Murder Suspect: Boy Charged in Tot Killing Was Terror of Neighborhood," Associated Press, March, 29, 2003.

Froonjian, John, "Office of the Child Advocate Stops Publishing Reports," *Press of Atlantic City*, August 3, 2009.

Hansen, Jane O., "Did 5-year-old Terrell Have to Die? Child Protection System Failed Him—and Covered Up the Truth," *Atlanta Journal-Constitution*, October 17, 1999.

Kocieniewski, David, "Abuse Complaints Filed on Father in Murder-Suicide," *New York Times*, July 11, 2003.

Lipka, Mitch, "Optimism on DYFS Overhaul Remains, Despite Slow Progress," *Philadelphia Inquirer*, May 3, 2004.

Litsky, Frank, "Giant Is Seen Facing Charge in Boy's Death," *New York Times*, May 15, 2001.

Livio, Susan K., "DYFS Fails 4 Starving Children. Camden County Couple Arrested, 5 State Workers Suspended in Case," *Newark Star-Ledger*, October 26, 2003.

———, "Davy's Swearing-in Is Called Good News for DYFS Children," *Newark Star-Ledger*, April 15, 2004.

———, "Abuse Claims Involving Parent's Partner Would Get 'High-Risk' Label," *Newark Star-Ledger*, April 29, 2004.

———, "Settlements Restore Jobs of 9 Fired DYFS Workers," *Newark Star-Ledger*, May 27, 2004.

———, "Four Boys to Share $12.5M Settlement in Starvation Case; Payout Is Jersey's Biggest for Child Abuse Lawsuit," *Newark Star-Ledger*, October 1, 2005.

Navarro, Mireya, "Florida Will Tighten Child Welfare Policies After Father's Killing of Girl, 6," *New York Times*, December 5, 1998.

"No Blame Assigned to Agency in Case of Boy Charged in Killing," *New York Times*, April 6, 2003.

Rothman, Carly J., "Camden Boy's Death Spurs More Doubts about DYFS Reforms," *Newark Star-Ledger*, April 12, 2009.

Schneider, Craig, "Georgia's Child Welfare Chief Resigns," *Atlanta Journal-Constitution*, March 3, 2008.

Stainton, Lilo K., "Boy's Death Puts DYFS on the Spot," *New Brunswick Home News Tribune*, April 22, 2004.

Stein, Rob, "Report Cites Abuse of 91,000 Babies Under 1," *Washington Post*, April 4, 2008.

Wald, Jonathan, "Report Slams N.J. Child Welfare System," *CNN*, June 12, 2003.

Studies and Reports

Alan Guttmacher Institute, "State Policies in Brief: Infant Abandonment," June 2005.

Bolling, I. M., "Adoption Trends in 2003: Infant Abandonment and Safe Haven Legislation," October 21, 2005.

Websites

Administration for Children and Families, Child Welfare and Neglect: http://www.childwelfare.gov/can/

Child Abuse Statistics: http://aia.berkeley.edu/publications/fact_sheets/boader_defs.php

DENGUE

Articles

"Dengue Fever a Risk in South Texas, US CDC Says," Reuters, August 9, 2007.

Stevenson, Mark, "Dengue Surging in Mexico, Latin America," Associated Press, March 30, 2007.

———, "Lethal Type of Dengue Fever Hits Mexico," Associated Press, April 1, 2007.

Wade, Betsy, "Dengue Fever Alert in Parts of Texas," *New York Times*, November 10, 1996.

Studies

Centers for Disease Control, "Underdiagnosis of Dengue—Laredo, Texas, 1999," February 2, 2001.

———, "Dengue Fever Seroprevalence and Risk Factors, Texas–Mexico Border, 2004," *Emerging Infectious Diseases*, October 2007.

Websites

World Health Organization Dengue Fever Information Page: http://www.who.
int/mediacentre/factsheets/fs117/en/

GUN-FREE ZONES

Books

Lott, John R., *The Bias Against Guns: Why Almost Everything You've Heard about Gun Control Is Wrong* (Chicago, 2003).

Articles

Archibold, Randal C., "Arizona Weighs Bill to Allow Guns on Campuses," *New York Times*, March 5, 2008.

Boccella, Kathy, "Student Group Pushes for Right to Carry Concealed Weapons on Campus," *Philadelphia Inquirer*, January 3, 2008.

Bowman, Rex, "Helping to Stop a Killer: Students Went After Law School Gunman," *Richmond Times Dispatch*, May 5, 2002.

Dewan, Shaila, and Liz Robbins, "A Previous Death at the Hand of Alabama Suspect," *New York Times*, February 13, 2010.

Dewan, Shaila, and Katie Zezima, "Twists Multiply in Alabama Shooting Case," *New York Times*, February 14, 2010.

"'Inexcusable' Actions in Va. Tech Killings Report," Associated Press, December 5, 2009.

Kopel, David B., "Gun-Free Zones," *Wall Street Journal*, April 18, 2007.

Meyer, Jeremy P., "7,000 at New Life Church When Shots Fired," *Denver Post*, December 10, 2007.

Schulte, Brigid, and Tim Craig, "Unknown to Va. Tech, Cho Had a Disorder: Fairfax Helped Student Cope with Anxiety," *Washington Post*, August 27, 2007.

Suchetka, Diane, "Ex-Charlottean: I Helped Nab Suspect," *Charlotte Observer*, January 18, 2002.

Sullum, Jacob, "The Gun Ban and the Gunman: Virginia Tech's Gun-Free Zone Left Cho Seung-Hui's Victims Defenseless," *Reason*, April 18, 2007.

Supreme Court Case

United States v. Lopez, 514 U.S. 549 (1995).

FDA

Articles

"FDA Issues Final Rules to Help Patients Gain Access to Investigational Drugs," *Oncology*, September 11, 2009.

Goldstein, Jacob, "Judge Rules PTC Therapeutics Must Give Experimental Drug to Teen," *Wall Street Journal*, August 21, 2008.

Groopman, Jerome, "The Right to a Trial: Should Dying Patients Have Access to Experimental Drugs?" *New Yorker*, December 18, 2006.

Trowbridge, Ronald L., and Steven Walker, "The FDA's Deadly Track Record," *Wall Street Journal*, August 14, 2007.

Walker, Steven, "A Different 'Right to Life,'" *Wall Street Journal*, January 11, 2008.

Willman, David, "How a New Policy Led to Seven Deadly Drugs," *Los Angeles Times*, December 20, 2000.

Court Case

Abigail Alliance for Better Access to Developmental Drugs v. von Eschenbach

Legislation

ACCESS (Access, Compassion, Care, and Ethics for Seriously Ill Patients) Act

Website

www.Abigail-alliance.org

CHAPTER 8: KISS TOMORROW GOOD-BYE

NEUROLAW

Articles

Rosen, Jeffrey, "The Brain on the Stand," *New York Times,* March 11, 2007.

Schulz, Kathryn, "Brave Neuro World," *The Nation*, January 9, 2006.

Tallis, Raymond, "Why Blame Me? It Was All My Brain's Fault; The Dubious Rise of 'Neurolaw,'" *Times* (London), October 24, 2007.

EUTHANASIA

Books

Betzold, Michael, *Appointment with Doctor Death* (Royal Oak, Michigan, 1993).

Sereny, Gitta, *Into That Darkness: An Examination of Conscience* (New York, 1983).

Smith, Wesley J., *The Culture of Death: The Assault on Medical Ethics in America* (New York, 2000).

———, *Forced Exit: Euthanasia, Assisted Suicide, and the New Duty to Die* (New York, 2006).

Articles

Burleigh, Michael, "Nazi 'Euthanasia' Programs," in Dieter Kuntz and Susan Bachrach, eds., *Deadly Medicine: Creating the Master Race* (Chapel Hill, North Carolina, 2004).

"Body Found in Van Registered to Kevorkian," CNN, January 29, 1996.

Fearon, Peter, "Prison Hasn't Mellowed Dr. Death," *New York Times*, June 4, 2007.

Gerber, Leslie, "From Mengele to Kevorkian? The Significance of Nazi Euthanasia for the Contemporary Right-to-Die Debate," *Issues in Integrative Studies*, 2000.

Goodnough, Abby, and Maria Newman, "Schiavo's Feeding Tube Removed at Judge's Order," *New York Times,* March 18, 2005.

Granberry, Michael, "Kevorkian to Sue to Keep Medical License. Euthanasia: 'Dr. Death,' Who Helped a Costa Mesa Man and 19 Other People End Their Lives, Will Also Challenge State Law Prohibiting Physician-Assisted Suicide," *Los Angeles Times*, July 29, 1994.

Hentoff, Nat, "Terri Schiavo's Lifesaving Legacy," *Jewish World Review*, April 3, 2008.

"Jury Gets Kevorkian Case," CNN, March 7, 1996.

"Kevorkian Charged with Murder in Euthanasia Case: Prosecutors Take Doctor Up on Challenge," CNN, November 25, 1998.

Lessenberry, Jack, "Death Becomes Him," *Vanity Fair*, July 1994.

Lyons, Patrick J., "Dr. Death Is Released," *New York Times*, June 1, 2007.

McNeil, Donald G., Jr., "In Feeding-Tube Case, Many Neurologists Back Courts," *New York Times*, October 26, 2003.

Nizza, Mike, "Thousands Back Kevorkian Candidacy," *New York Times*, July 8, 2008.

Parker, Laura, "As House Passes Bill to Delay Schiavo Case, Senate Unsure," *USA Today*, March 17, 2005.

Roscoe, Lori A., et al., "A Comparison of Characteristics of Kevorkian Euthanasia Cases and Physician-Assisted Suicides in Oregon," *Gerontologist*, 2001.

Smith, Wesley J., "Euthanasia World: The Worst Culture," *National Review*, October 17, 2003.

———, " 'Human Non-Person': Terri Schiavo, Bioethics, and Our Future," *National Review*, March 29, 2005.

———, "Awakenings: The Schiavo Case Revisited," *Weekly Standard*, November 5, 2007.

Sullivan, Sarah, "Kervorkian: The Rube Goldberg of Death," *Cornerstone Magazine*, 1997.

SOROS

Articles

Arnold, Robert, et al., "Pioneer Programs in Palliative Care: Nine Case Studies," Milbank Memorial Fund and Robert Wood Johnson Foundation, October 2000.

Barra, Paul A., "How We Die Today: Medicine and the End of Life in the 21st Century," *North Carolina Register*, October 7–13, 2007.

Goldberg, Carey, "Major Work on End of Life Is Dying Now: Big Donors Move On after $200 Million in Studies, Programs," *Boston Globe*, November 16, 2003.

McConnell, Kathryn, "U.S. Specialists Bring Palliative Care Training to Ukraine," *Voice of America*, December 24, 2008.

"Mourning the Loss of End-of-Life Funding," *Florida Hospices and Palliative Care*, June 20, 2005.

Speeches, Interviews, and Press Releases

"An Interview with Kathleen M. Foley," *Memorial Sloan-Kettering Cancer Center*, October 2002.

"Project on Death in America Awards 1 Million Dollars to the Arts and Humanities," *Project on Death in America*, August 1, 2000.

Speech by George Soros for the Alexander Ming Fisher Lecture Series at Columbia Presbyterian Medical Center, November 30, 1994.

STEM CELLS

Articles

Ackerman, Todd, "Stem Cells Put to the Test in Stroke Treatment," *Houston Chronicle*, March 31, 2009.

Anderson, Ryan T., "The End of the Stem-Cell Wars: A Victory for Science, for the Pro-life Movement, and for President Bush," *Weekly Standard*, December 3, 2007.

Condic, Maureen L., "What We Know about Embryonic Stem Cells," *First Things*, January 2007.

Conner, Steve, "British Scientists to Create 'Synthetic' Blood," *The Independent*, March 23, 2009.

Fumento, Michael, "The Great Stem-Cell-Research Scam," *New York Post*, July 15, 2009.

Jamieson, Alistair, "Stem Cells are More Flexible Than Previously Thought, Research Suggests," *Daily Telegraph*, November 23, 2008.

Kolata, Gina, "Man Who Helped Start Stem Cell War May End It," *International Herald Tribune*, November 11, 2007.

Krauthammer, Charles, "President Bush Got It Right Regarding Embryonic Stem Cell Research," *Washington Post*, December 1, 2007.

Lefkowitz, Jay P., "Stem Cells and the President—An Inside Account," *Commentary*, January 2008.

Randerson, James, "Surgeons Attempt to Repair Hearts with Stem Cell Injections," *The Guardian*, January 23, 2008.

Ritter, Malcolm, "SD Scientists Produce Embryo Clones of Two Men, Using Skin Cells," Associated Press, January 17, 2008.

Stein, Rob, "Advance Could Quiet Stem Cell Controversy: Scientists Able to Transform Adult Cell," *Washington Post*, August 28, 2008.

———, "Scientists Find Way to Regress Adult Cells to Embryonic State: Researchers Hopeful That Recent Breakthroughs Could Lead to Clinical Applications," *Washington Post*, September 25, 2008.

———, "Researchers Find Safer Way to Produce Stem Cell Alternative: Skin Cells Transformed Without Worrisome Use of Viruses," *Washington Post*, March 2, 2009.

CHAPTER 9: "LET ME BE CLEAR"

CAFE STANDARDS

Articles

Broder, John M., "Obama Directs Regulators to Tighten Auto Rules," *New York Times*, January 26, 2009.

Feller, Ben, "Obama Orders Push to Cleaner, More Efficient Cars," Associated Press, January 27, 2009.

Power, Stephen, and Christopher Conkey, "U.S. Orders Stricter Fuel Goals for Autos," *Wall Street Journal*, May 19, 2009.

ABORTION

Articles

Alonso-Zaldivar, Ricardo, "Obama to Rescind Bush Abortion Rule, Official Says," Associated Press, February 27, 2009.

Conlon, Michael, "U.S. Bishops Warn Obama on Abortion Issues," Reuters, November 12, 2008.

Connolly, John P., "D.C.-Area Bishops to Enforce Communion Ban on Sebelius," *The Bulletin* (Philadelphia), April 1, 2009.

Neuhaus, Richard John, "Obama and the Bishops," *First Things*, November 7, 2008.

Wilson, Reid, "Sebelius to Face Questions over Abortion," *The Hill*, March 1, 2009.

STEM CELLS

Articles

Aldhous, Peter, "Stem Cell Spinal Injury Trial Put on Hold," *New Scientist* August 24, 2009.

George, Robert P., and Eric Cohen, "The President Politicizes Stem-Cell Research: Taxpayers Have a Right to Be Left Out of It," *Wall Street Journal*, March 10, 2009.

Malkin, Bonnie, "MS Sufferer Walks After Stem Cell Treatment," *Daily Telegraph*, December 14, 2009.

Saletan, William, "Winning Smugly: You Just Won the Stem-cell War: Don't Lose Your Soul," *Slate*, March 9, 2009.

Stolberg, Sheryl Gay, "Obama Puts His Own Spin on Mix of Science with Politics," *New York Times*, March 9, 2009.

Vergano, Dan, "NIH Prohibits Stem Cells from Embryos Created for Science," *USA Today*, April 17, 2009.

CAP AND TRADE

Articles

Barton, Joe L., "Sending Us Back to 1875. Reducing our Carbon Footprint," *Washington Times*, May 10, 2009.

Broder, John M., "House Passes Bill to Address Threat of Climate Change," *New York Times*, June 26, 2009.

Legislation
H.R. 2454—American Clean Energy and Security Act of 2009

HEALTH CARE: U.K.

Articles
Asman, David, "There's No Place Like Home," *Wall Street Journal*, June 8, 2005.
Boseley, Sarah, "NHS Accused of 17,000 Unnecessary Deaths," *The Guardian*, January 18, 2008.
Devlin, Kate, "Barack Obama Healthcare: NHS Patients Missing Out, British Expert Warns," *Daily Telegraph*, August 12, 2009.
———, "Sentenced to Death on the NHS," *Daily Telegraph*, September 2, 2009.
Donnelly, Laura, "Patients Forced to Wait Hours in Ambulances Parked Outside A&E Departments," *Daily Telegraph*, May 30, 2009.
Fleming, Nic, "190,000 Patients Harmed by Hospital Safety Lapses," *Daily Telegraph*, July 22, 2005.
Hall, Celia, "One NHS Patient in 10 'Is Harmed in Hospital,'" *Daily Telegraph*, July 6, 2006.
Hannan, Daniel, "Americans! Don't Copy the British Healthcare System!" *Daily Telegraph*, April 6, 2009.
Hawkes, Nigel, "Go Private or Wait 80 Weeks, Patient Told," *Times* (London), June 18, 2005.
Lea, Michael, "Starved to Death in an NHS Hospital: Damning Inquiry Highlights Case of Patient Left Without Food for 26 Days," *Daily Mail*, January 9, 2009.
Light, Donald W., "Universal Health Care: Lessons from the British Experience," *American Journal of Public Health*, January 2003.
Marsh, Beezy, and Tom Harper, "Blunders by NHS Kill Thousands of Patients Each Year," *Daily Telegraph*, August 28, 2006.
Martin, Daniel, "Organs of 50 NHS Donors Are Sold to Foreigners Who Pay £75,000 for Each Operation," *Daily Mail*, January 4, 2009.
Martin, Nicole, "UK Cancer Survival Rate Lowest in Europe," *Daily Telegraph*, August 24, 2007.
Moore, Matthew, "Mistakes on Maternity Wards Put Mothers at Risk," *Daily Telegraph*, October 8, 2008.
Murphy, Joe, "London Suffering from Shocking Rise in Rare 'Victorian' Diseases," *Daily Mail*, April 15, 2009.
Rice-Oxley, Mark, "British Healthcare in Crisis Despite Massive Investment," *Christian Science Monitor*, October 19, 2007.
Smith, Rebecca, "Hospital Blunders 'Kill 90,000 Patients,'" *Daily Telegraph*, November 30, 2007.
Swaine, Jon, "Deaths Caused by Hospital Mistakes 'Up 60 Per Cent in Two Years,'" *Daily Telegraph*, January 6, 2009.

Templeton, Sarah-Kate, "Experts Push NHS to Use US-Style Cancer Care," *Times* (London), August 26, 2007.

Weaver, Claire, and Linda Simalis, "Our Health System Basically 'Broke,'" *Daily Telegraph*, February 1, 2009.

Winnett, Robert, "Patients 'Should Not Expect NHS to Save Their Life if It Costs Too Much,'" *Daily Telegraph*, August 12, 2008.

HEALTH CARE: CANADA

Articles

Esmail, Nadeem, "'Too Old' for Hip Surgery," *Wall Street Journal*, February 9, 2009.

Fekadu, Mesfin, "Doctor: Lack of Medical Helicopter Cost Actress," Associated Press, March 21, 2009.

Gratzer, David, "The Ugly Truth about Canadian Health Care," *City Journal*, Summer 2007.

Harrop, Froma, "Don't Use Canada for Health-Care Model," *Real Clear Politics*, February 27, 2007.

"Incoming Director of Canadian Healthcare System Says System Is in Trouble," *Canadian Press*, August 17, 2009.

Krauss, Clifford, "Canada's Private Clinics Surge as Public System Falters," *New York Times*, February 28, 2006.

Talaga, Tanya, "Patients Suing Province over Wait Times," *Toronto Star*, September 6, 2007.

Vadum, Matthew, "Did Canada's Universal Health Care Kill Natasha Richardson?" *American Spectator*, March 21, 2009.

HEALTH CARE: AUSTRALIA

Articles

Carty, Lisa, "Wait for It: Surgery List Now Even Longer," *Sydney Morning Herald*, June 7, 2009.

Guan, Lilia, "Australian Healthcare Lags in IT, Service Providers Critical," *CRN*, March 14, 2008.

Hedge, Mike, "Australian Healthcare 'Still in the 80s,'" *The West Australian*, March 29, 2008.

HEALTH CARE: JAPAN

Articles

Yamaguchi, Mari, "Injured Man Dies After Rejection by 14 Hospitals," Associated Press, February 4, 2009.

OBAMACARE

Articles

Atlas, Scott, "ObamaCare: Kiss Your Access Good-bye," *Real Clear Politics*, June 23, 2009.

Brown, Carrie Budoff, "Barack Obama's Health Plan Takes Shape," *Politico*, June 1, 2009.

Carlson, Heather J., "Mayo Clinic Leery of Public Health Plan," *Rochester Post-Bulletin*, July 10, 2009.

Catron, David, "Obamacare Could Kill You," *American Spectator*, January 15, 2009.

Hillyer, Quin, "Death Panels by Proxy," *American Spectator*, August 24, 2009.

Lucas, Fred, "Arizona Moves to Oppose Obama's Expected Health Care Mandates," CNS News, June 30, 2009.

Meckler, Laura, "Tough Questions Dog Health-Care Overhaul," *Wall Street Journal*, March 3, 2009.

Pear, Robert, "Shortage of Doctors an Obstacle to Obama Goals," *New York Times*, April 26, 2009.

Pipes, Sally, "Bam's Bad Medicine: Health-Care Rationing Ahead," *New York Post*, March 2, 2009.

Reisner, Rebecca, "End-of-Life Benefit Ignites Health-Care Rhetoric," *Business Week*, July 30, 2009.

Troy, Tevi, "The End of Medical Miracles?" *Commentary*, June 2009.

Tully, Shawn, "4 Reasons Why Obama's Health Plan Is No Bargain," *Fortune*, June 11, 2009.

HEALTH CARE: MASSACHUSETTS

Articles
Barr, Andy, "Romney a Victim in Health Care Debate," *Politico*, September 26, 2009.

Kowalczyk, Liz, "Waits to See Hub Doctors Grow Longer," *Boston Globe*, May 15, 2009.

Trapp, Doug, "Access-to-Care Problems Are Resurfacing in Mass.," *American Medical News*, June 29, 2009.

HEALTH CARE: HAWAII

Articles
Niesse, Mark, "Hawaii Ending Universal Child Health Care," Associated Press, October 17, 2008.

Studies
Sheldon, Trevor, et al., "Error Management," *Quality and Safety in Health Care*, December 2007.

Legislation
H.R. 3200. America's Affordable Health Choices Act of 2009.

GREENS

Books

Ehrlich, Paul, Anne Ehrlich, and John Holdren, *Human Ecology: Problems and Solutions* (San Francisco, 1973).

Hardin, Garrett, *Living within Limits: Ecology, Economics, and Population Taboos* (Oxford, 1993).

Lomborg, Bjorn, *The Skeptical Environmentalist. Measuring the Real State of the World* (Cambridge, U.K., 2001).

Lovelock, James, *The Revenge of Gaia. Why the Earth Is Fighting Back—and How We Can Still Save Humanity* (New York, 2008).

Articles

Bolt, Andrew, "Green Obsession Puts Deadly Heat on Elderly," *Melbourne Herald Sun*, April 8, 2009.

Brown, Lester, "Moving to a Stable World Population," Earth Policy Institute, January 22, 2009.

Duke, Steven, "Earth Population 'Exceeds Limits,'" BBC, March 31, 2009.

"EPA in Contempt for Destroying Files," Associated Press, July 23, 2003.

Fredosso, David, "Obama's Science Czar Suggested Compulsory Abortion, Sterilization," *Washington Examiner*, July 14, 2009.

Garber, Kent, "Browner: Climate Change Law Would Bolster U.S. Role at Global Warming Talks," *U.S. News & World Report*, April 13, 2009.

Gardiner, Anne Barbeau, "Human Sacrifice on the Altar of Gaia," *New Oxford Review*, June 2008.

Neefus, Christopher, "In the 70s, Obama's Science Adviser Endorsed Giving Trees Legal Standing to Sue in Court," CNSNews, July 30, 2009.

Smith, Robert J., "Ecoterrorism Kills: But Not Necessarily the Way You Think," *National Review*, October 30, 2007.

Tapscott, Mark, " 'Put Nothing in Writing,' Browner Told Auto Execs on Secret White House CAFE Talks; Sensenbrenner Wants Investigation," *Washington Examiner*, July 8, 2009.

———, "Browner Has History of Deceit on Government Files," *Washington Examiner*, July 9, 2009.

Interviews

AtKisson, Alan, "Introduction to Deep Ecology: An Interview with Michael E. Zimmerman," *Global Climate Change* (Summer 1989).

Websites

http://www.Dieoff.com

Pentti Linkola: http://www.penttilinkola.com/

http://www.newworldencyclopedia.org/entry/Deep_ecology

http://www.treehugger.com

Voluntary Human Extinction Movement: http://www.vhemt.org/

INDEX